The New Spinoza

Edited by

Sandra Buckley

Michael Hardt

Brian Massumi

THEORY OUT OF BOUNDS

...UNCONTAINED

BY

THE

DISCIPLINES,

INSUBORDINATE

11   **The New Spinoza**   Warren Montag and Ted Stolze, editors

10   **Power and Invention:
Situating Science**   Isabelle Stengers

9   **Arrow of Chaos:
Romanticism and Postmodernity**   Ira Livingston

8   **Becoming-Woman**   Camilla Griggers

7   **Radical Thought in Italy:
A Potential Politics**   Paolo Virno and Michael Hardt, editors

6   **Capital Times:
Tales from the Conquest of Time**   Éric Alliez

5   **The Year of Passages**   Réda Bensmaïa

4   **Labor of Dionysus:
A Critique of the State-Form**   Michael Hardt and Antonio Negri

3   **Bad Aboriginal Art: Tradition,
Media, and Technological Horizons**   Eric Michaels

2   **The Cinematic Body**   Steven Shaviro

1   **The Coming Community**   Giorgio Agamben

PRACTICES OF RESISTANCE

...Inventing,

excessively,

in the between...

PROCESSES

OF

HYBRIDIZATION

Contents

Abbreviations   vii

Preface   ix

Part I: Spinoza: Our Contemporary

1   **The Only Materialist Tradition, Part I: Spinoza**   *Louis Althusser*   3

2   **Spinoza and the Three "Ethics"**   *Gilles Deleuze*   21

3   **The Envelope: A Reading of Spinoza, *Ethics*, "Of God"**   *Luce Irigaray*   37

Part II: Surfaces without Depth, Processes without End(s)

4   **The Birth of Modern Materialism in Hobbes and Spinoza**   *Emilia Giancotti*   49

5   **The Problem of the Attributes**   *Pierre Macherey*   65

6   **Fortune and the Theory of History**   *Pierre-François Moreau*   97

7   **The Empty Synagogue**   *Gabriel Albiac*   109

8   **Superstition and Reading**   *André Tosel*   147

Part III: From the Subject to Collectivities: The Politics of the Multitude

9   ***Jus-Pactum-Lex:* On the Constitution of the Subject in the *Theologico-Political Treatise***   *Etienne Balibar*   171

10   **The Theoretical Function of Democracy in Spinoza and Hobbes**   *Alexandre Matheron*   207

THEORY

11   *Reliqua Desiderantur:* **A Conjecture for a Definition of the Concept of Democracy in the Final Spinoza**   *Antonio Negri*   219

Works Cited and Select Bibliography   249

Contributors   255

Index   257

The New Spinoza

Warren Montag and Ted Stolze, editors

Theory out of Bounds   *Volume 11*

University of Minnesota Press

Minneapolis • London

Published by the University of Minnesota Press
111 Third Avenue South, Suite 290,
Minneapolis, MN 55401-2520
http://www.upress.umn.edu
Printed in the United States of America on acid-free paper

LIBRARY OF CONGRESS CATALOGING-IN-PUBLICATION DATA
The new Spinoza / Warren Montag and Ted Stolze, editors.
p.   cm. — (Theory out of bounds ; v. 11)
Includes bibliographical references and index.
ISBN 0-8166-2540-9 (alk. paper) — ISBN 0-8166-2541-7 (pbk. :
alk. paper)
1. Spinoza, Benedictus de, 1632–1677. I. Montag, Warren.
II. Stolze, Ted. III. Series.
B3998.N45   1998
199'.492 — dc21   97-27337

The University of Minnesota
is an equal-opportunity educator and employer.

Abbreviations

Throughout this collection we have used the following standard abbreviations for Spinoza's writings:

CM		*Metaphysical Thoughts (Cogitata Metaphysica)*
E		*Ethics (Ethica)*
	App	Appendix
	Ax	Axiom
	C	Corollary
	Def	Definition
	Def. Aff.	Definition of Affect
	D	Demonstration
	Exp	Explanation
	Lem	Lemma
	P	Proposition
	Post	Postulate
	Pref	Preface
	S	Scholium

NB: A comma within a citation from the *Ethics* means "and"; e.g., the abbreviation *E* VP20D, S indicates that both the demonstration and the scholium of proposition 20 of *Ethics*, part V, are being cited.

Ep	Letter *(Epistola)*
KV	*Short Treatise on God, Man, and His Well-Being (Korte Verhandeling)*
PPC	Descartes's *"Principles of Philosophy" (Principia Philosophiae Cartesianae)*
TdIE	*Treatise on the Emendation of the Intellect (Tractatus de Intellectus Emendatione)*
TP	*Political Treatise (Tractatus Politicus)*
TTP	*Theologico-Political Treatise (Tractatus Theologico-Politicus)*

Quotations from Spinoza's writings are based on (but usually modify) the following translations: Curley (*TdIE, KV, CM, E, Ep* 1–28), Shirley (*TTP*), Wernham (*TTP, TP*), and Wolf (*Ep* 29–84). For longer quotations we cite as well Gebhardt's standard Latin edition, which we abbreviate as, for example, G II/153 (volume 2, page 153).

We have also used the following abbreviations for Hobbes's writings:

DCi	*Philosophical Rudiments Concerning Government and Society (De Cive)*
Lev	*Leviathan*
DCo	*Elements of Philosophy Concerning Body (De Corpore)*

Quotations from Hobbes are taken from the following editions: Gert (*DCi*), Curley (*Lev*), and Calkins (*DCo*).

Preface

THE PHILOSOPHER Louis Althusser once complained that his critics called him a structuralist only because "structuralism was all the rage and one did not have to read about it in books to be able to talk about it."[1] Few, if any, of his readers ever suspected that he was instead a "Spinozist," for to recognize the presence of Spinoza, he quipped, "one must at least have heard of him."[2]

The essays collected here suggest that Althusser's words apply as much to his philosophical generation (or at least a significant part of it) as to himself.[3] Even if they would hesitate to refer to themselves as Spinozists, there is ample evidence of Spinoza's presence not only in the work of Deleuze (who produced a major study of Spinoza) but also in the work of Lacan, Foucault, and Derrida, for whom Spinoza is seldom an explicit point of reference. And while the influence of Hegel, Nietzsche, and Heidegger on the texts that are regularly categorized as structuralist or (in the Anglophone world) poststructuralist has been documented and analyzed at great length, the influence of Spinoza has hardly been suspected. And if Spinoza was unfamiliar to academic readers in France, which has a long history of Spinoza scholarship, and where Spinoza has for some time been a fixture on the *agrégation* (the standardized national exam for university teachers), what can we expect from readers in the United States, where few book-length studies of Spinoza's political philosophy have appeared in the last three decades and where Spinoza rarely figures in undergraduate philosophy courses? In fact, we must go even further and say that even after the translation of Deleuze's two books on Spinoza,[4] Negri's *The Savage Anomaly*, as well as shorter pieces by Althusser and Balibar,[5] Spinoza's importance for contemporary critical theory and French philosophy remains relatively unexplored.[6]

In addition, a number of valuable studies of Spinoza from the standpoint of analytic philosophy have appeared in the last fifteen years: Jonathan Bennett's *A Study of Spinoza's Ethics*, Edwin Curley's *Behind the Geometrical Method*, Douglas J. Den Uyl's *Power, State and Freedom*, and, recently, Genevieve Lloyd's *Part of Nature*. Yirmiyahu Yovel's *Spinoza and Other Heretics* offers a detailed historical reading that situates Spinoza in the history of ideas. For all their interest, however, the orientation of these studies is quite distinct from that of the essays making up the present collection.

But how precisely are we to understand Spinoza's "importance for" or "influence on" contemporary thought? One way would be to seek the citations, the references, and the borrowings (acknowledged and unacknowledged) that bind contemporary Continental thought to the texts of Spinoza and that would thus put him in the position of a predecessor or forebear whose thought "anticipated" the concerns if not the conclusions of critical theory. Another way, the inverse of the first, would be to situate the contemporary "reception" of Spinoza in the history of Spinoza studies, as the most recent in a series of "readings" of Spinoza from the atheistic Spinoza of the seventeenth century to the pantheist Spinoza of the eighteenth and early nineteenth centuries to the monist of the twentieth century.

The texts collected here will help us define yet a third way to understand Spinoza's presence: neither as a historical figure whose thought could be captured once and for all, grasped definitively in the ideological context in which he lived and died, an author, a person; nor as an object of study whose texts, while fixed, provide a mirror in which succeeding centuries or even generations see their respective dilemmas. Spinoza's works constitute a philosophy that never definitively closes upon itself, that is never strictly identifiable with a finite set of propositions or arguments that would allow it to be categorized once and for all as "rationalist" or even "materialist." It is rather a philosophy characterized by an inexhaustible productivity that is thus capable, as Pierre Macherey has argued, of producing, and not simply reproducing, itself endlessly.[7] Spinoza's philosophy provides the best illustration of the concept of the immanent cause, a concept that, during the late seventeenth century, was one of its most scandalous postulates: it is a philosophy that exists in its effects, not prior to them or even independently of them, effects that may remain dormant or deferred for decades or even centuries, (re)activated only in an encounter with unforeseeable theoretical elements that arrive from beyond its boundaries. God, the immanent cause with which Spinoza is concerned in the *Ethics*, exists entirely in its own movement, the infinite productivity and dynamism that alone make it what it is.

      The openness of Spinoza's thought, its capacity to renew itself incessantly in irreducibly dispersed and diverse forms, is all the more surprising in the light of the stark singularity of Spinoza's individual itinerary. Born in 1632 to Portuguese Jewish parents who had fled to Amsterdam to escape the Inquisition, the young Spinoza was raised in the Jewish tradition. He learned Hebrew as a child and studied the *Tanach*. Although he left school as a teenager to enter his father's import-export firm, he continued to attend courses given by some of the great intellects of Amsterdam's Jewish community, including such figures as Menasseh ben Israel and the heretical Juan de Prado (who was twice excommunicated for freethinking). During this period, Spinoza appears to have continued to observe the religious customs, while reading widely in medieval Jewish philosophy, as well as Hebrew translations of Greek and Latin texts. Soon after his father's death in 1654, Spinoza ceased fully to observe Jewish ritual and apparently began professing heterodox ideas in conjunction with other Jewish freethinkers. By this time Spinoza had also learned Latin and perhaps some modern languages, becoming acquainted with Scholastic and early modern philosophical, political, and theological writing. After the alarmed leaders of the community tried and failed to convince Spinoza once again to resume religious observances, he was excommunicated on July 27, 1656.

      From henceforth completely isolated from the Jewish community (whose members were forbidden to communicate with him in oral or written form), Spinoza elected to join the loose and extremely cosmopolitan community of religious heretics and political radicals (many of whom were themselves exiles from other countries) that flourished in the *relatively* open atmosphere of Amsterdam. Within his circle, the ideas of Descartes and Hobbes were vigorously discussed and debated, while developments in mathematics and the sciences were closely followed. Several years after his excommunication he was forced to leave Amsterdam, living for the next decade among like-minded thinkers in outlying villages. During this period, Spinoza produced several works. The unfinished *Treatise on the Emendation of the Intellect*, a treatise on method, begins with an autobiographical account of the philosopher's search for the true good. The *Short Treatise on God, Man, and His Well-Being*, a treatise on metaphysics, contains certain quasi-mystical elements that are absent from Spinoza's later works, especially the *Ethics*, which covers much of the same ground. In 1663, he published the only text to which he would publicly attach his name. Ironically, it was his exposition of Descartes's *Principles of Philosophy* in geometric form.

In 1670 Spinoza moved to The Hague, where he would remain until his death. In the same year he published the *Theologico-Political Treatise*, taking great precautions to conceal his authorship and the place of publication. At this time Spinoza was a supporter of the republican cause in Holland, a cause that he saw embodied in the leadership of the De Witt brothers and several other representatives of the urban and maritime bourgeois class who stood for religious and intellectual tolerance and the predominance of state over church. A series of wars and economic crises, however, deprived the republicans of the mass support without which they could not survive. The urban masses in particular shifted their support to an alliance between the Prince of Orange and the Calvinist church. In 1672, the republicans were overthrown in a mass uprising to restore church and monarchy. From this point on, Spinoza shifted the focus of his political investigations from the attempt to furnish the principles of a state whose laws and customs would lead all people to conduct themselves rationally to the attempt to delineate the centrality of the multitude or the masses to any political system. The result was the unfinished *Political Treatise*. Spinoza's greatest work, a work on which he labored for over a decade but which he decided not to publish during his lifetime, was the *Ethics*. Spinoza died in 1677 at the age of forty-four, after having delivered, in the words of Althusser, "the greatest lesson in heresy the world has ever known."

Few philosophical oeuvres have given rise to such utterly divergent and even opposed "readings," readings not confined to a single commentator but common to entire centuries. Thus, the phrase, probably the most famous Spinoza ever wrote, "Deus sive natura" (God, that is, nature) (*Ethics* IV, preface) was generally taken by his contemporaries to mean that God was nothing more than nature, even that God was a thing. A century later, Spinoza could be described as a "God-intoxicated man," and "Deus sive natura" could be understood as establishing the presence of God everywhere and in all things, and thus as the foundation of a pantheist or even mystical doctrine. And the history of the reception of Spinoza's philosophy yields little that would appear to have prepared the way to the texts gathered here. Indeed, there was little in French Spinoza scholarship itself before the 1960s that would have allowed one to predict the orientation that emerged after 1968, with the publication of major studies of Spinoza by Gueroult, Deleuze, and Matheron. While Spinoza's thought occupied the attention of many of the major academic philosophers, the names of whom will most likely not be familiar to schol-

ars outside of France, the interpretations they offered (and despite certain diver-
gences, there were key points of unity among them) may surprise those familiar
with the Spinoza scholarship of the last several decades. Such figures as Lagneau,
Alain (Émile Chartier), Delbos, and Brunschvicg all produced major studies of Spinoza that were, to varying degrees, influenced by the French spiritualist tradition
(not the least important of whose expressions was existentialism) with its emphasis
on the freedom of the mind or spirit (*esprit*). Brunschvicg, for example, who argued
that Spinoza's work was dominated by the influence of Descartes,[8] saw in the *Ethics*
a theory of the "conquest of consciousness by the intellect that, in each of us, thanks
to the relational immanence of God, is endowed with an unlimited power of expansion."[9] This tradition persisted into our own time through the work of Ferdinand
Alquié, whose lectures and course notes from the 1950s and 1960s were finally gathered together and published in 1981 as *Le rationalisme de Spinoza*. Alquié found Spinoza's philosophy, despite the immense interest that it held for him, finally "incomprehensible." Unlike Descartes (still the counterpoint to Spinoza), who "never promised
anything that he did not deliver or at least allow us to discover" because "he never
sought to surpass the human condition,"[10] Spinoza's thought seemed not to correspond to any conceivable "internal experience," including that of comprehension itself. Even the notion of God as nature could never correspond to a clear and distinct
idea in the Cartesian sense. Alquié measured Spinoza against human experience and
found him wanting.

Even as Alquié developed his reading through his lectures at the
Sorbonne, another Descartes scholar, Martial Gueroult, turned his attention to Spinoza, finally producing a textual monument that arguably opened the way to the understanding of Spinoza that the essays collected here represent. In 1968, the first
volume of Gueroult's study of the *Ethics*,[11] which discussed only part I (approximately
thirty pages of text in English translation), appeared: it came to nearly six hundred
pages. A second volume on part II was slightly longer.[12] Gueroult died shortly after
beginning a projected third and final volume on parts III–V.[13] If Alquié's work was
marked by the spiritualist tradition of French philosophy, including, perhaps, existentialism, Gueroult's procedure had much in common with the emergent structuralism of the 1950s and 1960s. Indeed, Foucault declared the influence of Gueroult on
his own work in the introduction to *The Archaeology of Knowledge*, referring specifically to Gueroult's analysis of "the architectonic unities of systems . . . which are concerned not with the description of cultural influences, traditions, and continuities,
but with internal coherences, axioms, deductive connections, compatibilities."[14] And,
in the case of his study of the *Ethics*, as earlier in his study of Descartes's *Meditations*,

Gueroult showed not the slightest inclination to determine the adequacy of Spinoza's theses to human consciousness or experience, and even less to something called "reality" considered as inert and pregiven. Rather, Gueroult, explicitly rejecting any account of a philosophical work that returned only occasionally to the text itself, sought, with an unrivaled attention to the facts of Spinoza's text, to reconstruct the structure or system internal to the *Ethics*, holding that it would prove far more valuable to understand what Spinoza's text actually is than what it is not. Deleuze, in his extended review of Gueroult's study of Spinoza, hailed it as having made possible for the first time "a truly scientific study of Spinozism."[15] Gueroult had, according to Deleuze, "renewed the history of philosophy through a structural-genetic method that he elaborated well before structuralism emerged in other domains."[16] His method permitted the identification of the structure proper to a given philosophical work, "the order of reasons" or "the differential and generative elements of a system."[17] Gueroult's structuralist method was resolutely opposed to any notion of interpretation: there were no hidden meanings to discover, no latent content to make manifest. The order of reasons existed solely on the surface of the text(s); structure was not to be extracted from the rest of the text, leaving behind an unexplained and inexplicable remainder, but was identical with what was actually said.[18]

Deleuze's *Expressionism in Philosophy: Spinoza* (the original French title has a different meaning: *Spinoza and the Problem of Expression*), also published in 1968, represented his secondary thesis for the *Doctorat d'état* (*Difference and Repetition*, the primary thesis, was published the same year). At first glance, Deleuze's praise for Gueroult's "structural-genetic" method seems not to have resulted in the slightest imitation of it. In fact, Deleuze is the only figure of this generation of Spinozists to regard Alquié as a predecessor (although even then he is not very faithful to the original). There is no reconstruction of a system or an order of reasons. The notorious difficulty of Deleuze's study results, no doubt, from his effort instead to "think in Spinoza," as Macherey put it, "dynamically to produce rather than reproduce the intellectual movement by which" Spinoza's philosophy "became what it is."[19] And yet Deleuze is not as far from Gueroult as one might think. Like Gueroult, Deleuze's attempt to produce the intellectual movement through which Spinoza thought the problem of expression postulates a unity and even a coherence that earlier readings missed to the extent that they strayed from the textual surface in some hermeneutic quest.

The next year, 1969, another scholar inspired by Gueroult, Alexandre Matheron, published his comprehensive account of Spinoza's political thought: *L'individu et communauté chez Spinoza* (Individual and Community in Spinoza). Examining parts III-V of the *Ethics* and the *Tractatus Politicus*, Matheron reconstructs the propositional structures of parts III-V to reveal an architectonic unity to which the system internal to the *Tractatus Politicus* is homologous.

The philosophical effects of these three works can hardly be overestimated, not only for the study of Spinoza but for the history of philosophy in general. As Deleuze himself suggested, however, they cannot be understood in isolation from other developments in French intellectual life, especially the structuralist movement that dominated the sixties in France. These studies exhibited all the characteristics of other well-known "readings" of the time, which sought to return to the letter, that is, the materiality, rather than the spirit of (or behind or in) texts, reading them line by line with a scrupulosity that critics (and an older generation of scholars) found pedantic and even scholastic, a tedious examination of words and even letters that had, it was charged, all but abandoned the search for meaning and significance.

Of course, the first practitioner of such a procedure was none other than Spinoza himself, a fact not lost on Althusser, who in his *Reading Capital* identified Spinoza as "the first man ever to have posed the problem of *reading* and in consequence, of *writing*."[20] Spinoza's rule for the reading of the Scripture, that it must be approached like nature, without seeking its final causes or transcendental essences, thus not only served as the stimulus for *Reading Capital* but even more surprisingly for the recovery of his own text. One had, in a manner of speaking, to have already understood Spinoza in order to read him. And it is perhaps only through this paradox that one can grasp the astonishing influence of Althusser himself on contemporary Spinoza studies. Astonishing, because Althusser's influence is as pervasive as it is difficult to grasp. Althusser wrote no more than fifty pages on Spinoza, mainly in two essays: "On Spinoza" from *Essays in Self-Criticism* and a posthumous essay originally written as part of his autobiography, *The Future Lasts Forever* (the essay is included in the present collection). Significantly, Althusser's comments on Spinoza do not even amount to scholarly studies in the strict sense. There are no direct references to texts, and the formal character of the two essays is both elliptical and impressionistic: they provide a stark contrast to the attention to the letter of the text characteristic of Althusser's earlier work. Further, although he gave several courses in the 1960s and 1970s on Spinoza, none of Althusser's lecture notes have been found (while lecture notes ranging from handwritten outlines of a few pages to elaborate and polished manuscripts from similar courses on Machiavelli, Hobbes, Locke, and Rousseau have been recovered). Thus, it appears that Spinoza's relation to Althusser, like Althusser's relation to the present generation of French Spinoza studies, is, perhaps appropriately, that of an immanent cause, a cause present only in its effects. And, in turn, the number of contemporary Spinozists whose discovery or rediscovery of Spinoza's writing is indissociable from their encounter as student, colleague, or friend with Althusser the philosopher is striking. To name only those included in this volume who have produced full-length studies: Etienne Balibar (*Spinoza et la politique*), Pierre Macherey (*Hegel ou Spinoza*, *Avec Spinoza*, and *Introduction á l'Ethique de Spinoza/V*), Pierre-François Moreau (*Spinoza* and *Spinoza: L'expérience et l'éternité*), André Tosel (*Le crépuscule de la servitude* and *Du matérialisme de Spinoza*), and Gabriel Albiac (*La sinagoga vacía*). Although each philosopher has his own philosophical itinerary and personality, Althusser's notion of the symptomatic reading, the idea that to read a philosophical text is to grasp the conflicts that constitute it, the specific and determinate disorder that makes it what it is, has undoubtedly marked their endeavors.[21]

Finally, the publication of Antonio Negri's *L'anomalia selvaggia* in 1981 (the French translation equipped with no less than three separate prefaces by Deleuze, Macherey, and Matheron appeared the following year) provoked enormous debate. The book, written in one year during Negri's incarceration as a political prisoner in his native Italy, traces the development of Spinoza's thought from the Neoplatonism of the early works to the materialism of the *Tractatus Politicus*. Resident in France for over ten years, Negri's work (including his recent *Spinoza sovversivo*) forms an inseparable part of the encounter that has made French Spinozism what it is.

But what exactly is it, beyond a set of names and texts, and their filiations? Or, to put the question another way, what are the forms of Spinoza's actuality, the theoretical effects of which he is an immanent cause?

The first site of Spinoza's immanence is a network of problems around the concepts of expression and representation (if it is necessary to attach names to this highly complex and differentiated field, we might mention those of Derrida, Foucault, Deleuze, and perhaps even Althusser). Derrida's statement concerning the precise form of the problematization of the linguistic sign might be taken as an index: "the age of the sign is essentially theological."[22] Theories of signification are rooted in theology (specifically the notion of creation) to the extent that they seem inescapably to refer to a hierarchy of being, according to which the original term, that which is expressed or represented, is more real than the second term, that which expresses or represents, which must be seen as inescapably derivative or secondary, as a repetition that is somehow less than what it repeats. Deleuze in particular has identified the way that Spinoza has radicalized this relation in his discussion of substance and the attributes and modes in which it is expressed.[23] For it is not simply that Spinoza makes all schemes of expression and representation appear even more radically unsatisfactory with his thesis that there exists only one substance, indivisible and consisting of infinite attributes: God (and how could parts of God be less real than others, how could body pertain less to the divine essence than mind; in short, how could ontological hierarchies be possible?). It is even more that Spinoza seems to open the possibility of thinking otherwise, in a new way. For Spinoza, substance is not prior, logically or chronologically, to its attributes: the cause does not precede its effects; the whole, its parts; or unity, division. Rather substance is "its" infinite diversity itself; it is realized in this diversity and is nothing other than the process of production without beginning or end (beyond teleology, without goals or direction) of itself through the infinity of its attributes. In opposition to Hegel, who saw Spinoza's philosophy as an "Oriental theory of Absolute Identity,"[24] a "negation of all that is particular,"[25] Macherey reveals to us a Spinoza who is the thinker of a universe composed of singular essences, which are in turn composed of and themselves compose combinations of singular essences to infinity. As Spinoza argued in the final part of the *Ethics*, the way to know God is through the knowledge of singular things. For Luce Irigaray, Spinoza's questioning of the problematic of expression destabilizes the traditional hierarchization of the male-female opposition according to which woman functions as a kind of envelope for man, covering his essence while remaining external to it and therefore an outside, a surface, a beyond, coming into existence, if at all, by accident rather than by necessity. Spinoza's affirmation of surfaces allows the singularity of woman to be thought. It is around this set of problems that Spinoza appears to think at the limit, not of the thought of his time, but of ours, revealing the limit as a limit and thus making possible the crossing of a line that once appeared as an absolute horizon.

Another nodal point of theoretical inquiry and debate in the last decades has been the notion of the individual as sovereign subject. The work of Lacan and his school, Althusser's famous essay "Ideology and Ideological State Apparatuses," and Foucault's *Discipline and Punish* are some of the more notable moments in the process that opened an interrogation of the notion, central to legal, political, philosophical, and aesthetic reflection since the seventeenth century, that the individual (whose existence is a given) is the origin of desire, thought, speech, and action. So anomalous in his own time that his efforts could not be fully understood until ours, Spinoza denounced the illusion that the human individual was a kingdom within a kingdom, outside of the order of nature and master of his own desires and thoughts. Here, Spinoza overturns two hierarchies, both of which may be said to be historically constitutive of the notion of the subject. First, the thesis that the mind governs and determines the body. He counters this notion with the objection that our assumption of the mind's mastery over the body has prevented us from asking the fundamental question: what do bodies accomplish as bodies alone, determined merely by other bodies, without the intervention of the mind? Secondly, Spinoza denies that the mind can achieve mastery over the emotions, which, for him, must be studied according to the relations of force and necessity proper to them, without reference to a transcendent cause. But the double illusion of the individual as subject, master of himself and author of his actions, is not simply an effect of the imagination (the first of three kinds of knowledge, according to Spinoza), it is also the center of the system of superstition (with its apparatuses and practices—Althusser identifies Spinoza as the first to conceive of discipline in Foucault's sense) that determines the people not only to obey priests and despots but to live their obedience as freedom and to desire nothing but what was commanded. How else could we explain the fact that men so often "see the better and do the worse,"[26] that they fight and die for the tyrant who oppresses them as fervently as if they were fighting for their own well-being, and that they sacrifice their powers and pleasure to the supreme and original Subject, God, whose love for them, they imagine, increases with their suffering? (One will recognize some of the major themes of Althusser's "Ideology and Ideological State Apparatuses" here.)

Finally, the realm of political theory has recently seen a massive revival of liberalism: the notions of society as a voluntary association of originally free and equal individuals whose consent alone is the legitimate foundation of any collectivity, of autonomous individuals rationally calculating unique utilities, and of a politics of law and rights have seen a resurgence on both the Right and the Left. In particular, Anglo-American academic Marxism has embraced the apparatus of seventeenth- and eighteenth-century politico-juridical thought with great enthusiasm. The state, which once represented, to some at least, that which must be abolished if human liberation were to be achieved, has now become a perpetual necessity, no longer an impediment to real democracy but, according to political philosophers such as John Rawls, the institution whose mediation of the conflicting interests of the individuals and groups that constitute civil society will alone guarantee democratic freedom and justice.

Here Spinoza remains an anomaly, but one whose radical exteriority to the problematic of liberalism makes possible a critique of it. First, Spinoza rejects any dissociation of right and power: it makes no sense to speak of having the right to do what we have not the power to do. Once we conceive of politics as power, the individual ceases to be a meaningful unit of analysis. For the power of the individual considered as separate and autonomous is theoretically negligible. But Spinoza's critique of liberalism is less a wholesale rejection of its postulates than, as Balibar has argued, a working through of the conflicts constitutive of liberal political theory. Thus in the *Tractatus Theologico-Politicus* Spinoza speaks of a contract or pact (*Pactum*) between the sovereign and the people even as he deprives the notion of the contract of any normative function or ideal existence. The contract becomes for him an explanatory concept that allows us to understand the precise relationship of forces on which a given society at a given historical moment rests: every contract is singular in that it explains the specific relations of force that constitute a given society. Whether this was a case of turning the language of the enemy against that enemy, as Althusser suggests, subverting juridical thought by means of juridical concepts, or a necessary stage in Spinoza's development, it is difficult to say. We can, however, say with certainty that the notion of the contract is utterly absent from his last work, the unfinished *Tractatus Politicus*. There can be no contract because there can be no presocial state, a state of nature inhabited by the dissociated individuals imagined by Hobbes. Because isolated individuals do not possess sufficient power even to ensure their own survival, society in some form always already exists. There is thus no transition from a state of nature to the social state, nor any founding or constitutional moment in the life of a society. Politics is no longer centered on the relation, harmonious or antagonistic, between the individual and the state; not because individuals have disappeared into the dark night of the social but because individuals inescapably combine with other individuals, whether through the "imitation of the affects" that bind them together or through the collectivizing effects of religious and political apparatuses (both of which processes operate independently of the individuals' will) to form new, more powerful entities or individuals. The force of Negri's work lies in his identification of Spinoza as the first philosopher to see society as "constituted" by the power of the masses (*multitudo*) and thus the first to undertake an investigation rather than a denunciation of the multitude. For better or for worse, it is the multitude, subject to all the variability of fortune, whose struggles will determine the possibility of historical progress (the diminishing of superstition, the tendential dominance of active over passive emotions, and the increasing of the power and pleasure of the body) in the absence of any goal, end, or destiny and, most important, without any guarantees. Thus, according to Matheron, democracy, the "people's power" (in the physical sense, the force that the people, if only by virtue of their numbers, actually exercise), is the immanent cause of any society whatever: even the fate of a tyrant rests in the hands of the multitude whose approbation or acquiescence alone permits him to rule.

These three nodal points seem to define the problematic specific to Spinoza as he is constructed in our time: a new Spinoza.

W.M.

Notes

1. Althusser (1976, 132).

2. Ibid.

3. I would like to thank Etienne Balibar, Pierre Macherey, and Pierre-François Moreau for their generosity in helping me to understand twentieth-century French Spinoza studies. Needless to say, I alone am responsible for the interpretation advanced here.

4. Deleuze (1988, 1990).

5. Althusser's "On Spinoza" appeared in English translation in 1976 in *Essays in Self-Criticism*. A translation of Balibar's long essay "Spinoza, the Anti-Orwell: The Fear of the Masses" (1994) was first published in 1989.

6. There is, of course, Christopher Norris's *Spinoza and the Origins of Modern Critical Theory*, which suggests a number of links between Spinoza's method for the interpretation of Scripture and trends in contemporary literary theory and the philosophy of language. Norris, however, seldom refers to contemporary Continental Spinoza scholarship, a fact that is unfortunate, given that his work often retraces what others have done before him: Negri, Matheron, Tosel, Moreau, Gueroult, and Jean-Pierre Osier, to name only a few of the more obvious.

7. Macherey (1992, 31).

8. Brunschvicg (1951, 162).

9. Ibid., 168.

10. Alquié (1981, 11).

11. Gueroult (1968).

12. Gueroult (1974).

13. Gueroult (1977).

14. Foucault (1972, 5).

15. Deleuze (1969, 437).

16. Ibid., 426.

17. Ibid.

18. Ibid., 427.

19. Macherey (1992, 238).

20. Althusser (1970, 16).

21. Although further research may indeed show that "Althusser" as the name of an author, at least in the sixties, may correspond more to a collective effort than to the activity of the single individual who bore the name Louis Althusser.

22. Derrida (1974, 14).

23. Deleuze (1990).

24. Hegel (1983, 3:252).

25. Ibid., 257.

26. *E* III P2S.

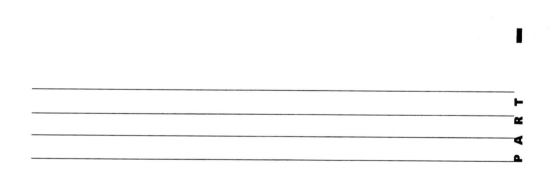

PART I

Spinoza: Our Contemporary

O   N   E

The Only Materialist Tradition, Part I: Spinoza

Louis Althusser

I

BEFORE COMING to Marx himself, I must speak of the detour I made, had to make (now I understand why), through Pascal, Spinoza, Hobbes, Rousseau, and perhaps especially Machiavelli.

      I had duly read Pascal in captivity (the only book I possessed). I was still a believer, but that was not the reason. What fascinated me was certainly Pascal's theory of justice and force, his theory of relations among men, but especially his theory of the apparatus of the body: "Kneel and pray," which was later to inspire my "theory" of the materiality of ideology (see what Michel Foucault appropriately calls the "disciplines of the body" in the seventeenth century; they have obviously not disappeared since), of the *semblance* I was to rediscover later, that is, further on, in Machiavelli. The theory of the skillful and semiskillful, like the theory of recognition and misrecognition that unbeknownst to me I was to rediscover later in my own sketch of a theory of ideology. What do I not owe to Pascal! and in particular to that astonishing sentence on the history of science, in which the moderns are said to be greater than the ancients only because they stand on the latters' shoulders. But this was not the most beautiful thing there. I found in this sentence a theory of scientific experimentation related not to its conditions of possibility (as later in Kant) but to its material conditions of historical existence, thus the essence of a genuine theory of history: when Pascal, speaking of new experiments that contradict those of the ancients, utters this extraordinary sentence: "*Thus it is that without contradicting [the ancients] we can advance the contrary of what they said*"! Without contradicting them: because the conditions of our scientific experiments have changed and are no longer the same as those of the ancients. They only made the theory of their own experiments and of the material conditions of experimentation within their own limits. We know of other conditions, that is, limits, certainly much larger, for time has passed and technology has expanded, and we state results and theories quite differently, but without ever contradicting the ancients, quite simply because the conditions of our experiments and our experiments themselves are different from theirs. I did not stop reflecting on this sentence, infinitely more profound than all that the philosophers of the Enlightenment were able to say (which was ultimately very simple-minded, because teleological) about history.

II

But Spinoza, whom I read for a long time without understanding him well, in any case without ever managing to embrace him, was to hold quite different revelations in store for me. I see now, if not what Spinoza really wanted to think and say, then the profound reasons for my attraction to him.

I discovered in him first an astonishing contradiction: this man who reasons *more geometrico* through definitions, axioms, theorems, corollaries, lemmas, and deductions — therefore, in the most "dogmatic" way in the world — was in fact an incomparable liberator of the mind. How then could dogmatism not only result in the exhaltation of freedom but also "produce" it? Later I was to formulate the same remark regarding Hegel: again a dogmatic thinker, but one who had led to Marx's radical critique, which Hegel had in a certain way produced or induced. How was this possible? I only understood it later while elaborating my personal little "theory" of philosophy as the activity of the positing of theses to be demarcated from existing theses. I noted that the truth of a philosophy lies entirely in its *effects*, while in fact it acts only at a distance from real objects, therefore, in the space of freedom that it opens up to research and action and not in its form of exposition alone. This form could be systematic or not, but in any event it was in itself "dogmatic" to the extent that every philosophy *posits*, not without reason, but without any possible empirical *verification*, apparently arbitrary theses, which in reality are not arbitrary, since they are a function of the space of freedom (or servitude) that the philosophy intends by *its effects* to open up at the heart of the space of theses already posed by existing philosophies within a given theoretical conjuncture. Under these conditions, systematic exposition in no way contradicts the philosophical *effects* produced; on the contrary, it can, through the rigor of the chain of its reasons, not only constrict more tightly the space it intends to open, but make the consistency of its own production infinitely more rigorous and more sensible and fruitful (in the strong sense) to the freedom of the mind. And, also following Hegel himself in this matter, I had to understand the reason of Spinoza's theses as theses *antithetical* to those of Descartes, whose *effects* he intended to combat by stepping back, just as Hegel, within the apparently "dogmatic" exposition of his philosophy, intended to combat the effects of Kant's philosophical theses by means of theses opposed to his, and finally to open up a new space of freedom.

Thus I established a rather strict parallel between Spinoza against Descartes and Hegel against Kant, showing that in the two cases what was in play and in struggle was a *transcendental subjectivist* conception of "truth" and knowledge. The parallel went quite far: no more *cogito* in Spinoza (but only the factual proposition *homo cogitat*, "man thinks"), no more transcendental subject in Hegel, but a subject as process (I pass over its [immanent] teleology). No theory of knowlege (that is, no theory of an a priori guarantee of truth and its scientific, social, moral, and political effects) in Spinoza, no theory of knowledge in Hegel, either, whereas Descartes presents in the form of a divine guarantee a theory of the guarantee of every truth and, therefore, of every knowledge — whereas Kant produced a juridical theory of knowledge under the "I think" of the transcendental Subject and the a priori conditions of every possible experience. In the two cases, Spinoza and Hegel managed — and little matter, or rather all the better, that their demonstration was rigorous and therefore apparently "dogmatic" — to disentangle the mind from the illusion of transcendent or transcendental subjectivity as a guarantee or foundation of every meaning or every experience of possible truth. I understood, then, the reason for this apparent paradox, which, if I can say it, comforted me against the host of accusations of "dogmatism" that had been thrown in my face. To know that a philosophy called "dogmatic" and actually having the form of a dogmatic exposition can produce effects of freedom: I had never sought anything else.

From what, then, did Spinoza liberate the human mind — and not through the terms of his theses but through the *effects* of his philosophy? From the illusions of what he called the imagination. The imagination not only rules over the first kind of knowledge, but also over the second, since the "intermediate generalities" — for example, the abstraction of the tree from the reduction of all the impressions of individual trees — are still relatively contaminated by the imagination and the *word* that utters them. The "intermediate" abstractions of the second kind of knowledge were thus still partially caught up in the illusion of the imagination and of the language directly tied to it.

What, then, became of the first kind of knowledge? I maintained that it had nothing to do with the first degree of a "theory of knowledge," Spinoza never having wanted in that way to guarantee but simply "to state the facts," "stripped of every foreign addition" (Engels). But in order to state the facts, it was truly necessary to strip them of every foreign addition, that of the imagination, which, however — and this is all the difference with Engels — is not presented at all as a foreign *addition* but as the immediate truth of the very meaning of the given and lived world. This is why I maintained that the first kind of knowledge is not a knowledge at all (the imagination is not a knowledge), but is the immediate world such as we perceive it, that is, as we live (perception itself being an element abstracted from life) under the domination of the imagination, in truth not *under* the imagination but so imbued with the imagination that the immediate world such as we perceive it is strictly indissociable and inseparable from the imagination, the imagination constituting *its very essence*, the internal connection of all its determinations. Perhaps it was forcing Spinoza a little to say that the first kind of knowledge, therefore, the imagination, was the immediate *Lebenswelt* — but this is how I interpreted him.

What, then, was the imagination that thus constituted the essence of our common *Lebenswelt*? Spinoza explained it with exemplary clarity in the appendix to part I of the *Ethics*. The imagination is (1) to put the (human) subject at the center and origin of every perception, of every action, of every object, and of every meaning, but (2) to reverse in this way even the real order of things, since the real order *is explained* (and not "*comprehended*," a subjective if not subjectivist notion *completely foreign to Spinoza*) solely by the determination of causes, while the subjectivity of the imagination explains everything by means of ends, by the subjective illusion of the ends of its desire and its expectations. This is, strictly speaking, to *reverse* the order of the world, to make it walk, as Hegel and Marx will say, "*on its head.*" It is to put to work, as Spinoza superbly said, an entire "*apparatus*" (a formula that was to speak volumes when I rediscovered it in proper terms in Marx and Lenin regarding the state), *an apparatus of reversal of causes into ends*. This "apparatus" is truly the world of the imagination, the world as such, the *Lebenswelt* lived in the *apparatus* of the reversal of causes into ends, those of the illusion of subjectivity, of the man who believes himself to be the center of the world and becomes "an empire within an empire," master of the world's meaning (the *cogito*), although he is entirely submitted to the determinations of the world: as a simple determinate part of the world, a finite mode of substance (as mode of extension and mode of thought, rigorously "*parallel*" modes).

It is in the appendix to part I of the *Ethics* that Spinoza developed his admirable critique of religious ideology, in which the human subject endowed with finalized desires projects himself into God as the original and final cause of the Universe, as the cause (in truth not the cause at all but the origin) of all meaning, that is, of every finality, of the Universe. That every meaning is an *end*, that is, an *eschatology of an imaginary meaning*—what critical depth! I saw in it immediately the matrix of every possible theory of ideology and profited from it, with the difference that I put first (but Spinoza did so, too, in the *Tractatus Theologico-Politicus*) not individual subjectivity alone but, if I can say it, social subjectivity, that of a conflictual human group, that is, of a class and therefore of antagonistic classes, what Spinoza, I must admit, doesn't say in so many words, but which he allows to be understood in his history of the Jewish people.

III

What then became of the famous and obscure, in any case misunderstood if not incomprehensible, "knowledge of the third kind"? Spinoza speaks of the *amor intellectus Dei* and of *beatitudo*, and these are no doubt philosophical effects in the head and body of man; but he didn't give—or so it seemed—any concrete example of this so-called "intuitive" knowledge. Now I found an example that was, in my opinion, perfect (and on this point I believe I am perhaps going to surprise people) in the *TTP* in which Spinoza dealt with history, and very precisely the history of the Jewish people. I considered in fact that with this example Spinoza gives us a "case" of knowledge of the "third kind," that is, of the knowledge of an object that is both singular (a historical individual: a determinate people, without precedent or sequel) and universal (we shall soon see in what sense). Spinoza could have given us other examples to consider, for example, a certain singular individual, Socrates (or his wife) or himself (or his spiders). But how is a singular individual also a universal? One might obviously think immediately of Hegel, of the universality that is truly constituted by a determinate people within universal history and not by a certain singular individual who, outside of the community of these people, cannot, unless he is himself the last philosopher (and it is still his belonging to the final individuality of a historical people that confers on him this privilege), attain concrete universality. Now I thought that Spinoza could consider every singularity, including that which took place in the *Lebenswelt* of the imagination, as universal singular individuality. As a *case*, almost in the sense in which the Wittgenstein of the *Tractatus* writes, "Die Welt ist alles was der Fall ist," an untranslatable sentence but one that more or less means "the world is everything that is the case." What is the "case" if not that which comes to pass, if not purely and simply that which "befalls," as if by accident, that is, without origin or end? That which befalls in existence and in being, in the world constituted by similar "falls," by similar "cases," to infinity. That every case (medical or otherwise) is singular, everyone will admit with no difficulty. But that a singular *case* is at the same time *universal* is what constitutes *both* a problem *and* a scandal! Now this is indeed the challenge to which it was necessary to respond theoretically. I would take a detour in order to confront it: the detour of medicine or, if one prefers, that of analysis, but it can just as well be the detour of a people and its singular history, as Spinoza took, for is there anything as singular as the conjunctural case of a historical people that knew a history and absolutely singular conditions from which one cannot by *abstraction* draw out any universal knowledge? It is here that from very far away, I well understood later, it was necessary to confront the simple-minded theses of Karl Popper, for whom history (and Marxism, which presumes to have knowledge of history) and psychoanalysis are not at all knowledges, for they are not empirically verifiable; that is, they are nonfalsifiable!

    Let us speak, then, of history, since Spinoza personally invites us to do so, and also of psychoanalysis, since Popper summons us. In history and psychoanalysis there are only "*cases*"; each of them will be suitable without difficulty. And how could it be said better than by Marx himself, who wrote that there is never production *in general*, labor *in general*, and so forth, and that every history is always a singular "*case*"—and likewise for analysts: they never encounter "the same case" again, but always and uniquely *singular and, therefore, different "cases."* How, then, to pretend to draw out consequences that are *general*, that is, abstract, since every case is concrete and, as opposed to concrete objects (oak trees, beech trees, plum trees, pear trees, etc., as realizations of the concept "tree"), one can never abstract from individual singularities in order to reach the abstract concept of the thing itself? Worse than that: how can one claim to speak about singularity itself in general if one has no previous knowledge of it, if the fact of singularity is not and can never be a "concept," even its own concept? And Spinoza would himself warn us: he speaks of an *intuitio* in the case of "knowledge of the third kind," just as later doctors will speak of a "chronic intuition"; analysts, of *Einsicht* or *insight* (intuitions); and politics, of the meaning of the conjuncture. How to abstract from whatever singular and therefore not comparable intuitions there are? We see that everything in this objection holds up quite well.

Yet Spinoza ignores this objection, just as Marx and psychoanalysis so blithely take exception to Popper. I would simply say something that seems to respond to Popper's objection and to Spinoza's concern: it is only in the individual and social life of singularities (nominalisms), really singular — but universal, for these singularities are as if traversed and haunted by repetitive or constant invariants, not by generalities but repetitive constants — that one can rediscover under their singular variations in other singularities of the same species and genus. Thus, Spinoza rediscovers quite naturally in the singular history of the Jewish people a *constant* that he has treated "in general" in the appendix of part I regarding religion in general, and yet there never exists religion in general in Spinoza, no more than does production in Marx. He rediscovers generic constants or invariants, as one wishes, which arise in the existence of singular "cases" and which permit their *treatment* (whether theoretical or practical, it hardly matters); generic and not "general" constants and invariants, *constants and not laws*, which obviously do not constitute the object of a will to *verification* in an abstract renewable experimental *dispositif*, as in physics or chemistry, but whose repetitive insistence permits us to mark the form of singularity in presence and, therefore, its treatment. It is obviously a question here of a *test* (*épreuve*), which has nothing to do with experimental proof (*preuve*) in the physical sciences, but which possesses its rigor, whether it be in the knowledge and treatment of individual singularity (medicine, analysis) or social singularity (history of a people) and action over history (politics).

Now this is precisely what I thought I had discovered in the *TTP*, which is a knowledge and elucidation of a singular history: that of a singular people, the Jewish people. And it is not an accident if Spinoza can invest in it as the exemplification of a repetitive constant his theory of religious ideology, his theory of language, his theory of the body, and his theory of the imagination, which I thought to be perhaps the first historical form of a theory of ideology.

For at the foundation, in the "third kind of knowledge," we are never faced with a *new* object but simply a new form of relation of appropriation (the word is Marx's) of an object that is *always already there* since the first kind of knowledge: the "world," the *Lebenswelt* of the first kind, is elevated while remaining the same, a concretion of universal singularities in itself, all the way up to the universe or nature and its substantial cause (God). What changes is never the being itself of things (what is a finite mode if not a universal singularity in its kind?) but the relation of appropriation that the human subject enters into with others. In this sense, which will be taken up again by Hegel and Marx, every process of knowledge indeed proceeds from the abstract to the concrete, from abstract generality to concrete singularity. In my language I had called that very roughly the passage from Generalities I to Generalities III by means of Generalities II; I deceived myself in that the reality aimed at by knowledge (of the third kind) is not that of a generality but of a universal singularity. But I was indeed on Spinoza's "line" by insisting with Marx and Hegel on the distinction between the "real concrete," therefore, the universal singular (all the "cases" that constitute the world from the beginning of knowledge of the first kind), and the concrete-in-thought that constitutes knowledge of the third kind.

The *TTP*, then, held wonders in store for me—the history of this singular people, living under a singular religion, the Torah, the observances, the sacrifices, and the rituals (I was later to rediscover in it what I then called the *materiality of the very existence of ideology*), with a language determined socially and precisely with these incredible prophets, men who climb the mountain at the summons of the Lord but who only understand in the thunder crash and lightning flash some partially comprehensible words. Then they go back down to the plain in order to submit to their brothers, who themselves know the message of God. The prophets have not understood anything that God has said to them: it is explained to them carefully, and then generally they understand the message of God; except that imbecile Daniel who knew how to interpret dreams but who not only understood nothing of the messages received from God (it was, however, the common lot of all) but, what is worse, would never comprehend any of the explanations the people gave him of the messages he had received! I saw in Daniel the prodigious proof of the stubborn resistance of every ideology to its clarification (and that against the naive theory that was to be the Enlightenment's). Later, following Spinoza and Pascal along this theme, I was to insist strongly on the material existence of ideology, not only on its material social *conditions* of existence (its connection with interests blinded by the imagination of a social group), which one finds first in Rousseau and in Marx and in a number of authors, but also on the *materiality* of its very existence. But I was not going to make an exposition on this admirable *TTP*.

What also fascinated me in Spinoza was his philosophical strategy. Jacques Derrida has spoken a lot about strategy in philosophy, and he is perfectly right, since every philosophy is a *dispositif* of theoretical combat that disposes of theses as so many strongholds or prominent places so as to be able, in its aim and strategic attacks, to take over the theoretical places fortified and occupied by the adversary. Yet Spinoza began with God! He began with God, and deep down inside (I believe it, after the entire tradition of his worst enemies) he was (as were da Costa and so many other Portuguese Jews of his time) an atheist. A supreme strategy: he began by taking over the chief stronghold of his adversary, or rather he established himself there as if he were his own adversary, therefore not suspected of being the sworn adversary, and redisposed the theoretical fortress in such a way as to turn it completely around, as one turns around cannons against the fortress's own occupant. This redisposition consisted in the theory of infinite substance identical to God *"causa sui"* (therefore, without exterior) and in the infinite omnipotence of God effecting his existence in the infinite attributes (infinite in number, but we have access only to two of them, thought and extension) and are parallel (that which identifies the *ordo rerum* and the *ordo idearum* — the order of things and the order of ideas — with one and the same *connexio*), being effected themselves into infinite modes and these finite modes into an infinity of finite modes. An infinite substance (God) that cannot even be called *unique*, for it has nothing else to compare with it in order to distinguish from it and to call it unique (Stanislaus Breton), therefore, without exterior, being effected in itself without ever leaving itself, therefore, without this other classical exteriority (in the illusion of creation) that is the world or universe. Generally this is not the way that philosophers proceed: they always oppose from a certain *exterior* the forces of their theses, which are destined to take over the domain protected and defended by previous theses, which already occupy the terrain. Militarily speaking, this revolutionary philosophical strategy recalls more than anything else the theory of the urban guerrilla and the encirclement of cities by the countryside dear to Mao or certain forms of politico-military strategy of Machiavelli (his theory of fortresses in particular). I was fascinated by this unparalleled audacity, which came to me as the idea of the *extreme* essence of every philosophical strategy, its acknowledged *limit*-essence, the one that could never be surpassed. Thus it reminded me of the thought of a Machiavelli, who always thinks "in extremes," "at the limits." And no doubt this strategy comforted me in my personal philosophical and political strategy: to take over the Party from inside its own positions . . . but what pretensions!

Yet I was not through with Spinoza. Not only had he rejected every theory of original foundation of every meaning and every truth (the *cogito*) always functioning as a guarantee of every established order, be it scientific, moral, or in the last resort *social* (mediated through other elements guaranteed by Truth), but he was a *nominalist*! I had read in Marx that nominalism is the "royal road" to materialism. To tell the truth, I really believe that nominalism is not the royal road to materialism but *the only conceivable materialism in the world*. How did Spinoza proceed? Without ever sketching a transcendental genesis of meaning, truth, or the conditions of possibilities of every truth, of whatever meaning and truth there might be, he established himself within the factuality of a simple claim: "We have a true idea," "We hold a norm of truth," not by virtue of a foundation lost in the beginnings, but because it is a fact that Euclid, thank God—God knows why—has existed as a factual universal singularity, and [that there is not] *even* a question, as Husserl will want to "reactivate the original meaning," [that] it suffices to think within the factual result of Spinoza's thought, within its crude result, in order to dispose of the power of thinking. This *factual nominalism* was rediscovered—and with what genius!—in the famous distinction, internal to every concept, between the *ideatum* and the *idea*, between the thing and its concept, between the dog that barks and the concept of the dog, which does not bark, between the circle that is round and the idea of the circle, which is not round, and so on. Thereby was opened and justified (always in fact) the distinction between inadequate knowledge of the first kind, that is, the passage, in the interplay and the space, of this crucial distinction, and a more and more adequate knowledge, up to "knowledge of the third kind," that is, the passage from the imagination-world to the world of the concept of this imaginary inadequation, up to the intuition of the universal singularities that exist from the beginning in every finite mode, but are then caught up and misrecognized in the imagination.

Should I add an extraordinary theory? Yes, that of the body, based on the famous parallelism of attributes. This body (our material organic body) of which we don't know "all the powers," but of which we know that it is animated by the essential power of the *conatus*, which is rediscovered in the *conatus* of the state of what corresponds to the *mens* (an untranslatable word: *mens* is neither the soul nor the mind but instead the power, the *fortitudo*, the *virtus* of thinking). Now this body—Spinoza thinks of it as *potentia* or *virtus*, that is, not only as *fortitudo*, but also as [*generositas*], that is, *élan*, opening to the world, free gift. I was to rediscover it later as the astonishing anticipation of the Freudian libido (less, to tell the truth, as the crucial sexual connotation), just as I found in Spinoza an astonishing theory of ambivalence, since—to give a single example—*fear is the same thing as hope, its direct opposite*, and they are both "sad passions," passions of slavery under the imagination, therefore, a kind of "death instinct," apt to destroy the joyous *élan* in all life and expansion of the *conatus* that unites the vital effort, that seals the effective unity of the *mens* and the body brought together as are "lips and teeth."

One can imagine how wonderful this theory of the body seemed to me. In it I rediscovered, in fact, my own vital experience, in the beginning a slave of a fear and a hope that were excessive, but that were liberated in the recomposition and appropriation of their forces during my grandfather's exercise of social labors and later in a prisoner-of-war camp.[1] That one can thus liberate and recompose one's own body, formerly fragmented and dead in the servitude of an imaginary and, there-fore, slavelike subjectivity, and take from this the means to think liberation freely and strongly, therefore, to think properly with one's own body, in own's own body, by one's own body, better: that *to live freely within the thought of the* conatus *of one's own body was quite simply to think within the freedom and the power of thought* — all that dazzled me as the incontestable saying of an unavoidable experience and reality I had lived, which had never become my own. It is so true, as Hegel said, that one re-ally only knows what one recognizes either to be *false* (knowledge of the illusion of the imaginary) or to be *true* (intuitive knowledge of one's *virtus*, knowledge of the third kind).

In this fantastic philosophy of the necessity of the factual stripped of every transcendent guarantee (God) or transcendental guarantee (the "I think"), I rediscovered one of my old formulas. I thought, then, using a metaphor — for what it was worth — that an idealist philosopher is like a man who knows in advance *both* where the train he is climbing onto is coming from *and* where it is going: what is its station of departure and its station of destination (or again, as for a letter, its final destination). The materialist, on the contrary, is a man who takes the train *in motion* (the course of the world, the course of history, the course of life) but without know-ing where the train is coming from or where it is going. He climbs onto a train of chance, of encounter, and discovers in it the *factual* installations of the coach and of whatever companions he is *factually* surrounded with, of whatever the conversations and ideas of these companions and of whatever language marked by their social mi-lieu (as the prophets of the Bible) they speak. All that was for me, or rather became little by little, as if inscribed in filigree in Spinoza's thought. It is then that I loved to quote Dietzgen, speaking of philosophy as the "Holzweg der Holzwege," antici-pating Heidegger, who no doubt knew this formula (which I owe to Lenin for hav-ing discovered, then to the beautiful translation by Jean-Pierre Osier), "the path of the paths that lead nowhere." I have known since that Hegel had previously forged the prodigious image of a "*path that proceeds all alone*," opening its own way to the extent of its own advancement in the woods and fields. What "encounters"!

It is assuredly through the encounter with Machiavelli that I was to experience the fascination of fascinations. But this occurred much later. One will not be astonished that once again I anticipate in my associations, for I am not inter-ested at all in the chronological sequence of anecdotes of a life, which interest no one — not even me — but in the repeated insistence of certain affects, whether they be psychic or theoretical or political, which are truly grasped and experienced only after the fact and whose order of appearance matters little, since most of the time it is a *subsequent affect* that not only gives meaning to a previous affect, but even reveals it to consciousness and to memory. I would never have finished meditating on this word of Freud's: "*an affect is always in the past.*" One may wish, therefore, indeed to follow me in this new retrospective anticipation.

IV

I discovered Machiavelli for the first time in August 1964, at Bertinoro, in an extraordinary old and large house on a hill dominating the whole plain of Emelia. Franca lived there, and I had known her for hardly a week. A woman of dazzling Sicilian beauty, black-haired (in Sicily it is called "mora"), who had been introduced to me by her sister-in-law Giovanna, the companion of Crémonini, the great painter, who was one of my old friends. Franca had a splendid body, a face of extreme mobility, and above all she displayed a freedom as a woman I had never known — and in Italy! She introduced me to her country, and our intense loves were sometimes dramatic (but of my doing rather than hers). In short, I was dazzled by her, by her love, by the country, the marvel of its hills and towns. I became an Italian, easily as always, and we often went down to Cesena, a large town on the plain at the foot of the hills. One day she taught me that Cesena was the little town from which César Borgia had left for his great adventure. I began to read a little Gramsci (on the intellectuals) but quickly interrupted my reading in order to engage myself in reading Machiavelli.

Ever since I have tried to read Machiavelli, to understand him, I have ceaselessly returned to him. I had several courses on him at the Ecole Normale. He is, without doubt, much more than Marx, the author who has most fascinated me. I do not intend here to give a talk on Machiavelli, about whom perhaps I should speak thoroughly one day, but I would like to indicate why he seems to have fascinated me. In addition I am told that there are even today, after Lefort's great book,[2] a good dozen theses being completed on him! What a success.

I came to Machiavelli by means of a word, ceaselessly repeated, of Marx's, saying that capitalism was born from the "*encounter between the man with money and free laborers*," free, that is, stripped of everything, of their means of labor, of their abodes and their families, in the great expropriation of the English countrysides (this was his preferred example). *Encounter.* Again a "*casus,*" a "case," a factual accident without origin, cause, or end. I would rediscover the same formula in Machiavelli when he speaks of the "encounter" between the good occasion (*fortuna*, or good conjuncture) and the man of *virtù*, that is, a man having enough intelligence (intuition) to comprehend that the good occasion presents itself, and above all having enough energy (*virtù*) or excess vigorously to exploit it for the benefit of his vital project. What is most astonishing in Machiavelli, in the theory that he made of this new prince before founding a new principality, is that this new man is a man *of nothing, without past, without titles or burdens*, an anonymous man, alone and naked (that is, in fact free, without determination — again the solitude, first of Machiavelli, next of his prince — that bears down on him and could impede the free exercise of his *virtù*). Not only is he like a naked man, but he finds himself intervening in one place as anonymous and as stripped of every outstanding social and political determination, which could impede his action. Whence the privileged example of César Borgia. Of course he was the son of a pope, but one who did not love him and, in order to extricate himself from him, bequeathed to him a plot of land in Romagne, really in Cesena — a part of the papal estates. Yet, one knows, Machiavelli sufficiently insisted on it: the church estates were absolutely not governed, without any political structure, governed only and still, he says, by religion, in any case not by the pope, nor by any serious politician: it was the total political void, another nakedness, in short an empty space without genuine structure able to obstruct the exercise of *virtù* of the future new prince (Hobbes will say: freedom is an empty space without obstacle). It is from this encounter of a man of nothing and naked (that is, free in his internal and external movements) and of an empty space (that is, without obstacle to oppose César's *virtù*) that his fortune and success arise. César knew how to recognize in this encounter the occasion of a fortune he knew how to seize, as one seizes "a woman by the hair" (Machiavelli). In this void he knew how to build structures, and he constructed for himself a kingdom that grew and, for Machiavelli, would have created Italian national unity if César had not fallen ill with fever in the pestilential marshes of Ravenna, and he found himself absent from Rome, where another decisive "occasion" would occur, at the time of the pope's death. This bad fortune (the fever) prevented him from seizing the distant good fortune (Rome where the pope died), and his destiny was sealed. César will vanish from the history that he was going to forge, and this exceptional man, but from now on deprived of "fortune," was left to die in an obscure Spanish place with the anonymity of a simple soldier one last time deserted by fortune (because of a bullet or an arrow). Anonymity again: at the beginning and the end.

But how to guide one's *virtù* in order to produce a real continuation of fortune, that is, to maintain *in a lasting way* (Machiavelli's problem: "a principality which *lasts*") a favorable conjuncture well beyond the moment when the "feminine" fantasy of fortune is offered to her conqueror? This is the whole problem of the prince as head of a state. I do not want to enter here into detail, where a number of specialists are more competent than I. I only want to note what follows.

We know that Machiavelli, taking up again the classical image of the half-beast, half-man centaur, says that the prince must be such a being: half-beast through the violent force of which he must be capable (the lion) and half-man through the human morality with which he must be stamped. But it is too often overlooked that *the beast is divided in Machiavelli*, who by this fact completely abandons the metaphor of the centaur to forge an entirely different one. In fact, the beast is divided into a lion and a fox.

What is the fox? The ruse, one might think. But this is too simple. In fact, it appears that the fox is indeed in reality something like a third instance that governs the other two. In other words, it is the fox's instinct (a kind of half-conscious, half-unconscious intuition) that indicates to the prince what attitude he must adopt in such and such a conjuncture in order to rally to himself the people's assent. Sometimes to be moral, that is, clothed with virtues (in the moral sense, which has nothing to do with *virtù*, this *virtus* whose concept Spinoza obviously borrows from Machiavelli and which is *potentia*), and sometimes to be violent, that is, to make use of force. Or rather, and this point is decisive, *to know how sometimes to be moral and sometimes to be violent.* Or rather, for this point is even more decisive, to know how *to appear* to be moral or to know how *to appear* to be violent, in all the cases that he is one or the other or the one and the other, to know how to *appear* to be it at the decisive moment in order to win for oneself the continuation of fortune, to render fortune *lasting*.

It is here that this quiet instinct of the fox intervenes. It is that, in the last resort, which inspires in the prince the appearance of such and such conduct, that of the virtuous man or that of the violent man. This instinct is in fact the *instinctive* intuition of the conjuncture and of possible fortune to be seized: a new "encounter," but this time controlled and prepared as in advance.

Thereby the prince constitutes for himself a kind of *lasting image*. Machiavelli says that the prince must be neither loved nor hated but only feared, that is, always at the correct *distance*, which at the same time maintains him above the people and great men and their perpetual antagonism, above and beyond the immediate reaction that such and such of his regular initiatives can arouse (those which, contrary to his image, *do not last*), and definitely *at a distance from himself, from his own desires, drives, and impulses, and therefore*, in the language of the time, from his passions. His image forces him to some extent to remain always faithful to this image of himself, therefore, to restrain his own "passions" for him to conform to them *in a lasting way*, for without it he could not render fortune and therefore the friendship of his peoples *lasting*. For Machiavelli indeed wants, too, to call the people's fear a kind of friendship—but never love—for the prince.

If he provokes hate or love, the prince appears to be submitted to the passions he can no longer control either in himself or in the people, passions without internal limitation. Thus, Savonarola's demagogy of love has unleashed in the people a true passion of love, which has entailed horrible struggles in the people and finally—the so-called prince not being able to control them—his own execution. Thus, such people's *hate* for its tyrant and his continual violences always ends by throwing the people either into the nothingness of stunned silence (see later Montesquieu: the silence of despotism) or into the insurrectional revolt of riots, which lead inevitably to the death of the tyrant and to the loss of his regime.

Thus, there exists an extremely profound connection between the "passions" of the prince and the "passions" of the people. If the prince doesn't control his passions, he cannot control the passions of the people—worse, he unleashes them and winds up being their first victim, and his state perishes with him. Everything happens, then, as if the absolute condition of the reign that *lasts*, of fortune governed by the prince in order that it *last* in his favor, proceeded by means of this fundamental *distance* through which, even if its being inside of him makes everything different, the prince must *know how to appear to be*, conforming to his lasting image: a head of state who maintains his subjects at a distance from himself, maintains them at the same time at a distance from their mortal passions, whether it be love or hate (what a beautiful ambivalence!).

Certainly, Machiavelli is completely silent on the internal nature of the fox, unless one of his texts has escaped me on this point. He thinks of the fox not in terms of its internal nature as "*cause*" but only in its *effects* of semblance. To think that certain people harp on the "theater" of politics as if its reality and its discovery were new things!

Having presupposed that this man exists, the prince must assume in his own behalf "*the emptiness of a distance taken*" (which is how I provisionally defined philosophy in *Lenin and Philosophy*). The question is whether or not the prince is capable of doing so, but Machiavelli is equally silent on this point, that is, on the appropriate means to produce this distance, which is the mastery in the prince of his own passions, and the distance with respect to every passion—we would say today of every *transference* and especially *countertransference* (for the countertransference not to be harmful, it must, while neutralizing it, anticipate the transference, in this case, of the people's passional reactions). But perhaps here I could turn back to Spinoza, for he is not at all silent on this question.

One knows, in fact, that for Spinoza, in the Cartesian tradition of the *Treatise on the Passions of the Soul* (but in an entirely different sense), it is a question of giving to man the mastery of his passions, of passing from the domination (of the imagination) of "sad passions" over "joyous passions" to the contrary domination of "joyous passions" over "sad passions" and through this *displacement* of guiding man to freedom. The current interpretation, resting on certain of Spinoza's formulas isolated from their meaning, believes that this mastery of the passions is the effect of an "emendation of the intellect," that is, of a simple intellectual knowledge. This is the position of the philosophy of the Enlightment, which saw in knowledge and its public diffusion the solution to all personal and social contradictions, including the dissipation of all ideological illusions. But Spinoza does not at all share this opinion. And the root of the mistake in this interpretation can be found very precisely in the total neglect of the *mens* in Spinoza. We have seen that the soul (the *mens*, the activity of the mind) is in no way separate from the activity of the organic body; that, quite the contrary, the soul only thinks to the extent that it is affected by the impressions and movements of the body, that therefore it thinks only with the body but *in it*, consubstantially united with it before any separation, since this union, which is never a problem, contrary to what happens in Descartes, is based in the infinity of attributes of substance and their strict parallelism. The mastery of the passions in Spinoza, far from being able to be interpreted as an "intellectual" liberation of the negative efficacy of the passions, on the contrary consists in their subsumption united with the internal *displacement* of the "sad passions" into "joyous passions." Just as later in Freud no fantasy ever disappears but—and this is the effect of the cure—*is displaced from a dominant position into a subordinate position*, so too in Spinoza no passion ever disappears but is displaced from a position of "sadness" into a position of "joy." The *amor intellectus Dei* is in no way an "intellectual" love; it is the love of the entire individual, which is a finite mode of infinite substance—a love of the body substantially united (from the moment of constitutive substance, that is, God) with the love of the *mens*, and bringing about in the movements of the *mens* the very movements of the body, those of the fundamental *conatus*: "The more power the body has, the more freedom the mind has" (Spinoza). It is here that one could bring together Spinoza with Freud: for this *conatus*, torn between sadness and joy, what is it therefore by anticipation if not the libido torn between the instincts of death and life, between the sadness of Thanatos and the joy of Eros?

So it is that I laboriously advanced, across my own fantasies, across Spinoza and Machiavelli, toward Freud and Marx, whom I had never dissociated from my preoccupations. And so each follows his own path, and it would be interesting to compare our respective paths. But will it ever be possible? In any case, for my account, my cards are on the table. Make of them what you will. But I owe it to my friends and others to help them understand what has befallen me—both success, perhaps, and drama, surely.

Translated by Ted Stolze

Notes

1. Althusser (1992).
2. Lefort (1972).

T W O

Spinoza and the Three "Ethics"

Gilles Deleuze

"I'm not going to dance about like some sort of Spinoza"
—Chekhov, "The Wedding"[1]

ON A first reading, the *Ethics* can appear to be a long, continuous movement that goes in an almost straight line, with an incomparable power and serenity, passing and passing again through definitions, axioms, postulates, propositions, demonstrations, corollaries, and scholia, carrying everything along in its grandiose wake. It is like a river that sometimes spreads out and sometimes branches into a thousand streams, sometimes speeding up and sometimes slowing down, but always maintaining its radical unity. And Spinoza's Latin, so scholarly in appearance, seems to constitute the ageless ship that follows the eternal river. But as emotions invade the reader, or after a second reading, these two impressions prove to be erroneous. This book, one of the greatest in the world, is not what it first seems: it is not homogeneous, rectilinear, continuous, serene, navigable, a pure language without style.

The *Ethics* sets forth three elements, which are not only contents but forms of expression: signs or affects; notions or concepts; essences or percepts. They correspond to the three kinds of knowledge, which are also modes of existence and expression.

A sign, according to Spinoza, can have several meanings, but it
is always an *effect*. An effect is first of all the trace of one body upon another, the
state of a body insofar as it suffers the action of another body. It is an *affectio*, for example, the effect of the sun on our body, which "indicates" the nature of the affected
body and only "envelops" the nature of the affecting body. We know our affections
through the ideas we have, sensations or perceptions, sensations of heat and color,
the perception of form and distance (the sun is above us, it is a golden disk, it is two
hundred feet away...). We will call them, out of convenience, *scalar* signs, since
they express our state at a moment in time and are thus distinguished from another
type of sign. This is because our present state is always a slice of our duration (*durée*),
and as such determines an increase or decrease, an expansion or restriction of our
existence in duration in relation to the preceding state, however close it may be. It
is not that we compare the two states in a reflective operation, but that each state of
affection determines a passage to a "more" or a "less": the heat of the sun fills me
or, on the contrary, its burning repulses me. Affection is therefore not only the in-
stantaneous effect of a body upon my own, but also has an effect on my own duration, a pleasure or pain, a joy or sadness. These are passages, becomings, rises and
falls, continuous variations of power (*puissance*) that pass from one state to another.
We will call them *affects*, properly speaking, and no longer affections. They are signs
of increase and decrease, signs that are *vectorial* (of the joy-sadness type) and no longer
scalar like the affections, sensations, or perceptions.

   In fact, there is an even greater number of types of signs. The
scalar signs have four principal types. The first, which are sensory or perceptive physical effects that merely envelop the nature of their cause, are essentially *indicative*,
and indicate our own nature rather than something else. In a second case, our nature, being finite, simply retains some selected character from what affects it (man
as a vertical animal, or a reasonable animal, or an animal that laughs). These are *abstractive* signs. In the third case, the sign always being an effect, we take the effect
for an end, or the idea of the effect for the cause (since the sun heats, we believe
that it was made "in order to" warm us; since the fruit tastes bitter, Adam believes
that it "should not" be eaten). These are moral effects or *imperative* signs: Do not
eat this fruit! Get out in the sun! The last of the scalar signs, finally, are imaginary
effects: our sensations and perceptions make us conceive of suprasensible beings
who would be their final cause, and conversely we imagine these beings in the inor-
dinately enlarged image of what affects us (God as an infinite sun, or as a Prince or
Legislator). These are *hermeneutic or interpretive* signs. The prophets, who are the
greatest specialists in signs, marvelously combine the abstractive, imperative, and in-

terpretive signs. In this regard, a famous chapter of the *Tractatus Theologico-Politicus* joins together the power of the comic with the depth of its analysis. There are thus four scalar signs of affection, which could be called sensible indices, logical icons, moral symbols, metaphysical idols.

There are in addition two kinds of vectorial signs of affect, depending on whether the vector is one of increase or decrease, growth or decline, joy or sadness. These two sorts of signs could be called augmentative powers (*puissances*) and diminutive servitudes. We could also add to these a third sort: ambiguous or fluctuating signs, when an affection increases or diminishes our power at the same time, or affects us with joy and sadness at the same time. There are thus six signs, or seven, which ceaselessly combine with each other. In particular, the scalars are necessarily combined with the vectorials. Affects always presuppose the affections from which they are derived, although they cannot be reduced to them.

The common characteristics of all these signs are associability, variability, and equivocality or analogy. The affections vary according to the chains of association between bodies (the sun hardens clay and softens wax, the horse is not the same for the warrior and for the peasant). The moral effects themselves vary according to peoples, and the prophets each have personal signs that appeal to their imaginations. As for interpretations, they are fundamentally equivocal depending on the variable association that is made between a given and something that is not given. It is an equivocal or analogical language that ascribes to God an infinite intellect and will, in an enlarged image of our own intellect and our own will: this is an equivocity similar to the one found between the dog as a barking animal and the Dog as a celestial constellation. If signs, like words, are conventional, it is precisely because they act on natural signs and simply classify their variability and equivocity: conventional signs are Abstractions that fix a relative constant for variable chains of association. The conventional-natural distinction is therefore not determinative for signs, any more than is the distinction between the social State and the state of nature; even vectorial signs can depend on conventions, as rewards (augmentation) and punishments (diminution). Vectorial signs in general, that is, affects, enter into variable associations as much as do affections: what is growth for one part of the body can be a diminution for another part, what is servitude for one part is power for another, and a rise can be followed by a fall and conversely.

Signs *do not have objects as their direct referent*. They are states of bodies (affections) and variations of power (affects), each of which refer to the other. Signs refer to signs. They have as their referent confused mixtures of bodies and obscure variations of power, following an order which is that of Chance or the fortuitous encounter between bodies. Signs are effects: the effect of one body upon another in space, or affection; the effect of an affection on a duration, or affect. Like the Stoics, Spinoza breaks causality into two distinct chains: effects among themselves, on the condition of in turn grasping causes among themselves. Effects refer to effects as signs to signs: consequences separated from their premises. We must also understand "effect" optically and not merely causally. Effects or signs are *shadows* that play on the surface of bodies, always between two bodies. The shadow is always on the border. It is always a body that casts a shadow on another. We know bodies only through the shadow they cast upon us, and it is through our own shadow that we know ourselves, ourselves and our bodies. Signs are *effects of light* in a space filled with things colliding into each other at random. If Spinoza differs essentially from Leibniz, it is because the latter, close to a Baroque inspiration, saw the Dark ("fuscum subnigrum") as a matrix or premise, out of which chiaroscuro, colors, and even light will emerge. In Spinoza, on the contrary, everything is light, and the Dark is only a shadow, a simple effect of light, a limit of light on the bodies that reflect it (affection) or absorb it (affect). Spinoza is closer to Byzantium than to the Baroque. In place of a light that emerges by degrees from the shadow through the accumulation of red, we instead have a light that creates degrees of blue shadow. Chiaroscuro is itself an effect of the brightening or darkening of the shadow: it is the variations of power or vectorial signs that constitute degrees of chiaroscuro, the augmentation of power being a brightening, the diminution of power, a darkening.

If we consider the second aspect of the *Ethics*, we see a determining opposition to signs emerge: *common notions are concepts of objects*, and objects are causes. Light is no longer reflected or absorbed by bodies that produce shadows; it makes bodies transparent by revealing their intimate "structure" (*fabrica*). This is the second aspect of light, and the intellect is the true apprehension of the structures of the body, whereas the imagination merely grasped the shadow of one body upon another. Here again it is a question of optics, but it is now an optical geometry. The structure is geometrical and consists of solid lines, but they are constantly being formed and deformed, acting as cause. What constitutes the structure is a composite relation of movement and rest, of speed and slowness, which is established between the infinitely small parts of a transparent body. Since the parts always come in larger or smaller infinities, there is in each body an infinity of relations that compose and decompose themselves, in such a way that the body in turn enters into a more vast body under a new composite relation or, on the contrary, makes smaller bodies come out from under their composite relations. Modes are geometric but fluid structures that are transformed and deformed in the light at variable speeds. Structure is rhythm, that is, the linking of figures that compose and decompose their relations. It causes disagreements between bodies when the relations decompose, and agreements when the relations compose a new body. But the structure moves in both directions simultaneously. Chyle and lymph are two bodies determined by two relations that constitute blood under a composite relation, although a poison may decompose the blood. If I learn to swim or dance, my movements and pauses, my speeds and slownesses, must take on a rhythm common to that of the sea or my partner, following a more or less durable adjustment. The structure always has several bodies in common, and refers to a concept of the object, that is, to a common notion. *The structure or object is formed by at least two bodies*, each of which in turn are formed by two or more bodies, to infinity, while in the other direction they are united into ever larger and more composite bodies, until one reaches the unique object of Nature in its entirety, an infinitely transformable and deformable structure, universal rhythm, *Facies totius Naturae*, infinite mode. Common notions are universals, but they are "more or less" so depending on whether they form the concept of at least two bodies, or that of all possible bodies (to be in space, to be in movement and at rest...).

Understood in this way, modes are projections. Or rather, the variations of an object are projections that *envelop* a relation of movement and rest as their invariant (involution). And since each relation involves all the others to infinity, following an order that varies with each case, this order is the profile or projection that in each case envelops the face of Nature in its entirety, or the relation of all relations.[2]

Modes, as projections of light, are also colors, *coloring causes*. Colors enter into relations of complementarity and contrast, which means that each of them, at the limit, reconstitutes the whole, and that they all merge together in whiteness (infinite mode) following an order of composition, or stand out from it in the order of decomposition. What Goethe said about whiteness must be said of every color: it is the opacity characteristic of pure transparency.[3] The solid and rectilinear structure is necessarily colored in, because it is the opacity that reveals itself when light renders the body transparent. In this way, a difference in kind is established *between color and shadow, between the coloring cause and the effect of shadow*: the first adequately "delimits" the light, while the second abolishes it in the inadequate. Vermeer is said to have replaced chiaroscuro by the complementarity and contrast of colors. It is not that the shadow disappears, but it remains as an effect that can be isolated from its cause, a separated consequence, an extrinsic sign distinct from colors and their relations.[4] In Vermeer, one sees the shadow detach itself and move forward, so as to frame or border the luminous background from which it origi-nates (*The Maidservant Pouring Milk, The Young Lady with a Pearl Necklace, The Love Letter*). This is the way in which Vermeer opposed himself to the tradition of chia-roscuro, and in all these respects Spinoza remains infinitely closer to Vermeer than to Rembrandt.

The distinction between signs and concepts thus seems irre-ducible and insurmountable, much as in Aeschylus: "He is going to express himself, no longer in a mute language, nor through the smoke of a fire burning on a peak, but in clear terms."[5] Signs or affects are inadequate ideas and passions; common notions or concepts are adequate ideas from which true actions ensue. If one refers to the cleavage in causality, signs refer to signs as effects refer to effects, following an *associative chain* that depends on the order of the simple chance encounter between physical bodies. But insofar as concepts refer to concepts, or causes to causes, they follow what must be called an *automatic chain*, determined by the necessary order of relations or proportions, and by the determinate succession of their transforma-tions and deformations. Contrary to our initial thesis, it therefore seems that signs or affects are not and cannot be a positive element in the *Ethics*, and even less a form of expression. The kind of knowledge they constitute is hardly a knowledge but rather an experience in which one randomly encounters the confused ideas of bodily mixtures, brute imperatives to avoid this mixture and seek another, and more or less delirious interpretations of these situations. Rather than a form of expres-sion, it is a material and affective language, one that resembles cries rather than the discourse of the concept. It seems then that if signs-affects intervene in the *Ethics*, it is only to be severely criticized, denounced, and sent back to their night, out of which light either reappears or in which it perishes.

This cannot, however, be the case. Book II of the *Ethics* sets out the common notions by beginning with "the most universal" (those which agree with all bodies). It presumes that concepts are already given; hence the impression that they owe nothing to signs. But when one asks *how* we manage to form a con-cept, or how we rise from effects to causes, it is clear that at least certain signs must serve as a springboard for us, and that certain affects must give us the necessary vi-tality (book V). Out of the random encounter of bodies, we can select the idea of those bodies that agree with our own and give us joy, that is, that increase our power. And it is only when our power has sufficiently increased, to a point that un-doubtedly varies with each case, that we come into possession of this power and be-come capable of forming a concept, beginning with the least universal (the agreement of our body with *one* other), even if we subsequently attain ever larger concepts following the order of the composition of relations. There is thus a *selection* of the passional affects, and of the ideas on which they depend, which must release joys, vectorial signs of the augmentation of power, and ward off sadnesses, signs of diminution. This selection of the affects is the very condition for leaving the first kind of knowledge and for attaining the concept through the acquisition of a sufficient power. The signs of augmentation remain passions and the ideas that they presuppose remain inadequate, yet they are the precursors of the notions, the dark precursors. Furthermore, even when we have attained common notions, as well as the actions that follow from them as active affects of a new type, the inadequate ideas and passional affects (i.e., signs) will not disappear entirely, nor even the inevitable sadnesses. They will subsist, they will double the notions, but will lose their exclusive or tyrannical character to the profit of notions and actions. There is thus something in signs that at the same time prepares for and doubles the concepts. The rays of light are both prepared for and accompanied by these processes that continue to operate in the shadows. *Values of chiaroscuro are reintroduced* in Spinoza, because joy as a passion is a sign of brightening that leads us to the light of the notions. And the *Ethics* cannot dispense with this passional form of expression that works through signs, for it alone is capable of bringing about the indispensible selection without which we would remain condemned to the first kind.

This selection is extremely hard, extremely difficult. The joys and sadnesses, increases and decreases, brightenings and darkenings are often ambiguous, partial, changing, intermixed with each other. And above all, there are those who can only establish their Power (*Pouvoir*) on sadness and affliction, on the diminution of the power of others, on the darkening of the world. They act as if sadness were a promise of joy, and already a joy in itself. They institute the cult of sadness, of servitude or impotence, of death. They never cease to emit and impose signs of sadness, which they present as ideals and joys to the souls they have made ill. Hence the infernal couple, the Despot and the Priest, terrible "judges" of life. The selection of signs or affects as the primary condition for the birth of the concept does not merely imply the personal effort each person must make on their own behalf (Reason), but a passional struggle, an inexpiable affective combat one risks dying from, in which signs confront signs and affects clash with affects in order that a little joy might be saved that could make us leave the shadow and change kind. The cries of the language of signs are the mark of this battle of the passions, of joys and sadnesses, of increases and decreases of power.

The *Ethics*, or at least most of the *Ethics*, is written in common notions, beginning with the most general and ceaselessly developing their consequences. It presupposes that the common notions are already acquired or given. The *Ethics* is the discourse of the concept. It is a discursive and a deductive system, which is why it can appear to be a long, tranquil, and powerful river. The definitions, axioms, postulates, propositions, demonstrations, and corollaries form a grandiose course. And when one or the other of these elements deals with inadequate ideas or passions, it does so in order to denounce their insufficiency, to repress them as far as possible like so many sediments on the riverbanks. But there is another element that only ostensibly has the same nature as the preceding ones. These are the "scholia," which are nonetheless inserted into the demonstrative chain, even though the reader quickly realizes that they have a completely different tone. They have another style, almost another language. They operate in the shadows, trying to distinguish between what prevents us from reaching common notions and what, on the contrary, allows us to do so, what diminishes and what augments our power, the sad signs of our servitude and the joyous signs of our liberations. They denounce the personae that lie behind our diminutions of power, those that have an interest in maintaining and propagating sadness, the despot and the priest. They herald the sign or condition of the new man, one who has sufficiently augmented his power in order to form concepts and convert his affects into actions.

The scholia are ostensive and polemical. If it is true that the scholia most often refer to other scholia, we can see that in themselves they constitute a specific chain, distinct from that of the demonstrative and discursive elements. Conversely, the demonstrations do not refer to the scholia, but to other demonstrations, definitions, axioms, and postulates. If the scholia are inserted into the demonstrative chain, it is therefore less because they form a part of it than because they intersect and reintersect with it, by virtue of their own nature. It is like a broken chain, discontinuous, subterranean, volcanic, which at irregular intervals comes to interrupt the chain of demonstrative elements, the great and continuous fluvial chain. Each scholium is like a lighthouse that exchanges its signals with the others, at a distance and across the flow of the demonstrations. It is like a language of fire that is distinguishable from the language of the waters. It is undoubtedly the same Latin in appearance, but one could almost believe that the Latin of the scholia is translated from the Hebrew. On their own, the scholia form a book of Anger and Laughter, as if it were Spinoza's anti-Bible. It is the book of Signs, which never ceases to accompany the more visible *Ethics*, the book of the Concept, and which only emerges for its own sake at explosive points. Nonetheless, it is a perfectly positive element and an autonomous form of expression in the composition of the double *Ethics*. The two books, the two *Ethics*, coexist, the one developing the free notions conquered in the light of transparencies, while the other, at the most profound level of the obscure mixture of bodies, carries on the combat between servitudes and liberations. At least two *Ethics*, which have one and the same meaning but not the same language, like two versions of the language of God.

Robert Sasso accepts the principle of a difference in kind between the chain of scholia and the demonstrative linkages. But he notes that there is no reason to consider the demonstrative linkage itself as a homogeneous flow, continuous and rectilinear, whose progress would be sheltered from turbulences and accidents. This is not only because the scholia, by interrupting the course of the demonstrations, happen to break its flow at various points. It is the concept in itself, says Sasso, that passes through extremely variable moments: definitions, axioms, postulates, demonstrations that are sometimes slower, sometimes more rapid.[6] And certainly Sasso is correct. One can discern *stations, arms, elbows, loops*, speedings up and slowings down, and so on. The prefaces and appendices, which mark the beginning and end of the great parts, are like the stations along the river where the ship takes on new passengers and drops off old ones; they often mark the juncture between the demonstrations and the scholia. Arms appear when a single proposition can be demonstrated in several ways. And elbows appear when the flow changes direction: a single substance is posited for all the attributes by means of an elbow, whereas upstream each attribute could have one and only one substance. In the same way, an elbow introduces the physics of bodies. The corollaries, for their part, constitute derivations that loop back onto the demonstrated proposition. Finally, the series of demonstrations attests to relative speeds and slownesses, depending on whether the river widens or narrows its course: for example, Spinoza will always maintain that one cannot begin with God, with the idea of God, but that one must reach it *as quickly as possible*. One could identify many other demonstrative figures. Yet whatever their variety, there is a single river that persists throughout all its states, and forms the *Ethics* of the concept or of the second kind of knowledge. This is why we believe that the difference between the scholia and the other elements is more important, because in the final analysis it is what accounts for the differences between the demonstrative elements. The river would not have so many adventures without the subterranean action of the scholia. It is they that give emphasis to the demonstrations, and ensure the turnings. The entire *Ethics* of the concept, in all its variety, has need of an *Ethics* of signs in their specificity. The variety in the course of the demonstrations does not correspond term by term to the jolts and pressures of the scholia, and yet it presupposes and envelops them.

But perhaps there is yet a third *Ethics*, represented by book V, incarnated in book V, or at least in the greater part of book V. Unlike the other two, which coexist throughout the entire course, it occupies a precise place, the final one. Nonetheless it was there from the start as a focus, the focal point that was already at work before it appeared. Book V must be conceived as coextensive with all the others; we have the impression of arriving at it, but it was there all the time, for all time. It is the third element of Spinoza's logic: no longer signs or affects, or concepts, but Essences or Singularities, Percepts. It is the third state of light: no longer signs of shadow or of light as color, but light in itself and for itself. The common notions (concepts) are revealed by the light that traverses bodies and makes them transparent; they therefore refer to geometrical structures or figures (*fabrica*), which are all the more alive in that they are transformable and deformable in a projective space, subordinated to the exigencies of a projective geometry like that of Desargues. But essences have a completely different nature: *pure figures of light* produced by a substantial Luminosity (and no longer geometrical figures revealed by light).[7] It has often been noted that Platonic and even Cartesian ideas remained "tactilo-optical": it fell to Plotinus in relation to Plato, and to Spinoza in relation to Descartes, to rise to a purely optical world. The common notions, insofar as they concern relations of projection, are already optical figures (although they still retain a minimum of tactile references). But essences are pure figures of light: they are in themselves "contemplations," that is to say, they contemplate as much as they are contemplated, in a unity of God, the subject or the object (*percepts*). The common notions refer to relations of movement and rest that constitute relative speeds; essences on the contrary are absolute speeds that do not compose space by projection, but occupy it all at once, in a single stroke.[8] One of the most considerable of Jules Lagneau's contributions is to have shown the importance of speeds in thought, as Spinoza conceives of it, although Lagneau reduces absolute speed to a relative speed.[9] These are nonetheless the two characteristics of essences: *absolute and no longer relative speed, figures of light and no longer geometric figures revealed by light.* Relative speed is the speed of the affections and the affects: the speed of an action of one body upon another in space, the speed of the passage from one state to another in duration. What the notions grasp are the relations between relative speeds. But absolute speed is the manner in which an essence surveys (*survole*) its affects and affections in eternity (speed of power [*puissance*]).

For book V alone to constitute a third *Ethics*, it is not enough for it to have a specific object; it would also have to adopt a method distinct from the two others. But this does not seem to be the case, since it presents only demonstrative elements and scholia. Yet the reader has the impression that the geometric method here assumes a strange and wild demeanor, which could almost make one believe that book V was only a provisional version, a rough sketch: the propositions and demonstrations are traversed by such violent hiatuses, and include so many ellipses and contractions, that the syllogisms seem to be replaced by simple "enthymemes."[10] And the more one reads book V, the more one realizes that these features are neither imperfections in the working out of the method nor shortcuts, but are perfectly adapted to essences insofar as they surpass any order of discursivity or deduction. They are not simple operations of fact, but an entire procedure in principle. This is because, at the level of concepts, the geometric method is a method of exposition that requires completeness and saturation: this is why the common notions are expounded for themselves, starting with the most universal, as in an axiomatic, without one having to wonder how in fact we attain even a *single* common notion. But the geometric method of book V is a method of invention that will proceed by intervals and leaps, hiatuses and contractions, somewhat like a dog searching rather than a reasonable man explaining. Perhaps it surpasses all demonstration inasmuch as it operates in the "undecidable."

When mathematicians are not given over to the constitution of an axiomatic, their style of invention takes on strange powers, and the deductive links are broken by large discontinuities or on the contrary are violently contracted. No one denies Desargues's genius, but mathematicians like Huygens or Descartes had difficulty understanding him. His demonstration that every plane is the "polar" of a point, and every point the "pole" of a plane, is so rapid that one has to fill in everything it skips over. No one has described this jolting, jumping, and colliding thought, which grasps singular essences in mathematics, better than Evariste Galois, who himself encountered a good deal of incomprehension from his peers: analysts "do not deduce, they combine, they compose; when they arrive at the truth, it is by crashing in from all sides that they happen to stumble on it."[11] Once again, these characteristics do not appear as simple imperfections in the exposition, so that it can be done "more quickly," but as powers of a new order of thought that conquers an absolute speed. It seems to us that book V bears witness to such thought, which is irreducible to that developed by the common notions in the course of the first four books. If, as Blanchot says, books have as their correlate "the absence of the book" (or a more secret book made of flesh and blood), book V could be this absence or this secret in which signs and concepts vanish, and things begin to write by themselves and for themselves, crossing the intervals of space.

Consider proposition 10: "As long as we are not torn by affects contrary to our nature, we have the power of ordering and connecting the affections of the body according to the order of the intellect."[12] There is an immense rift or interval that appears here between the subordinate and the principal. For affects contrary to our nature above all prevent us from forming common notions, since they depend upon bodies that do not agree with our own; on the contrary, every time a body agrees with our own and increases our power (joy), a common notion of the two bodies can be formed, from which an active order and an active linking of the affections will ensue. In this voluntarily opened rift, it is the ideas of the agreement between bodies and of the restricted common notion that have only an implicit presence, and both of them appear only if one reconstitutes a missing chain: a double interval. If this reconstitution is not made, if this white space is not filled in, not only will the demonstration be inconclusive, but we will always remain undecided about the fundamental question: How do we come to form any common notion at all? And why is it a question of the least universal of notions (common to our body and *one* other)? The function of the interval or hiatus is to bring together to the maximum degree terms that are distant as such, and thereby to assure a speed of absolute survey (*survol*). Speeds can be absolute and yet have a greater or lesser magnitude. The magnitude of an absolute speed is measured in precise terms by the distance it covers at one stroke, that is, by the number of intermediaries it envelops, surveys, or implies (here, at least two). There are always leaps, lacunae, and cuts as positive characteristics of the third kind.

Another example can be found in propositions 14 and 22, where one passes, this time by contraction, from the idea of God as the most universal common notion to the idea of God as the most singular essence. It is as if one jumped from a relative speed (the greatest) to absolute speed. Finally, to limit ourselves to a few examples, demonstration 30 traces, but along a dotted line, a kind of sublime triangle whose summits are the figures of light (Self, World, and God) and whose sides, as distances, are traversed by an absolute speed, which is in turn revealed to be the greatest. The special characteristics of book V, the way it surpasses the method of the preceding books, always comes down to this: the absolute speed of figures of light.

The *Ethics* of the definitions, axioms, postulates, demonstrations, and corollaries is a river-book that develops its course. But the *Ethics* of the scholia is a book of fire, subterranean. The *Ethics* of book V is an aerial book of light, which proceeds by flashes. A logic of the sign, a logic of the concept, a logic of essence: Shadow, Color, Light. Each of the three *Ethics* coexists with the others and is taken up in the others, despite their differences in kind. It is one and the same world. Each of them sends out bridges in order to cross the emptiness that separates them.

Translated by Daniel W. Smith and Michael A. Greco

Notes

1. Anton Chekhov, "The Wedding," in *Complete Plays*, trans. Julius West (London: Duckworth, 1915), p. 61, translation modified.

2. Yvonne Toros, in *Spinoza et l'éspace projectif* (thesis, University of Paris-VIII, St.-Denis), makes use of various arguments to show that the geometry that inspires Spinoza is not that of Descartes or even Hobbes, but a projective optical geometry closer to that of Desargues. These arguments seem decisive, and entail, as we shall see, a new comprehension of Spinozism. In an earlier work, *Espace et transformation: Spinoza* (Paris-I), Toros compared Spinoza with Vermeer, and sketched out a projective theory of color as a function of the *Treatise on the Rainbow* (in *Spinoza's Algebraic Calculation of the Rainbow; and, Calculation of Chances*, ed. M. J. Petry [The Hague: Nijhoff, 1985]).

3. Johann Wolfgang von Goethe, *Goethe's Color Theory*, trans. Herb Aach, ed. Rupprecht Matthaei (New York: Van Norstrand Reinhold, 1971), §494. On the tendency of each color to reconstitute the whole, see §§803–15.

4. See Guiseppe Ungaretti, *Vermeer*, trans. Phillipe Jaccottet (Paris: Echoppe, 1990; unpaginated): "Color that he sees as a color in itself, as light, and in which he also sees — and isolates when he sees it — the shadow...." See also Gilles Aillaud's theater piece, *Vermeer and Spinoza* (Paris: Bourgois, 1987).

5. Aeschylus, *Agamemnon*, 495–500.

6. See Robert Sasso, "Discours et non-discours de l'*Ethique*," in *Revue de synthèse* 89 (January 1978).

7. Science confronts this problem of geometrical figures and figures of light. (Thus Bergson can say, in chapter 5 of *Duration and Simultaneity*, that the theory of relativity reverses the traditional subordination of figures of light to solid, geometrical figures.) In art, the painter Robert Delaunay opposes figures of light to the geometrical figures of cubism as well as to abstract art.

8. Toros, in chapter 6 of *Spinoza et l'éspace projectif*, marks in precise terms two aspects or two principles of Desargues's geometry: the first, homology, concerns propositions; the second, which will be named "duality," concerns the correspondence of the line with the point, and of the point with the plane. This is a new understanding of parallelism, since it is established between a point in thought (the idea of God) and an infinite development (*déroulement*) in extension.

9. Jules Lagneau, *Célèbres leçons et fragments*, 2nd ed., revised and expanded (Paris: Presses Universitaires de France, 1964), pp. 67–68 (the "rapidity of thought," to which one finds an equivalent only in music, which rests less on the absolute than on the relative).

10. Aristotle, *Prior Analytics*, II, 27: the enthymeme is a syllogism of which one or the other premise is assumed, hidden, suppressed, or elided. Leibniz takes up the question in *New Essays*, I, chap. 1, §4 and §19, and shows that the hiatus is not only made in the exposition, but in our thought itself, and that "the force of the conclusion consists in part in what one suppresses."

11. See the texts by Galois in André Dalmas, *Evariste Galois* (Paris: Fasquelle, 1956), p. 121. And p. 112 ("one must constantly indicate the progress of the calculations and foresee the results without ever being able to carry them out"); p. 132 ("in these two memoirs, and especially in the second, one often finds the formula, *I don't know*"). There thus exists a style, even in mathematics, which would be defined by modes of hiatus, elision, and contraction in thought as such. In this regard, one can find some invaluable comments in Gilles-Gaston Granger, *Essai d'une philosophie du style*, 2nd ed. (Paris: Odile Jacob, 1988), although the author has a completely different conception of style in mathematics (pp. 20–21).

12. Spinoza, *Ethics*, in *The Collected Works of Spinoza*, ed. and trans. Edwin Curley, p. 601.

THREE

The Envelope: A Reading of Spinoza, *Ethics*, "Of God"

Luce Irigaray

Definitions

"BY CAUSE of itself, I understand that, whose essence involves existence; or that, whose nature cannot be conceived unless existing" (Baruch Spinoza, *Ethics*, p. 335).[1] This definition of God could be translated as: *that which is its own place for itself,* that which turns itself inside out and thus constitutes a dwelling (for) itself. Unique and necessary. Solitary. But in itself. Sufficient. Needing no other in its reception of "space-time." Men may, perhaps, contemplate or seek to contemplate God in his place; men do not give God his place.

Which also means: that which by nature can be conceived only as existing, or *that which provides its own envelope* by turning its essence outward, must necessarily exist. That which provides its own space-time *necessarily* exists.

Hence:

We do not exist *necessarily* because we do not provide ourselves with our own envelopes.

Man would thus exist more necessarily than woman because he gets his envelope from her.

Twice over:

in or through his *necessary fetal existence,*

in his role as *lover.* Which is contingent? Except for happiness? And becoming necessary again for procreation.

That is, he is enveloped as fetus, as lover, as father.

But

Man *receives* that envelope. By nature, it is true! And the reversal can operate just as well. Man does not provide himself with his own envelope, unless it is his nature to be conceived in woman. By essence, to be conceived in woman.

Woman would theoretically be the envelope (which she provides). But she would have no essence or existence, given that she is the potential for essence and existence: *the available place.* She would be cause for herself—and in a less contingent manner than man—if she enveloped herself, or reenveloped herself, in the envelope that she is able to "provide." The envelope that is part of her "attributes" and "affections" but that she cannot use as self-cause. If she enveloped herself with what she provides, she could not but necessarily be conceived of as existing. Which, to an extent, is what happens: women's suffering arises also from the fact that man does not conceive that women do not exist. Men have such a great need that women should exist. If men are to be permitted to believe or imagine themselves as self-cause, they need to think that the envelope "belongs" to them. (Particularly following "the end of God" or "the death of God," insofar as God can be determined by an era of history in any way but through the limits to its thinking.) For men to establish this belonging—without the guarantee provided by God—it is imperative that that which provides the envelope should necessarily exist. *Therefore* the maternal-feminine exists necessarily as the cause of the self-cause of man. But not for herself. She has to exist but as an a priori condition (as Kant might say) for the space-time of the masculine subject. A cause that is never unveiled for fear that its identity might split apart and plummet down. She does not have to exist as woman because, as woman, her envelope is always *slightly open* (if man today thinks of himself as God, woman becomes, according to Meister Eckhart, an adverb or a quality of the word of God).

"That thing is called finite in its own kind [*in suo genere*] which can be limited by another thing of the same nature. For example, a body is called finite, because we always conceive another which is greater. So a thought is limited by another thought; but a body is not limited by a thought, nor a thought by a body" (p. 355).

From which it would follow that:

God is infinite and unlimited because nothing of the same nature exists;

man is finite and limited
    both by men of the *same nature*
    and by that which is *greater*, therefore

by the/his mother, even if he doesn't think so

by the/his woman, even if he doesn't think so, because of the extension of the place-envelope;

and by *God*: but he may be so ignorant that he does not want to know that universe and thought are always greater than he is at any given moment.

Does God, then, limit man by the creation and self-sufficiency of thought?

Within sexual difference, there would, it seems, be at once *finiteness and limit*, as a result of the meeting of two *bodies*, and two thoughts, and also infiniteness and unlimitedness if "God" intervenes.

If there are not *two* bodies and *two* thoughts, according to Spinoza, an evil infinite may occur: with the thought of the one limiting the body of the other and vice versa. There is no longer finiteness, or limits, or access to the infinite. At best, is matter made into form by the act? Which would virtually happen once, then once more, plus one, plus one, plus one... a multiplicity of feminine formations that have access neither to the finite nor to the infinite.

If man and woman are both body and thought, they provide each other with finiteness, limit, and the possibility of access to the divine through the development of envelopes. Greater and greater envelopes, vaster and vaster horizons, but above all envelopes that are qualitatively more and more necessary and different. But always *overflowing*: with the female one becoming a cause of the other by providing him with self-cause. The setup must always be open for this to occur. It must also afford a *qualitative* difference. Essence must never be completely realized in existence—as Spinoza might say? Perhaps, for men, the movement is made in reverse? It is through existence that they can discover essence? Men would not unfold their essence into existence, but by virtue of existence would, perhaps, successfully constitute an essence.

Within sexual difference, therefore, *finiteness*, *limit*, and *progression* are needed: and this requires two bodies, two thoughts, a relation between the two and the conception of a wider perspective.

Clearly, for Spinoza, a body is not limited by a thought or a thought by a body. The two remain "parallel" and never intersect. The question of sexual difference, a question to be thought out particularly after and with the "death of God" and the period of the ontic-ontological difference, requires a reconsideration of the split between body and thought. The whole historic or historical analysis of philosophy shows that being has yet to be referred to in terms of body or flesh (as Heidegger notes in "Logos," his seminar on Heraclitus).[2] Thought and body have remained separate. And this leads, on the social and cultural level, to important empirical and transcendental effects: with *discourse* and *thought* being the privileges of a *male* producer. And that remains the "norm." Even today, bodily tasks remain the obligation or the duty of a female subject. The break between the two produces rootless and insane thinking as well as bodies (women and children) that are heavy and slightly "moronic" because they lack language.

Does the act of love then mean that thinking about the body receives an infusion of flesh? Clearly, to take may be to give. And this is already a way out of parallelism. The two sexes would penetrate each other by means of theft or a rape, a more or less mechanical encounter whose goal would be to produce a child. To produce a body? Or just body? As long as our thinking is unable to limit the body, or vice versa, no sex act is possible. Nor any thought, any imaginary or symbolic of the flesh. The empirical and the transcendental have split apart (just like the roles fulfilled by man and woman?), and the body falls on one side, language on the other.

"By substance, I understand that which is in itself and is conceived through itself; in other words, that, the conception of which does not need the conception of another thing from which it must be formed" (p. 355). Here Spinoza is talking about God. Only God is in himself, conceived by himself; needing the concept of no other thing in order to be formed. Only God generates his existence out of his essence, which means also that he engenders himself in the form of concepts without having need of concepts different from himself in order to be formed.

God alone is *in self* [*en soi, par soi*], in an autodetermination that is linked to the in-itself [*en-soi*]. Does *in self by self* amount to a definition of place that develops itself? Does *in self conceived by self* mean capable of providing and limiting its place? Never to be determined and limited by anything but self. Itself autoaffecting itself, potentially, as in the middle-passive, but never passively affected by anything else. Not knowing passivity. Never power [*puissance*], body-extension, available to suffer the action of an other than self.

That said, if this definition can be applied to God alone, the definition is defined, and God is defined, by man and not by God himself. Therefore God determines himself conceptually out of man. He does not proffer his own conception, except through the mouth of man. Obviously, in certain traditions and at certain periods, God designates himself: in words, in the texts of the law, through incarnation in different modes. But, in most cases, it is man who names in the form of conceptions and who situates God in that space as far as the generation of conception goes.

It also seems that *Man* conceives himself without anyone else, except God, forming his conception. But the relation of man to God, of God to man, often seems circular: man defines God, who in turn determines man.

This would not be the case for *woman*, who would correspond to no conception. Who, as the Greeks saw it, lacks fixed form and idea, and lacks above all a conception that she provides for herself. As matter, or extension for the concept, she would have no conception at her disposal, would be unable to conceive herself or conceive the other, and, theoretically, she would need to pass through man in order to have a relation, for herself, to man, to the world, and to God. If indeed she is capable of any of this.

Axioms

"Everything which is, is either in itself or in another" (p. 355). Being is determined by the place that envelops it:

> Either the envelope is the essence of the existing thing or of existence (see "Of God," Definitions, I). That which is, is *in self.*

> Or else that which is, is *in something other,* depends on the existence of something other: is not cause of self.

That which is, is determined by that in which it is contained — by that which envelops it, envelops its existence.

"That which cannot be conceived *through* another must be conceived *through* itself" (p. 355). Refer to the commentary on the Definitions, III. Definitions of substance.

Not to be *in* self means being in something other. This is still the problem of place, of the need to receive place (unless one is God), as a result of the passage from middle-passive to passive, from autoaffection to heteroaffection, from autodetermination, autoengendering, to determination, creation, even procreation by someone other. From the necessary circularity and conceptional self-sufficiency of God to the difference of that which can be conceived *by*, or even *in*, something other.

"From a given determinate cause an effect necessarily follows; and, on the other hand, if no determinate cause be given, it is impossible that an effect can follow" (p. 355). Everything takes place in a chain of causalities, in a genealogical sequence of *there is*'s. There has to be a cause that is already given, already existing, if there is to be an effect, a necessary effect. But does the cause that is already given result from an essence that is not given as such? Not in the works of Spinoza? Where God and nature are coessentials?

What relation is there between the given cause and the revealed cause? The *data*, the *there is*, the problem of the neuter case, and the fact God will be referred to in the neuter as *indeterminatum, non datum*.

But, to return to my hypothesis, if the feminine does not manifest itself as cause, it can engender no effects. And yet the maternal-feminine is also *cause of causes*. Does that mean that it too is an *indeterminatum* in its way? Insofar as it always lies behind the *data*. Behind that which is already determined in the chain of causalities. Or else: the chain of causalities on the female side remains unrevealed. Still to be unveiled. The maternal-feminine would unfold, offer, manifest itself in the form of *data* that are not determined, not given *as such*. No effects would thereby ensue. And all this would remain possible for lack of any thought about the body and the flesh — for lack of a reciprocal determination of the one by the other, as opposed to the parallelism that prevents the maternal-feminine from being inscribed in duration as causes and effects. This in fact leaves the masculine *lost* in the chain of causalities as far as the male body, the male flesh, is concerned, as well as their relations to conception, the cause of self, except by means of the absolute causality that is God.

As for the feminine, this absence of inscription of its causes and effects in the chain of causalities leads, for example, to Aristotle's notion that woman is engendered as if by *accident*. A genetic aberration. An illness. A monstrosity. Or again, the notion that the child is engendered from the male seed alone. The female seed would not be necessary. It is not a cause and, if anything, *impedes* the possibility of generation. (See this strange quotation, among many others, from Aristotle, who was, nevertheless, a doctor: "Here is an indication that the female does not discharge semen of the same kind as the male, and that the offspring is not formed from a mixture of two semens, as some allege. Very often the female conceives although she had derived no pleasure from the act of coitus; and, on the contrary side, when the female derives as much pleasure as the male, and they both keep the same pace, the female does not bear—unless there is a proper amount of menstrual fluid [as it is called] present.")[3]

The female, it seems, is pure disposal "matter." Pure receptacle that does not stay still. Not even a place, then? Always belonging to a threatening primitive chaos. That even God should never approach. For fear he may suffer its obscure effects? Could the female be effect(s) without cause? Necessary cause. Raised as an issue only as the *accidental* cause of man? A genetic mistake. Or a divine whim? With God giving birth to the woman out of the body of the man.

"The knowledge [*cognitio*] of an effect depends upon and involves knowledge of the cause" (p. 355). Does knowledge of an effect envelop knowledge of the cause by a retroactive process? Which, however, by enveloping, hides the knowledge, veils it, and perhaps gives birth to it by a roundabout or return route to generation?

When knowledge of the effect envelops that of the cause, this can evoke the maternal-feminine, even in its most physical effects of generation as it doubles back on the "masculine" and its thought, and overwhelms it. Because it is not thought of as a cause, does the maternal-feminine mask cause? Overwhelm it with a veil (that of the illusion of flesh? or the veil of Maya?). Hide it? We shall need to decipher, work through, interpret the knowledge of *effects* in order to achieve knowledge of *causes*. Is this a reverse knowledge? Why is it that the *data* are not already thought of as effects? Why is *cause* already *caused*? Because it comes from God? With cause already being effect, but of God. We can agree that there should be no effects without cause, but cause is already a given effect, or even an effect of an effect. To the genealogy of causes corresponds a hierarchy of effects. Two parallel chains that do not always cross and yet mutually determine each other, in particular as they roll and unroll, reciprocally. That which is self-cause is an envelope for itself, which develops into existence(s), but is enveloped by our knowledge of its effects. As it reveals its existence to us, we envelop-veil it with the knowledge of its effects, on the basis of which we seek knowledge of its cause(s).

Does knowledge of the effect envelop knowledge of the cause? The effect overwhelms the cause from the point of view of knowledge. A double movement in "theology," moving up and down. Essence envelops existence if there is *cause of self*; knowledge of the effect envelops that of the cause if there is no cause of self. If I start with the creatures, I move up the chain of effects (until, perhaps, I reach an uncreated cause whose knowledge, or ultimate cause, escapes us?); if I start with God, I move down the chain of causes, on the basis of a *causa sui*.

There are no effects without an already given cause. And this is linked to the question of *miracles* for Spinoza. There might be effects without *data*: inexplicable, "miraculous" effects. Before deciding for a "miracle," Spinoza notes our inability to perceive the extension of the chain of causalities and, in particular, our inability to analyze the relation of contingency to necessity. A belief in "miracle" or in "chance" is often a result of weakness or narrowness in the field of conception.[4]

"Those things which have nothing mutually in common with one another cannot through one another be mutually understood, that is to say, the conception of the one does not involve the conception of the other" (p. 355). Conception means taking hold of, perceiving, and conceiving an available matter or power. Conception is more active than perception; or, more exactly, conception designates the active pole of the mind, and perception designates the passive pole. Whence the fact that, traditionally, the feminine, insofar as it has access to mind, remains in perception, while the conception is the privilege of the masculine.

I am often asked this question: if sexual difference exists, what path can there still be between man and woman? Which amounts to saying that in the past relations between men and women were not determined by sex. In Spinoza's terms, this is to assume that woman cannot conceive. Or else that man can't? (But that cannot be so, since Spinoza is conceiving his system. . . .)

If sexual difference exists, does that mean that man and woman hold nothing in common? There is at the very least the child as an effect, as we know. In our thinking, clearly, the child is still thought of as an effect of man's, of the male, seed, even if biology has established that this is not so. Our thinking still thinks of the ovum as passive, of the female body as passivity, of woman as remaining in the domain of perception, or even at times of the perceived.

What would man and woman have in common? Both conception and perception. *Both.* And without any hierarchy between the two. Both would have the capacity to perceive and conceive. *To suffer and to be active.* To suffer the self and to understand the self. To receive the self and to envelop the self. Becoming more open because of the freedom of each, male and female. Since freedom and necessity are correlated. With each giving the other necessity and freedom. In self, for self, and for the other.

If I exist, that would mean that I correspond to a necessity. Therefore that I should be free. For this to become so, the concept of the masculine would have to cease to envelop that of the feminine, since the feminine has no necessity if it is uniquely an effect of and for the masculine.

Between man and woman, whatever the differences may be and despite the fact that the concept of the one, male or female, cannot envelop that of the other, certain bridges can be built, through two approaches:

that of generation,

that of God.

But, historically, in Genesis, the feminine has no conception. She is figured as being born from man's envelope, with God as midwife. Whereas woman envelops man before his birth. Could it be that God is he who intervenes so that there should be a *reciprocal limitation* of envelopes for both? Which is why it is necessary to go through the question of God every time the sexual act comes under consideration.

The openings in the envelopes between men and women should always be mediated by God. Faithless to God, man lays down the law for woman, imprisons her in his conception(s), or at least in accordance, with his conceptions instead of covering her only for God, while awaiting God. Woman, who enveloped man before birth, until he could live outside her, finds herself encircled by a language, by places that she cannot conceive of, and from which she cannot escape.

It's nothing new for man to want to be both man and woman: he has always had pretensions of turning the envelope inside out. But by willing to be master of everything, he becomes the slave both of discourse and of mother nature.

Translated by Carolyn Burke and Gillian Gill

Notes

1. Page references following quotations are to Baruch (Benedict de) Spinoza, *Ethics*, Part I, "Of God," trans. W. H. White and Rev. A. H. Stirling, in *Great Books of the Western World*, vol. 31, *Descartes, Spinoza* (Chicago: Encyclopaedia Britannica, 1952), pp. 355–72.

2. Martin Heidegger, "Logos (Heraclitus, Fragment B 50)," in *Early Greek Thinking: The Dawn of Western*

Philosophy, trans. David F. Krell and Frank A. Capuzzi (New York: Harper and Row, 1975), pp. 59–78.

3. *Aristotle: Generation of Animals*, trans. A. L. Peck (Cambridge: Harvard University Press, 1963), pp. 97–98.

4. See, for example, Spinoza, *Ethics*, proposition 33, scholium 1: "But a thing cannot be called contingent unless with reference to a deficiency in our knowledge."

Surfaces without Depth,
Processes without End(s)

F O U R

The Birth of Modern Materialism in Hobbes and Spinoza

Emilia Giancotti

WHEN WE speak of the birth of modern materialism in Hobbes and Spinoza, we do not intend to turn them into the creators of modern materialism. We only want to emphasize the specific form that, at certain points of their theory, reveals the traces of an orientation, also present in other philosophers and scientists of the age, that will fully develop only during the following centuries.

By speaking of "traces of an orientation," we reject at the start every possibility of a univocal reading of the authors cited, whose richness and problematicity is well known — and it is historical documentation that authenticates it.

We say again that our interest here is not to establish the possible ties of dependence of one (Spinoza) vis-à-vis the other (Hobbes), but only to show briefly their participation in the nascent phase of modern materialism and determine the modes of this participation. If, for Hobbes, such participation is not in doubt — the debate being limited to the type of materialism of which he was the theorist — for Spinoza, on the other hand, the discussion can focus on the very legitimacy of a reading that attempts to define the modes and limits of this participation.

Therefore, the following questions will be taken up: sense and philosophy and the ontological impact of knowledge in Hobbes; and extension or matter as an attribute of substance, the theory of the *mens*, and the realism of the theory of knowledge in Spinoza.

Hobbes clearly distinguishes philosophy or science from original or sensible knowledge, by attributing, however, to the former the body as an object of analysis and by identifying the same body as a point of departure or cause of the latter. The body is thus either the immediate object of sensibility and the cause of its appearance, since by its action it determines the reaction of the body that, transmitted as far as the heart and the brain, extends into emotions and passions; or, on the other hand, the object on which reason or philosophy, across the operations of analysis and synthesis, of decomposition and composition, is exercised as calculation. It is thus that, despite the diversity of the respective modes of accomplishment and results, the body constitutes, in every state of cause, the point of reference that is common to two types of knowledge. As a knowledge of the *oti*, of the "what," of the "given," sense is limited to observing the existence of an external body; and, in the human subject, sense determines in its encounter with an external body sensations without which no concept is possible: "there is no conception in a man's mind, which hath not at first, totally, or by parts, been begotten upon the organs of sense."[1] The "phantasms" of sense, that is, the ideas produced by sensations, are the "first principles" (*principia prima*) of science.[2] Without them, no science is possible, just as it is also hardly possible if science is limited to them. Through sense we know the phenomena or effects of nature, that is, "such things as appear, or are shown to us by nature" (*quaecunque apparent sive a natura nobis sunt ostensa*).[3] And sensation itself is also the beginning of the knowledge of the principles that govern the domain of phenomena, objects of research for physics, principles that the human mind does not produce but finds "placed in the things themselves" (*in ipsis rebus posita*).[4] Thus, if the knowledge of matter necessarily has its point of departure in phenomena, identified as principles of knowledge of other things ("if the appearances be the principles by which we know all other things..." [*si phaenomena principia sint cognoscendi caetera...*]),[5] sensation is at the same time the beginning of knowledge and of these principles (the phenomena) and of the principles that govern its course and are situated in things themselves, and are not—let us repeat—products of the human mind but are observed by the human mind.

The logical premise of such a conception of natural phenomena is the very definition of the body as "that, which having no dependence upon our thought, is coincident or coextended with some part of space" (*quicquid non dependens a nostra cogitatione cum spatii parte aliqua coincidit vel coextenditur*).[6] This is an aspect that seems to us particularly important as an indicative sign of the Hobbesian realist point of view, a point of view that the hypothesis of the "annihilation of the world" (*annihilatio mundi*), in our opinion, does not wind up contradicting.

Accident of the body and channel of the relationship between knowing subject and external body: such is the motion that, as is well known, is the universal principle of explanation, the cause of every phenomenon, and the cause from which all other causes can be deduced. The validity of this principle and the general possibility of observing it are in themselves obvious for Hobbes; the intervention of reason later serves only to determine the particular quality of the motion, but the existence of the motion as such is immediately apparent.[7] In order to explain the motion of a body, one must find an external efficient cause,[8] that is, the presence of another body in motion, through application of the general principle according to which motion has no other cause than motion itself.[9]

Sensation — defined as "a phantasm, made by the reaction and endeavour outwards in the organ of sense, caused by an endeavour inwards from the object, remaining for some time more or less" (*ab organi sensorii conatu ad extra, qui generatur a conatu ab objecto versus interna, eoque aliquamdiu manente per reactionem factum phantasma*)[10] — is a particular aspect of motion. It is a typical example of action and reaction, action on the part of the external body (*conatus ab objecto versus interna*) and reaction on the part of the human body (*conatus ad extra*) — an action of the external body, which refers, as to its cause, to the motion of another body, the whole being placed inside of the general process of cause and effect, that is, at the heart of universal determinism. The *phantasma*, that is, the knowledge to which sensation gives a content, is always particular. The diversity of *phantasmata* corresponds to the diversity of the organs on which is exerted the action of the external body, an action that prompts another type of motion inside the human body: animal motion, whose progression causes "pleasure" (*voluptas*) and whose obstruction causes "pain" (*dolor*), whose difficulties cause "grief" (*aegritudo*) and, consequently, "appetite" (*appetitus*) in the first case and "aversion" (*aversio*) or flight in the second case, *appetitus* and *aversio* that — if they are preceded by a positive or negative decision, that is, if they proceed through reflection — are affirmed as the will, whose freedom is specified not as freedom from necessity, but only as the capacity to do what one has decided to do. More precisely, the will also enters into the general schema of determinism, since it is nothing other than the moment of consciousness that accompanies the motion of desire or rejection with which animal motion reacts to the action of the external body.

Reason works on the data offered by sensation, adopts them as valuable, then separates itself from them in order to construct its own system. Philosophy is identified with reason, whose essence is calculation, and develops in a double direction: either from the concepts of causes or generations to the knowledge of effects or phenomena (synthesis, composition), or else from known effects or phenomena to the identification of real or possible causes (analysis, decomposition).[11] Since science consists in the search for and determination of the causes of all things, and since the causes of all singular things are composed of the causes of universal things, it is above all necessary to know the causes of universal things, that is, the accidents common to all bodies, that is, to every material object, rather than the causes of singular things, that is, the accidents in the middle of which one thing distinguishes itself from another. Reason pursues this knowledge through analysis. The part of science, then, that includes the search for principles is "purely analytical" and starts with the idea or concept of a singular thing from which it arises, through decomposition, going all the way to universal principles, the first of which is motion. The idea or concept of the singular thing has no other origin than sensation, that is, original knowledge, without which—let us repeat—no science is possible even if, by limiting onself to it, one cannot construct science. A theory of the arbitrary, nominalism, the formal nature of truth within discourse—all these elements thereby characterize the Hobbesian theory of science. In order to mark the removal of original knowledge, Hobbes—as is well known—formulates the famous hypothesis of the *annihilatio mundi*, which has nourished the interpretation of the Marburg school (Natorp and Cassirer), taken up again recently in Italy (Pacchi),[12] according to which Hobbesian materialism is not ontological but hypothetical. This interpretation can appear suggestive, as can the accentuation in the phenomenalist sense that makes Hobbes a precursor of Kant. But, in our opinion, this interpretation is incompatible with the metaphor of the mirror present in the *De Principiis* (MS 5297 of the Bibliothèque Nationale de Galles, transcribed and published by Rossi in *Civiltà moderna* [1941] and dated by him between 1637 and 1640), not reproduced in other writings but never explicitly contradicted; with the affirmation of existence *in ipsis rebus* of principles on which natural phenomena depend, that is, laws according to which natural phenomena unfold, principles that (as we have already emphasized) "are not such as we ourselves make and pronounce in general terms, as definitions; but such, as being placed in the things themselves by the Author of Nature, are by us observed in them" (*non facimus nos, nec pronunciamus universaliter, ut definitiones, sed a naturae conditore in ipsis rebus posita observamus*);[13] and finally, with the ontological impact that is undoubtedly possessed by the original knowledge that is not science but without which science cannot proceed, since it alone supplies it with the principles on which it is based. Here and there Hobbes undoubtedly employs expressions of problematic appearance. The definition of "body"[14] in fact moves between a clearly realist position and a problematic foundation that seems to call the latter into question. The reference to the concept of imaginary, subjective space in which the body is situated seems to take away some consistency from the description of the body marked with the clearest realism. But the identification between real space and body that it brings about later replaces — in our opinion — the question in its correct terms:

> The extension of a body, is the same thing with the magnitude of it, or that which some call real space. But this magnitude does not depend upon our cognition, as imaginary space doth; for this is an effect of our imagination, but magnitude is the cause of it; this is an accident of the mind, that of a body existing out of the mind.

> [*Extensio corporis idem est quod magnitudo eius, sive id quod aliqui vocant "spatium reale"; magnitudo autem illa non dependet a cogitatione nostra, sicut spatium imaginarium, hoc enim illius effectus est, magnitudo causa; hoc animi, illa corporis extra animum existentis accidens est.*][15]

Real space, or magnitude, and body are identified; the body *is*, it does not seem that it is, nor is it supposed to be something not dependent on our thought, as opposed to the imaginary space that is *animi accidens*. A passage of *Leviathan*, concerning Holy Scripture and precisely the meaning of the word "mind," is equally quite explicit:

> The word *body*, in the most general acceptation, signifieth that which filleth, or occupieth some certain room, or imagined place; and dependeth not on the imagination, but is a real part of that we call the *universe*. For the *universe*, being the aggregate of all *bodies*, there is no real part thereof that is not also *body*; nor any thing properly a *body*, that is not also part of that aggregate of all *bodies*, the *universe*.[16]

The subjectivity of imaginary space does not take away reality from the body but reduces it to a mental category without ontological dimension, whose function is to lead back to unity and to organize every datum of sense, everything that is not a cause and, at the same time, an object of sensation governed by the laws of motion. On the other hand, the whole part that treats the body confirms the reality of the body as the ultimate foundation of every knowledge and does so despite the theory of the subjectivity of sensible qualities. It is only from the reality of the body, observed and experienced through sense, that reason is in a position to exercise its characteristic functions of calculation, whose practical goal is that of acting on the body in order to adapt it to our usefulness.[17] In the accomplishment of this operation, reason proceeds by hypothesis, formalizing the data acquired through sense or original knowledge, whose ontological aspect is outside of discussion. The clear separation between sensibility and intellect—a separation that Kant on the one hand reaffirms and on the other hand strives to go beyond, while maintaining the irremediable dualism in the world outside of the knowing subject—prevents Hobbes from attributing certainty to reason, the ontological impact of which sense makes use, while remaining incapable of theorizing it. Must one speak of "hypothetical" materialism? Certainly not, if one means to suggest that Hobbes doubted the existence of external bodies. Yes, if one wants to emphasize the proper function of Hobbesian reason, whose essence is purely formal and is realized in calculation, that is, in the operations of analysis and synthesis and in the elaboration of hypotheses that practice (recall that the goal of philosophy is practical) confirms or declares to be without foundation.

The role Hobbes attributes to the *annihilatio mundi* is that of marking the distance between original knowledge and philosophy or science, the former tied organically to matter (whether it be the external body or the subject-body of sensibility) and emerging from it, the latter separated from it but always dependent on it as the source of data on which its theoretical function is exercised. In the absurd hypothesis that the world could be annihilated and that a single man could survive with the inheritance of images that his previous relation with the external world had allowed him to acquire, this man could continue to exercise his own reason, to work with the names attributed to things before their disappearance, to pronounce "true" propositions, truth being an intrinsic property of discourse, and thus in succession, in full autonomy vis-à-vis the external world. This autonomy grows, however, on the basis of a previously established relation—through sense—with this world, today disappeared, from which he has drawn out the data for his operations.

In contrast with the progressive nature of his natural philosophy, Hobbes preserves intact, such as he receives it from the theologico-philosophical tradition, the concept of God as a person, all-powerful, creator of the world and separate from the world, object of cult and worship, father and sovereign to whom one owes obedience. Since we cannot go into detail at the heart of this question, we shall limit ourselves to indicating two possible responses—which are not necessarily mutually exclusive but which are perhaps concurrent—to the question posed by the persistence of this concept alongside a materialism whose critical dimension does not seem to us to call the systematic consistency into question. The maintenance of the concept of God as a person and the reverence vis-à-vis established religion, although within the framework of a theory that subordinates religious power to political power, are a cover for the freedom of research within the domain of natural philosophy; on the other hand, this concept serves to provide a foundation — as if it were necessary — for the theory of absolutism, for a totalizing conception of political power that Hobbes indicated as the only form of organization capable of confronting the threats of revolution and of ensuring the conditions necessary for the preservation of life and the free activity of a mercantile economy. The last page of *Leviathan* seems to justify these two responses.[18]

II

It is indeed on this terrain, in contrast, that Spinoza — some years later — will give a response that clearly challenges this concept of God, by leaving the door open to the supposition that only reasons of prudence (which all the same have no guarantee against the charge of atheism) have pushed him to preserve the name. It is on this terrain, certainly the most sensitive and exposed, that Spinoza leads — I would say audaciously, even if he does so with some contradictions — his struggle against superstition in defense of a clear intelligence of the real. It is not a question, in my opinion, of just the doctrinal aspect of Spinozism being able to situate its author along the line of development of, but not entirely within, modern materialism. But it is certainly a question of the most innovative and fruitful aspect. The terms of the question are well known, but it is worth recalling their essential lines.

At the conclusion of the statement of the theory of substance, after having emphasized one of its essential features, that of indivisibility, Spinoza proclaims again the identification between the concept of God and that of substance[19] and relates extension, as well as thought, to God as God's own attribute or as a modification of this attribute.[20] In a language that is even more precise and explicit, the first and second propositions of part II affirm that "thought is an attribute of God, or God is a thinking thing" (*cogitatio attributum Dei est, sive Deus est res cogitans*) and "extension is an attribute of God, or God is an extended thing" (*extensio attributum Dei est, sive Deus est res extensa*) (G II/86–7). Spinoza perfectly accounts for the objections to which he is exposed and the scandal that his theory is going to arouse. And in *E* IP15S he confronts these objections by demonstrating analytically that they are all based on an erroneous presupposition, that of the divisibility and thus the finitude of corporeal substance, and that once this presupposition is eliminated, all the imperfections that derive from it are also eliminated in such a way that nothing more is opposed to its attribution to the essence of God, an attribution that permits one, on the other hand, not to fall into what Spinoza regards as an absurdity, that is, the creation of matter from nothing. Always in line with a consistent definition of the unity and the systematic nature of the real, *E* IP25S asserts that "God must be called the cause of all things in the same sense in which he is called the cause of himself" (*eo sensu, quo Deus dicitur causa sui, etiam, omnium rerum causa dicendus est*) (G II/68), that is, the corollary adds, "particular things are nothing but affections of God's attributes, or modes by which God's attributes are expressed in a certain and determinate way" (*res particulares nihil sunt, nisi Dei attributorum affectiones, sive modi, quibus Dei attributa certo, et determinato modo exprimuntur*) (G II/68). Referring to this corollary, *E* IID1 asserts: "By body I understand a mode that in a certain and determinate way expresses God's essence insofar as he is considered as an extended thing" (*Per corpus intelligo modum, qui Dei essentiam, quatenus, ut res extensa, consideratur, certo, et determinato modo exprimit*) (G II/84). If any doubt remained regarding the supersession of every fracture and distance between God and the world, *E* VP25D eliminates it by asserting that "the more we understand singular things in this way, the more we understand God" (*quo magis res singulares intelligimus, eo magis Deum intelligimus*) (G II/296).

The definition of extension or matter as an attribute of God, that is — according to Spinoza's conception of the attribute — as a constitutive aspect of his essence (we shall not speak here about the discussion on the interpretation of the attributes in Spinoza, while stating that we accept the interpretation first proposed by Kuno Fischer), this definition is equivalent to raising matter to the level of the mind by recognizing the same dignity in it, that is, that this definition is equivalent to going beyond without possible hesitation what was regarded as an insurmountable distance, and no longer seeing in matter the source of evil and error. In the century in which Galileo was forced — despite the efforts at reconciliation he made in all good faith — to recant his scientific theories because they were incompatible with the truths sanctioned by Holy Scripture (Spinoza was born around a year after the scientist underwent his trial), only an unshakable confidence in the liberatory and progressive value of truth, of which he considered himself without the shadow of a doubt to be the depository, only such a confidence can have pushed Spinoza to sustain with as much clarity a thesis that reversed the sanctioned order of priorities and created an irrevocable presupposition for the definition of a materialist conception of the real.

While emphasizing the enormous importance that, in our opinion, Spinoza's conception of extension as an attribute of God has for the history of Western thought, all the same it must be said that Spinoza did not finish a complete elaboration of a scientific theory of matter. The little treatise on physics situated between *E* IIP13 and P14 offers few aspects that can be related to a mechanical conception of the relation between bodies and an organicist conception of corporeal nature in its totality. Certain aspects offered by letters 81 and 83 seem particularly interesting to us, for they confirm these lacunae. As is well known, Spinoza — responding in the first letter to Tschirnhaus, who asked him for clarifications regarding the possibility of demonstrating a priori the existence of bodies and regarding the concept of infinity — rejects the Cartesian concept of extension as inert mass, for he considers it unable to account for the existence of bodies:

> For matter at rest, insofar as it is in itself, will persevere in its rest, and will not be set in motion unless by a more powerful external cause. For this reason I did not hesitate, previously, to affirm that Descartes's principles of natural things are useless, not to say absurd.
>
> (*Materia enim quiescens, quantum in se est, in sua quiete perseverabit, nec ad motum concitabitur, nisi a causa potentiori externa, et hac de causa non dubitavi olim affirmare rerum naturalium principia Cartesiana inutilia esse, ne dicam absurda.*)
> (G IV/332)

In the second letter, again to Tschirnhaus, who continued to ask Spinoza for elucidations — by making him remark in addition that Descartes did not conceive of extension as an inert mass, since he sustained that motion was aroused in itself by God, and by allowing us to see that Spinoza did not want to reveal his thought to him — Spinoza responds by opposing the Cartesian theory, and does this in the same words employed in letter 83, his own conception of matter as an attribute:

> You ask whether the variety of things can be demonstrated a priori from the concept of extension alone. I believe I have already shown sufficiently clearly that this is impossible, and that therefore Descartes defines matter badly by extension, but that it must necessarily be defined by an attribute which expresses eternal and infinite essence.
>
> (*Quod petis, an ex solo extensionis conceptu rerum varietas a prior possit demonstrari, credo me iam satis clare ostendisse, id impossibile esse; ideoque materiam a Cartesio male definiri per extensionem; sed eam necessario debere explicari per attributum, quod aeternam, et infinitam essentiam exprimat.*) (G IV/334)

However, he fears not having provided an adequate elucidation, for he continues: "But perhaps I will treat these matters more clearly with you some other time, if life lasts" (*Sed de his forsan aliquando, si vita suppetit, clarius tecum agam*) (G II/334). And he is equally conscious of not having elaborated a clear theory on this subject, for he concludes: "For up till now I have not been able to set out anything concerning them in an orderly way" (*Nam huc husque nihil de his ordine disponere mihi licuit*) (G II/334). Less than one year later Spinoza died without having had the chance to deepen the question posed by Tschirnhaus, a question whose elucidation would have required, in our opinion, a revision or at least a clarification of one aspect of the theory. We are thinking of the concept of "motion." It is motion that oversees the relationship among bodies, that is, among the modes of extension, and itself belongs, just as finite modes, to Natured Nature. While belonging to Natured Nature, that is, to what derives from the necessity of God's nature but which is not his essence itself, motion occupies, however, a specific place in the general articulation of reality, within the relation between substance and modes: in the theological language of the *Short Treatise*, motion is a "Son of God"; in the more certain and less imaginative language of letter 44 to Schuller, motion is that which is immediately produced by God and that from which other things derive (the reference to *E* IPP21–2 is obvious). We are not going to confront here the complex and controversial problem of the role played by the infinite immediate modes (*intellectus infinitus, motus* and *quies*: *Short Treatise*, the *Ethics*, the letter cited) and the infinite mediate modes (*facies totius universi*: letter 44) at the heart of the totality of Spinoza's system, or the reason why Spinoza introduced them by situating them in an intermediate position between substance and finite modes, as if the concept of immanent causality seemed inadequate to him to clarify this relationship. We only want to draw attention to an aspect that seems to us not to be consistent with the part of the theory exposed until now. Extension is an attribute of God, that is, it forms part of God's essence, of Naturing Nature; extension must not be understood as inert matter but as an attribute, that is — and it is we who add to it by explaining it from Spinoza's text — as "actual essence" (*actuosa essentia*), a dynamic principle, immanent causality, hence, activity. Why, then, does motion not belong to the essence of substance as it is expressed under the attribute of extension, remaining situated at the level of effect, whereas it defines modality itself as the accomplishment of the causality of substance insofar as it is extension? A clear vision of the role of motion would perhaps have led Spinoza to a "radicalization" of what on the contrary remained simple "aspects" of materialism, whose importance, though, must not be underestimated.

The conception of the relationship between the human mind and body is strictly dependent on the conception of the relationship between extension and thought as attributes of substance: "the essence of a human being is constituted by certain modifications of God's attributes" (*essentiam hominis constitui a certis Dei attributorum modificationibus*) (G II/93).[21] And, more precisely, "a human being consists of a mind and a body, and... the human body exists, as we are aware of it" (*hominem mente et corpore constare, et corpus humanum, prout ipsum sentimus, existere*) (G II/96).[22] The problematic resonance that this relationship had in Descartes is also lost. The condition of the mode, common to the body and soul, annuls on the other hand the very roots of the substantiality of the soul and poses on other grounds the question of its possible survival out of the body: "The first thing that constitutes the actual being of a human mind is nothing but the idea of a singular thing which actually exists" (*Primum, quod actuale mentis humanae esse constituit, nihil aliud est, quam idea rei alicuius singularis actu existentis*) (G II/94);[23] "The object of the idea constituting the human mind is the body, or a certain mode of extension which actually exists, and nothing else" (*Obiectum ideae, humanum mentem constiuentis, est corpus, sive certus extensionibus modus actus existentis, et nihil aliud*) (G II/96).[24] For Spinoza the relationship between the body and the mind is thus so organic that it leads him to specify that in order to determine the superiority of a mind, in reality and in perfection, in relation to another mind, its object, that is, the human body, would have to be known more fully. In the absence of this knowledge, he limits himself to stating a general principle:

[I]n proportion as a body is more capable than others of doing many things at once, or being acted on in many ways at once, so its mind is more capable than others of perceiving many things at once. And in proportion as the actions of a body depend more on itself alone, and as other bodies concur with it less in acting, so its mind is more capable of understanding distinctly.

[*Quo corpus aliquod reliquis aptius est ad plura simul agendum, vel patiendum, eo eius mens reliquis aptior est ad plura simul percipiendum; et quo unius corporis actiones magis ab ipso solo pendent, et quo minus alia corpora cum eodem in agendo concurrunt, eo eius mens aptior est ad distincte intelligendum.*][25] (G II/97)

If the soul, then, is indeed the idea of the body, given that there can be no idea without its object, it follows that there cannot be a mind without the body whose idea it is. There can be no survival of the individual soul from the body; in other words, the immortality of the soul is denied. However, Spinoza asserts that "something of it remains which is eternal" (*aliquid remanet, quod aeternum est*) (G II/295).[26] According to popular opinion, this something eternal that remains after the body's death is confused with duration and is attributed to the imagination, that is, to the memory that is believed to persist after the body's death.[27] On the other hand, it is precisely the imagination, in which passion is rooted, that perishes, whereas it is the intellect that is eternal,[28] that is, the mind insofar as its essence is defined as intelligence and, as such, a part of the infinite and eternal intellect of God. If one frees one-self from what we shall not hesitate to regard as a metaphor, once the concept of im-mortality is denied, that is, the survival of the individual soul from the body—as a principle that is independent of, and separable from, it—the eternity that Spinoza attributes to the human mind does not seem to us to differ from the form of perma-nence obtained by every idea or knowledge that becomes—whether it is denied or later displaced by other acquisitions—a common inheritance of humanity's forms of knowledge. Which does not differ from the type of eternity that we can attribute to the body insofar as it is a mode of the attribute of extension, if it is true that "the whole of Nature is one Individual, whose parts, i.e., all bodies, vary in infinite ways, without any change of the whole Individual" (*totam naturam unum esse individuum, cuius partes, hoc est, omnia corpora infinitis modis variant, absque ulla totius individui mutatione*) (G II/102).[29] This assertion can arouse a certain perplexity and appear too simplistic, for it seems to ignore the problematic importance (either in the sense of theoretical influences, or in the sense of the internal consistency of Spinoza's sys-tem) of the concept of the infinite intellect of God, a concept that seems to be able to reintegrate the personal God that had been refuted with such vigor: it suffices to think of the discussion on divine freedom and the theorization of determinism. We do not want in any way to underestimate the importance of this problematic, but we have consciously chosen here to examine the texts with the intention of extracting from them aspects of a progression, those which are capable of a reading oriented in the direction of materialism.

In this sense, Spinoza's concept of *mens* seems to us to be impor-tant, for—since it is defined as pure intelligence, a cognitive function tied to the body—it is posed as the negation of the concept of the soul insofar as it is an au-tonomous spiritual principle vis-à-vis the body, seat of values and subject of respon-sibility, with an ultraterrestrial individual destiny.

There is still a point on which we should like to pause briefly before concluding these observations. It concerns the theory of knowledge insofar as it is true and adequate knowledge. "A true idea must agree with its object" (*Idea vera debet cum suo ideato convenire*) (G II/47);[30] an adequate idea is, on the other hand, an idea that "insofar as it is considered in itself, without relation to an object, has all the properties, or intrinsic denominations of a true idea" (*quatenus in se, sine rela-tione ad obiectum consideratur, omnes verae ideae proprietates, sive denominationes intrise-cas habet*) (G II/85).[31] Adequation, as is well known, concerns the formal aspect of an idea, whereas truth concerns its relationship with its object. An idea is true when there is a correspondence between it and that of which it is the idea, that is, when it reflects the reality in relation to which it is posed as knowledge. Letter 9 concerning the nature of definitions, after having distinguished between the definition of the thing of which one seeks only the essence, which one does not doubt, and the definition that is proposed only in order to be examined, that is, the definition in its purely formal aspect, specifies that the first must be "true," for it has a determinate object and offers the example of Solomon's temple, of which — if one asks me for a description of it — I must give a true description, that is, corresponding to the formal and material characteristics of this building. In other words, if I project "into my mind" some other temple, in all legitimacy, from this projection I deduce the quantity of terrain, the number of bricks, the purchase of other necessary materials, without which no one could challenge the validity of my calculations, since in this case the reference to an extra-mental reality, in relation to which alone this contestation would have a meaning, is missing. We are in the domain of the pure and simple possibility of conceiving something that has no relation to the criterion of truth, which concerns the idea or the definition of a thing that exists *extra intellectum*. The example of Solomon's temple, of a given building, provided with controllable formal and material structures, clarifies with exactness the meaning of Spinoza's concept of truth as an extra-mental mirror of reality, a faithful reflection of its objective characteristics. Although Spinoza emphasizes in the *Ethics*, as he had already done in the *Treatise on the Emendation of the Intellect*, the active nature of the concept, although he rejects the theory of the *influxus physicus* and every relation of causality from the body to the idea or vice versa, the process of determination of the finite being internal to the series of modifications of every attribute; nonetheless, the identity of the order according to which these mutually autonomous processes unfold (it is a question of the famous *E* IIP7: "the order and connection of ideas is the same as the order and connection of things" [*ordo et connexio idearum idem est, ac ordo, et connexio rerum*] [G II/89]) guarantees the correspondence of the true idea with its ideatum, that is, the fact that the idea is the authentic mirror of known reality. Reality whose structure is thus a possible object of true knowledge, of knowledge that provides a piece of information worthy of faith regarding it, which discovers in it the objective laws within which it recognizes its own laws.

It is undoubtedly a question of a metaphysical solution. The correspondence between idea and ideatum is not the result of a critical research regarding the real but is certain from the start by the metaphysical presupposition of the unity of substance, governed by the laws that unfold in parallel within its two spheres of expression that are known to us: matter and thought. However, once freed from its metaphysical envelope, this theory encloses a principle that was to prove fruitful and—barring error on our part—to be taken up again, developed, and systematized by dialectical materialism. Plekhanov, whose interpretation of the Spinoza-Marx-Engels relationship we do not share, for we consider it to be schematic and reductive vis-à-vis the latter two, had nonetheless correctly detected in Spinozism, beneath its "faded theological finery," a theoretical kernel contributing to progress.

Translated by Ted Stolze

Notes

1. *Lev* I.

2. *DCo* VI/1.

3. *DCo* XXV.

4. Ibid.

5. Ibid.

6. *DCo* VIII/1.

7. *DCo* VI/5.

8. *DCo* XV/1.

9. *DCo* VI/5.

10. *DCo* XXV/2.

11. *DCo* I/1, VI/1ff.

12. See especially Pacchi (1965).

13. *DCo* XXV/1.

14. *DCo* VIII/1.

15. *DCo* VIII/4.

16. *Lev* XXXIV; the emphasis is in the original.

17. *DCo* I/7.

18. "To conclude, there is nothing in this whole discourse, nor in that I writ before of that same subject in Latin, as far as I can perceive, contrary either to the Word of God, or to good manners; or to the disturbance of the public tranquility. And thus I have brought to an end my Discourse of Civil and Ecclesiastical Government, occasioned by the disorders of the present time, without partiality, without application, and without other design than to set before men's eyes the mutual relation between protection and obedience; of which the condition of human nature, and the laws divine, both natural and positive, require an inviolable observation. And though in the revolution of states, there can be no very good constellation for truths of this nature to be born under (as having an angry aspect from the dissolvers of an old government, and seeing but the backs of them that erect a new), yet I think it will be condemned at this time, either by the public judge of doctrine, or by any that desires the continuance of public peace. And in this hope I return to my interrupted speculation of bodies

natural; wherein, if God gives me health to finish it, I hope the novelty will as much please, as in the doctrine of this artificial body it useth to offend. For such truth, as opposeth no man's profit, nor pleasure, is to all men welcome" (*Lev*, "A Review and Conclusion").

19. *E* IP14C1.

20. *E* IP14C2.

21. *E* IIP10C.

22. *E* IIP13C.

23. *E* IIP11.

24. *E* IIP13.

25. *E* IIP13S.

26. *E* VP23.

27. *E* VP34S.

28. *E* VP40C.

29. *E* IIL7S.

30. *E* IA6.

31. *E* IID4.

F I V E

The Problem of the Attributes

Pierre Macherey

The Ambiguity of the Notion of "Attribute"

HEGEL'S OBJECTIONS on the question of the relation of the attributes to substance are formulated from the same perspective as his critique of the *more geometrico*, of which they are an elaboration. The previous discussion essentially concerned the conditions of a true knowledge, and thus put into play the position of thought in relation to the real. Yet the intervention of the categories of substance and attribute in the treatment of this problem causes an essential divergence to appear between Spinoza and Hegel. For Hegel, thought and the real are fundamentally united in that they arise from the same process in which the mind, the real, is to itself its own subject: beyond the presentation of the true as substance, which is unilateral, there is *also* its being grasped as a subject, that is, as a totality in movement. In contrast, when Spinoza presents thought, not even as substance, but as an attribute of substance, he once again admits that he falls short of a truly rational knowledge, of which his system would provide only an imperfect and incomplete sketch.

In this displacement—from thought as substance that has become a subject, to thought as an attribute of substance—what is at issue is first the status of thought. By presenting thought "outside" of substance and in some way dependent on it, Spinoza, according to Hegel, extracts thought from its position of eminence at the same time that he contests its universal vocation. In this sense,

Spinoza remains foreign to the idealist perspective, because he denies thought the character of a substance (which Descartes, however, granted to thought). Actually, it indeed seems that between substance, which is "absolutely infinite," and its attributes, which are "infinite *only* in their kind,"[1] there is a hierarchical difference, analogous to the difference separating the whole from its parts. If, then, thought is an attribute, which the Spinozist system undeniably asserts, and if the attributes occupy a subordinate position in relation to substance, which confers on them diminished, or incomplete, functions, thought is no longer that absolute process that affirms its necessity by realizing it. Rather, thought is only an aspect or a moment of that process, which does not have all its conditions in itself, and whose development is, if one considers it in itself, contingent insofar as it depends on an external cause. This is how Hegel speaks of the attributes, "that is, as not having a separate existence, a self-subsistent being of their own, but only as sublated, as moments."[2] But are the attributes parts of substance for Spinoza? And is the relation of dependence that links the attributes to substance, as Hegel interprets it, a hierarchical relation between essentially unequal elements? This is where the whole question lies.

It must be understood that, in this argument, Hegel moves from a difficulty that is for him primary, specifically concerning one of the Spinozist attributes, Thought, to a critical analysis of the nature of the attributes considered in general, to which he extends these first objections. It is not surprising, then, that he repeats, regarding the attributes, the same arguments that had in the first place concerned method. Here again, what Hegel reproaches Spinoza for is the latter's formalism and the abstraction that, according to Hegel, characterizes Spinoza's entire system. As a matter of fact, the attributes, as Spinoza defines them, are for Hegel abstract essences, points of view *on* substance, which remain external to substance and as a result only "represent" it in an incomplete manner, outside of every possibility of a concrete development:

> Spinoza's definition of the absolute is followed by his definition of the attribute, and this is determined as the manner in which intellect comprehends the essence of substance. Apart from the fact that intellect, in accordance with its nature, is postulated as posterior to attribute—for Spinoza defines it as mode—attribute, determination as determination of the absolute, is thus made *dependent on an other,* namely, intellect, which appears as external and immediate over against substance.[3]

What is at issue here is obviously Spinoza's definition of the attribute at the beginning of *E* I: "By attribute I understand what the intellect perceives of substance, as constituting its essence."[4] Apparently, Hegel follows this definition literally: if the attribute is *what* the intellect perceives of substance, it is thus that it does not exist by itself outside of the intellect that perceives it, and in which it appears as a representation, that is, an image or an idea, of substance, external to it, and by this fact is necessarily incomplete. Then the gap that separates the attribute from substance becomes obvious: it is only a point of view in which substance is reflected, not, however, in itself, in the proper movement of its internal reflection, since according to Hegel the Spinozist substance is essentially immobile; but it must be said instead that substance is reflected outside of itself, in the intellect that perceives *an* irreducible essence of it, which represents the totality of substance by mutilating it, by reducing it, to just one of its aspects or moments.

This objection by Hegel appears to be quite strong, because it casts doubt on a great contradiction in Spinoza's very statement: the attribute "expresses" substance and in a certain way is identical to it, it participates in its own infinity, it constitutes its own essence, one will say again that it is substantial; and yet it does not present substance in its intimate nature—but does it have only one nature? As a foundation, the Spinozist substance is for Hegel an abyss, a nothingness of determinations—but such as it appears, such as it is shown outside of itself, for an intellect that comprehends it.

But what is this intellect that perceives substance and on which the nature of the attribute is then found to depend? Whether it is a finite or infinite intellect—let us note that Spinoza's definition does not allow this distinction to arise—it is a mode, that is to say, an affection of substance through the intermediary of a single one of its attributes, which in this case is thought. It is thus that the circle in which the mode of abstract reasoning of Spinoza's system encloses itself clearly appears: in the "order" of the system, the attribute, as an essence of substance, precedes the mode, which is a final determination of substance; in its definition, however, the consideration of a mode, the intellect, intervenes. Better: this definition makes the nature of the attribute depend on the existence of this mode without which it would be not only incomprehensible but even impossible.

For Hegel the Spinozist system is essentially abstract, because it wants to think the absolute in a beginning, as a beginning: the determination of the absolute is then reduced to the regressive order of a manifestation of substance outside itself (since it has nothing in itself), first in its attributes, then in its modes. Yet because of its formal character, this order is reversed at the very moment that it unfolds: to the extent that it follows it, the mode depends on the attribute; and yet Spinoza thinks of, or rather defines, the attribute in terms of the mode, and thus as a mode; the result, then, is, at the minimum, that the distinction between the attribute and the mode becomes incomprehensible.

But this inconsistency cannot be attributed to a fault in reasoning; it has a meaning: it expresses the limitation characteristic of Spinoza's thought, which, according to the premises, the "principles" that it gives itself, cannot avoid falling into such difficulties. The absolute self-sufficiency of substance, its unity from the beginning, given in a foundation that absorbs into itself all reality but from which nothing can escape, except for appearances or "ways of being," gives its ontological guarantee to the system, but at the same time prevents it from being developed. In its development it must challenge these premises: the "passage" from substance to the attributes is the formal and arbitrary process through which substance is destroyed or exhausted and disperses its profound unity in a multiplicity of attributes that "comprise" it only by ignoring its true nature. The inconsistency, the weakness of Spinoza's notion of attribute expresses the necessary, or rather inevitable, self-exteriority of substance, which can be grasped in its essence only if this essence is opposed to it as a determination held over it from outside, which must therefore be inadequate to it. But this inadequation is only the defect of substance itself: as a universal and empty form, substance is capable of returning to itself in order to grasp itself in itself as true. This is why the inconsistency of Spinoza's system, such as it appears in its definition of the attributes, follows "logically" from its premises, of which it is the obligatory consequence: the vicious circle in which Spinoza turns is also his truth; it is the condition of possibility of his discourse and the obvious symptom of his failure.

Because he reasons abstractly, Spinoza can determine the absolute only by decomposing it, by "passing" from the point of view of an immediately given consistency to the point of view of an analysis of the elements, the "essences" that constitute it. As soon as one escapes the foundation so as to go toward what it founds, by envisioning its successive determinations, the attributes and then the modes, one sees its unity undone, or even disappear, and it is a multiplicity, a diversity that takes its place. In fact, not only are the attributes external to substance, and they thus manifest the self-exteriority of substance itself, which is incapable of actually being assembled in an intrinsic movement, but they are also external to one another, as aspects or points of view: irreducible essences that can only be posed alongside of one another and enumerated, without a genuine community capable of being established among them. And it is in fact an unequivocal affirmation in Spinoza that the attributes, which do not act on one another, which are not connected by a relation of reciprocal communication, are fundamentally independent.

In this separation of the attributes, Hegel correctly sees the symptom of their powerlessness to equal the absolute, which they partially "represent." Then the immediate and empty unity of substance scatters into a multiplicity of attributes that express it in incomplete forms, and these forms cannot be grasped together, included within an actual whole; but are only assembled, juxtaposed, added to one another, as pieces abstractly and arbitrarily held in a totality.

But—and here Hegel's critique reaches its crucial point—the attributes not only exist as separate entities, each posed in itself in the solitude of its abstraction, they are also opposed to one another. Since they are only points of view on the substance whose content they share and that they make appear in a mutilated way, they are in a way confronted with one another, like concurrent forms, each of which exists only in the absence of all the others, and against them.

Here a new argument is sketched, the one that takes as its pretext the well-known thesis *omnis determinatio est negatio*: the attributes determine substance negatively, that is, privatively. Thus, what gives form to an attribute is what all the others lack; this is why it is irreducible to them.

We shall consider this argument in its own right later. For the moment we retain only a consequence. We have seen that, posing the attributes after substance as its abstract determinations, the Spinozist system finds itself inevitably drawn into a regressive movement: part, but only part—for, let us recall, the root of Spinoza's error is found in his point of departure, from which he could only deviate—of the absolute knowledge of a unique substance, it next takes a step backward, *and it then finds Cartesian dualism.* Note how in his *Lectures on the History of Philosophy* Hegel presents what he calls the Spinozist idealism by reducing it to its main inspiration:

> Spinoza's philosophy is the objectification (*Objektivierung*) of that of Descartes in the form of absolute truth. The simple thought of Spinoza's idealism is this: What is true is quite simply the one substance, whose attributes are thought and extension (nature): and only this absolute unity is the real (*wirklich, die Wirklichkeit*), it alone is God. It is, as in Descartes, the unity of thought and being, or that which contains the principle of its existence in itself. In Descartes substance, the Idea, certainly has being included in its concept; but it is only being as abstract, not as real being (*reales Sein*) or as extension but corporealities, something other than substance, not one of its modes. In the same way, the 'I,' which thinks, is for itself also an autonomous being. This autonomy of the two extremes is done away with in Spinozism, and they become moments of absolutely one being. We see that, what is thus expressed, is that being must be grasped as the unity of opposites.[5]

At first glance, this text illuminates what separates Spinoza from Descartes: what the latter posits as autonomous substances, thought and extension (which Hegel assimilates to "nature," indeed to the "real"), are brought together, reconciled, in Spinoza by the absolute unity of substance, which is also the "unity of opposites." But we know that for Hegel this unity is abstract, that is, a false unity that decomposes by being determined, precisely in these very opposites that it had therefore only provisionally brought together, by "surpassing" their opposition. Such as Spinoza presents them, the oppositions that are only oppositions can only be surpassed in an illusory way; they are simply transposed. This is why, at the foundation of Spinoza's system, we find Cartesian dualism, even if in a modified form.

Hegel's commentary on the definition of the attributes in the same chapter of the *Lectures* has exactly this sense:

> What comes second, after substance, is the attributes; the latter belong to substance. "By attribute I understand what the intellect perceives of substance as constituting its essence," and to Spinoza this alone is true. This is a great determination; the attribute is at the same time a determinateness and a totality. Substance has only two attributes, thought and extension. The intellect grasps them as the essence of substance; essence is not more than substance, but it is only essence from the perspective of the intellect. This perspective is external to substance; the latter can be envisaged in two ways, as extension and as thought. Each is the totality, the entire content of substance, but only under a form; this is why the two sides are in themselves identical and infinite. This is the true perfection. In the attribute, the intellect grasps all of substance; but how substance passes over into the attribute is not said.[6]

If the entire content of substance is found in each attribute, it is to the extent that substance is already in itself devoid of all content: the attribute is only a form, which can certainly be autonomous and infinite; it remains no less deprived of all real movement, and thus of a concrete unity. The attributes are essences that confront one another, that are opposed, and their extrinsic relation reveals the powerlessness of substance, that is, of the absolute posed as immediate, to determine itself by itself.

But what is above all characteristic, in the two previous texts, is an extraordinary omission. Spinoza asserts that substance expresses itself in an infinity of attributes, of which we perceive only two: thought and extension. Yet when Hegel characterizes the nature of attributes, he acts as if there existed only the two attributes that we perceive: "It [substance] has only two: thought and extension." This restriction has extremely important consequences, for it is what allows Hegel to establish a relation of filiation between Spinoza and Descartes: it is also what authorizes him to present the unity of the attributes "within" substance as a unity of opposites.

Let us take up again the definition Spinoza gives of attributes: they are "what the intellect perceives of substance as constituting its essence." We have already remarked that Spinoza does not specify what is the intellect that here perceives substance: is it an infinite intellect, which perceives all its essences, or a finite intellect, which perceives only two? Why doesn't this distinction arise in the general definition of the attributes? It is clear in any case that Hegel has not taken any account of this lack of precision, and that he interprets the definition of the attributes in a very particular sense: for him the intellect that "constitutes" the attributes by perceiving substance is the finite intellect that apprehends the latter only under the two forms of thought and extension.

Gueroult has emphasized the Kantian inspiration of interpretation that Hegel proposes of Spinoza: it is really this implicit reference to Kant that justifies the accusation of formalism brought against Spinoza. The attributes are not just the "essences" of substance, they are its forms and, at the limit, its phenomena. The attribute is substance such as it appears, for an intellect that decomposes it depending on the very conditions of its perception, that is, that determines it by limiting it. In this sense, for Hegel the infinity of attributes, which express their identity with substance, is an infinity without content: it is the infinity of a form that, in itself, as form, in the limitation that constitutes it, from the point of view of the intellect that "perceives" it, is a finite form. Thus everything makes sense: Spinoza's inability concretely to think about the absolute results, from the fact that from the start he has situated himself at the point of view of the finite intellect, which is by its own nature incapable of grasping the infinite other than by decomposing it, that is, by reducing it to abstract essences. Let us note that, underlying all this argumentation the Kantian distinction between reason (devoted to the unconditioned) and the understanding (which determines its object only under its conditions) may be seen. What Hegel has not seen, has not wanted to see, in the definition of the attributes given by Spinoza, is precisely the anticipatory refusal of such a distinction. This refusal is expressed by the fact that the notion of the understanding figures in this definition in an absolutely general way, without there being room for some difference — whatever there may be — to arise among the several kinds of understanding.

From then on it is obvious that Hegel does not explain Spinoza's text but proposes an interpretation of it. Through this interpretation he finds

Descartes in Spinoza: the intellect that serves to determine the nature of the attributes being the finite intellect that perceives only two attributes, the unity of substance decomposes, comes apart, in the distinction of thought and extension, which reestablishes in it an unacknowledged duality. In this sense, Hegel can say that Spinozism is a failed effort to surpass the limits of Cartesianism: both rest on the same premises, and treat, even if in a different way, the same problem, that of the relation of two distinct entities, between which must be established the conditions of an agreement. Spinoza having posed from the beginning the unity of substance, which is then a unity without content, one thought and one extension into which this unity next decomposes come to confront one another, as opposites that must be reconciled, and that fail to be so other than in a formal way.

We are going to see that this interpretation completely *misses* what Spinoza actually argues in his demonstrations. For in him thought and extension do not confront one another as the terms of an opposition that should next be overcome; this is precisely what the thesis of their irreducibility means, which excludes every relation, even a relation of opposition, between them. Yet if one returns to the letter of the system, one perceives that the independence of the attributes, which are nonetheless identical in the substance of which they constitute the essences, is only comprehensible from the fact that substance expresses itself not in one, two, or any number of attributes, but in their infinity, which forbids establishing among them a term-by-term relation, whatever its form. But to understand this is to situate oneself within a mode of reasoning that has nothing to do with the one that Hegel imputes to Spinoza.

The Reality of the Attributes

Through his critique of Cartesianism, Spinoza invalidates in advance a Kantian type of problematic of knowledge, posed in terms of the relationship of subject/object or form/content. This is what Hegel, who himself nonetheless rejects this problematic and claims to surpass it, absolutely ignored: this lacuna governs his entire interpretation of Spinozism. What is astonishing here is that Hegel, on a point at which, between his philosophy and Spinoza's, an essential convergence appears, discovers on the contrary a motif of divergence. This reversal can only be explained in two ways: either Hegel uses irrefutable arguments that permit to be established that the Spinozist critique of the classical conception of truth is inadequate, and by this fact falls back into the shortcomings of this conception from which it remains inseparable, as he asserts. Or else this Spinozist critique is intolerable to Hegel because, still more radical than his own, it highlights its limits, and reveals the complicity that always links the Hegelian system with the previous conceptions he claims to invalidate by resolving all their contradictions. We are going to see that it is the latter interpretation that must be adopted.

Let us return to the problem of the attributes. The latter, according to Hegel, are "determinations," "forms" by which substance is reflected in the point of view of the intellect. In a way, substance is a content without form, immediately given in its absolute indetermination, in the manner of the empty Being of the Eleatists. It is next externalized in forms without content, which reflect it in the manner of Kantian categories. Yet this schema betrays Spinoza's doctrine at least on one point: if for Spinoza the attributes are forms, kinds of being, natures, or even essences, they are certainly not forms in opposition to a content, no more than they are predicates in opposition to a subject, or abstract categories in opposition to a concrete reality that would remain external to them. Or then one could as easily say that the attributes are themselves contents that hold good for a form, substance, for the latter "consists" in them, and comprehends them as "constituting" its essence. This means quite simply that the terms "form" and "content" are entirely improper to characterize the relation that links attributes to substance.

If the attributes are "what the intellect perceives of substance," they are not at all thereby dependent from the point of view of the intellect in which they would exist as reflected forms, nor even more so from the point of view of a finite intellect opposed to an infinite reason. Here the fact that in his definition of attributes Spinoza uses the word "perceive" (*percipere*) must be taken seriously: the intellect *perceives* the attributes as constituting the essence of substance. If we refer to the explanation of definition 3 at the beginning of book II of the *Ethics*, we observe that this term has a very precise meaning: regarding the idea that is a "concept of the mind," Spinoza writes that "I say concept rather than perception, because the word perception seems to indicate that the mind is acted on by the object. But concept seems to express an action of the mind." This indication can be turned around and applied to the definition of the attributes: Spinoza does not say that they are what the intellect "conceives" of substance, precisely because that would imply an activity of the intellect in relation to its "object," on which it would impose a modification, for example, by giving it a form, by "informing" it. The attribute is what the intellect "perceives" of substance, because, in the relation established here, there is on the contrary a passivity of the intellect vis-à-vis substance, which it accepts as such, in the essences that constitute it, that is, in its attributes.

The term "intellect," such as it appears in the definition of the attributes, thus cannot be interpreted in a Kantian sense. Even if it were a matter here of our own singular intellect, the finite intellect, the objection that Spinoza directed against Bacon would remain applicable:

> He supposes that in addition to the deceptiveness of the senses, the human intellect is deceived simply by its own nature, and feigns everything from the analogy of its own nature, not from the analogy of the universe, so that in relation to the rays of things it is like an uneven mirror, which mixes its own nature with the nature of things.[7]

Yet Hegel's interpretation of the role of the intellect in the definition of the attributes proceeds precisely in this sense: the intellect that reflects substance in the form of its attributes is indeed a kind of deforming, or informing, mirror, which impresses its own mark on the images it produces in such a way that it is the mirror that the latter allow to be seen instead of the object reflected in it. But, for Spinoza, if the intellect is a mirror—which is also questionable, since ideas are not images—it is certainly not such an active mirror that intervenes in reality, decomposing it in order to reconstruct it in its own measure: it must be, at least in the case that occupies us, a perfectly objective mirror, which "perceives" substance as it is, in the essences that actually constitute it. The definition of attributes that Spinoza offers clearly excludes all creativity by the intellect.

A remark is necessary here, which will take on all its meaning only by what follows. We have just shown that the relation of perception that ties the intellect to substance in the definition of attributes implies passivity instead of activity. But this idea of passivity, if one examines it a little more closely, also proves to be embarrassing: doesn't it mean that the attributes, as faithful images that are content to reproduce a model, are passive representations, corresponding exactly to the object that they allow to be seen, that is, that they are, to take up again a well-known expression, "mute paintings on a canvas"? What we would then have gained, on the one hand, by ceasing to consider attributes as forms engendered by the intellect, we would have obviously lost on the other, by reducing them to ideas that passively reflect an external reality. In order to dispose of this new difficulty, it must be added that attributes are neither "active" nor "passive" representations of the intellect, quite simply because they are not representations, images, or even ideas of the intellect or in the intellect: attributes are not in the intellect, as forms through which the latter would apprehend, objectively or not, a content given in substance; but they are in substance itself whose essences they constitute. This specification allows us to rid the definition of the attributes of any notion of passivity: attributes are active to the extent that substance is expressed in them, in all its essences.

Yet to renounce any consideration of the attributes as ideas of the intellect is by the same token to call into question another aspect of the interpretation proposed by Hegel. In order to present the abstract nature of the attributes, Hegel separates the attributes from substance, by presenting their relationship as a relationship of succession: *first* substance, *then* the attributes. The identity of the attributes and of substance, however clearly asserted by Spinoza, then becomes entirely problematic: outside of substance and after it, the attributes are really only the forms through which the intellect reflects it, by dissociating them from the foundation to which they refer. But this idea of a priority of substance in relation to its attributes, which establishes a hierarchical relationship between them, is completely contrary to the letter of Spinoza's doctrine.

Here, one would again have to take up the argumentation, even the irrefutable proof, on the contrary, of such commentators as Deleuze and Gueroult, who, after Lewis Robinson, have emphasized the "genetic" and not "hypothetical" nature of the first propositions of the *Ethics*, which result in the demonstration of the existence of God, that is, of the unique substance that includes an infinity of attributes. It is, in a general way, a largely received idea that Spinoza's *Ethics* "begins" with God: Hegel takes up again this idea in his own way, by holding it against Spinoza that he "begins," as if he were Chinese, with the absolute. Yet, if it is also entirely doubtful that Spinoza's system is erected on the basis of an absolute beginning, an attentive reading of the beginning of the *Ethics* shows that this beginning could not really be God, that is, the absolutely infinite unique substance: of the latter we only have first a nominal definition (definition 6), and we must wait until proposition 11 to discover that this definition corresponds to a real, actually unique, being. What has happened in the meantime?

If the first ten propositions of the *Ethics* are interpreted in the sense of a general ontology or a formal combinatory, which amounts to denying to them every real meaning, in order to turn them into a statement concerning only possibilities,[8] one will respond that nothing really happens in them at all; but they have only a preparatory value and serve as a methodological precondition for the actual discourse on substance, which will only come next, at the moment that the existence of the latter will have been really established, which puts an end to considerations on pure essences, considered outside of the taking of a position on their existence.

Let us note immediately that this interpretation is akin to Hegel's on an essential point: it turns the discourse about substance into a kind of absolute beginning; this is why, insofar as there is no question of substance itself, in a certain sense in person, that is, of God, Spinoza's demonstrations will be said only to have an introductory function; strictly speaking, they say nothing, since their object is "being in general," envisaged outside of the conditions of its existence. What reappears here is the formalist conception of the attributes, explained on the basis of a dualism of essence and existence, which Spinoza nonetheless explicitly rejects: "The existence of the attributes does not differ from their essence."[9]

Doesn't such a reading call into question again the necessity of reasoning, such as the *more geometrico* establishes it, within a synthetic, truly causal progression? According to Spinoza, true discourse is also, and by the same token, actual, which excludes any investigation of the possible, and also any submission to the precondition of a beginning or an introduction. One must thus take up again the totality of the propositions that precede the demonstration of the existence of God in order to identify their status.

Gueroult presents these propositions according to the following division:[10]

> Propositions 1 to 8 carry out the deduction of the constitutive elements of the divine essence, namely, substances with a single attribute.

> In the second section (propositions 9 to 15), it will be question of constructing God on the basis of his simple elements, substances with a single attribute... and of conferring on him the recognized characteristics of each of them.

We shall see that certain of these formulations arouse serious objections and cannot be maintained. However, even if they present it in an inaccurate discourse, which deviates at least at one point from the letter of the system, they allow a very important aspect of Spinoza's demonstration, an aspect that has never appeared as clearly before, to be highlighted.

In fact, if one follows the essentials of Gueroult's analysis, even if it also appears that it is inadmissible on certain points, one perceives, to take up again the terms of the question posed above, that something indeed occurs in the propositions that open book I of the *Ethics*. And this event is situated precisely at the intersection of propositions 8 and 9, at the moment when one "passes" from *substantia unius attributi* (let us set aside for the moment the translation of this expression, for it poses a problem) to absolutely infinite substance, which possesses all the attributes and necessarily exists, in such a way that no other substance can be conceived. Thus, to take up again Gueroult's expression, substance is "constructed" from the elements that compose it, that is, the attributes themselves insofar as they constitute substance (for the attributes are "substantial" if they are not strictly speaking substances). Substance appears, then, in its real process, and the discourse of this objective genesis does not express an empty knowledge to which the formal precondition of a combinatory would be reduced, but actively expresses the actual movement of its object, in some sense in its concrete history.

The essential merit of this analysis is to give to the notion of *causa sui* all its significance. If God is "cause of himself," it is not in the sense that Hegel interprets it of an immediate gift of the absolute in the gesture of an original foundation in which the latter is exhausted at the same time that it is entirely communicated in one fell swoop, in the irreducibility of an inalienable presence that could thus be determined only from outside. But the *causa sui* is nothing but the process within which substance engenders itself on the basis of the "essences" that constitute it, on which its existence is established: this movement leads to the moment in which it produces substance, as the product of its activity, as the result of its own determination. From this point of view, Spinozist substance has nothing to do with the Being of the Eleatics: in its immanent life—whereas Hegel does not cease to speak of "dead substance"—it is a movement toward self, affirmation of self, quite the contrary of an unreal content that should seek its forms outside of itself. Here again, we find ourselves "quite near" Hegel, whereas the latter has remained completely blind to this proximity.

It is this movement that the definition of God expresses that must be understood genetically and causally: "By God I understand a being absolutely infinite, i.e., a substance consisting of an infinity of attributes, of which each one expresses an eternal and infinite essence."[11] This definition is synthetic and geometrical, because it determines its object necessarily, by producing it: God, if he is *causa sui*, is not without a cause; but on the contrary he is absolutely determined by himself: the attributes are precisely the forms of this determination. On the basis of such a definition, one can deduce in a way that is also necessary all the properties of its object:

> When I define God as the supremely perfect being, since this definition does not express the efficient cause (for I conceive that an efficient cause can be internal as well as external) I shall not be able to discover all the properties of God from it; but when I define God as *a being*, etc. (see *E* ID6)[12]

Thus, engendered in its attributes, which are its internal efficient cause, substance is also cause of itself. It is clear from the start that substance is not an immediate absolute, since it must be deduced, even if from itself.

The relation of substance to its attributes is thus found to be profoundly modified. First, it is no longer possible to assert the exteriority of the attributes vis-à-vis substance: the attributes are in substance, as aspects or moments through which it is constituted. On the other hand, if one absolutely insists on establishing an order of succession between substance and the attributes, it is no longer at all certain that substance ought to be situated *before* the attributes, but it is rather the attributes that precede substance as the conditions of its self-production, since in the process of its constitution they play an essentially causal role. Thus is explained an often-noted anomaly: the *Ethics* does not "begin" with God but it leads to him, or at least reaches him, after a whole series of demonstrations, a difficulty that interpreters traditionally circumvent by emptying of all content the propositions that do *not yet* concern the unique and really existing substance, in order to turn them into just the formal preconditions of a discourse that really only begins after them.

However, as we shall see, it is no more satisfying to speak of a "priority" of attributes in relation to substance. This is why we shall be content for the moment to insist on another aspect of the argument, which is essential and which concerns the identity of the attributes and substance. If this identity is admitted, it is no longer possible to think between substance and the attributes this inequality that presupposes as much a chronological relation of succession as that of a hierarchical subordination. There is no more or less being or reality in substance than in its attributes, but there is exactly *as much*, or at least this is what one might say if this reality could be measured quantitatively. The attributes are no less than substance; for example, they are not essences that, taken in themselves, lack existence; but substance is precisely what they are. In *Descartes's "Principles of Philosophy"* Spinoza already wrote:

> Again, when he [Descartes] says: *it is greater to create or preserve a substance than to create or preserve its attributes,* he can surely not understand by attributes what is contained formally in substance and is distinguished from substance itself only by reason. For then creating a substance is the same as creating its attributes.[13]

But God, a substance that includes all the attributes, "creates" neither substance nor the attributes, what Descartes can no longer "understand."

Letter 9 to Simon de Vries, if it is read correctly, establishes that "attribute" and "substance" are different names for the same thing, just as the names "Israel" and "Jacob" designate the same being. It is true that this letter has usually been read in the wrong way: as if it were the attributes themselves that were different *names* for this identical and unique *thing* that would be substance. The persistence of this error[14] can only be explained in one way: in his letter Spinoza speaks of *two* names for the same thing, and the example he uses develop this hypothesis. Everything happens as if the gaze of his readers remained fixed on this number, which in itself has no significance; the occasion is then ready-made to mark an ordinary fantasy in metaphysics, of which Hegel has already given us a good example: "two" seems to indicate only a single thing, the duality of thought and extension, according to the Cartesian division of substances; this is what leads one to consider the attributes, identified once for all with the two attributes that our finite intellect perceives, as names, that is, forms external to a content that they designate in an extrinsic manner. But, on this point, Spinoza is perfectly clear: the attributes are essences, hence, realities. The attributes are therefore absolutely not in themselves names, that is, designations of substance through the intermediary by which the latter would be decomposed abstractly into a multiplication of perspectives or appearances.

In order to grasp this real identity that connects the attributes and substance, it will suffice again to bring together two texts, whose cross-referencing excludes any equivocation:

> By attribute I understand whatever is conceived through itself and in itself, so that its concept does not involve the concept of another thing.[15]

> By substance I understand what is conceived through itself and in itself, i.e., that whose concept does not involve the concept of another thing.[16]

Attribute and substance arise from one and the same definition, which concerns an identical reality: the fact is here immediately readable. Spinoza could have written just as easily: "By substance and attribute I understand one and the same thing."

Again:

> By God's attributes are to be understood what... expresses [*exprimit*] an essence of the Divine substance, i.e., what pertains [*pertinet*] to substance. The attributes themselves, I say, must involve [*involvere*] it itself.[17]

Exprimit: the attributes express substance; this absolutely does not mean that they represent it in the form of a predicate, a property, or a name. Rather, it means that they constitute it, in what can be called its concrete being. *Pertinet*: the attributes are included within substance, and, just as much, it is included in them; they are not at all external and arbitary manifestations, dependent on the free will of an intellect that would reflect it according to its own categories: let us note that the definition that we are in the process of commenting on no longer refers to the intellect. *Invol-*

vere: attributes and substance are inseparable in that they cannot be conceived without one another, outside of one another; and this reciprocal dependence expresses nothing but the fact of their real unity.

One more remark to conclude. Perhaps the equivocations that have accumulated around the interpretation of the initial definition of the attributes (*E* ID4) could have been avoided if Spinoza had written this definition in a slightly different way: "By attribute I understand what constitutes the essence of substance, and it is thus that the intellect perceives it (such as it is)," a formulation that suppresses every species of dependence of the attributes in relation to the intellect. After all, to admit the rigorous nature of Spinoza's text does not necessarily mean to consider his letter as inviolable, nor to turn it into an object of adoration, by considering it as a receptacle in which great mysteries sleep, mysteries that it would be necessary only to contemplate at a distance, taking great care not to awaken them. The *Ethics* must be explained by the *Ethics*, as Spinoza elsewhere explained Scripture by Scripture, that is, to determine the system of the material constraints that organize its text, and that permit it actually to fulfill its objectives; on the basis of this, it must be possible eventually to identify its lacunae.

The Diversity of the Attributes

The attributes are thus identical to substance, and likewise substance is the same thing as its attributes: it is only from the point of view of the intellect that a distinction between substance and attribute can be established, which means that this distinction has no real nature but is only a distinction of reason.

However, care must be taken not to interpret the relation of substance and the attributes in the sense of a formal reciprocity. If there is incontestably identity among them, the latter is not an abstract and empty equality; without it, one would no longer understand what is the role of the notion of attribute in the necessary economy of the demonstration, which one might be tempted purely and simply to suppress. In this sense, apparently, Spinoza asserts that "in Nature there is nothing except substances and their affections, as is evident from A1, D3, and D5";[18] and again: "Except for substances and accidents, nothing exists in reality, *or* outside the intellect, for whatever there is, is conceived either through itself or through another, and its concept either does or does not involve the concept of another thing."[19] In the real, that is, outside of the intellect, and we are referred back to the point of departure, it seems: if the attributes have no real existence, if they are detached from substance only from the point of view (*perspectu*) of the intellect, aren't they beings of reason, intellectual fictions external to every content, that is, pure forms of representation?

Let us recall that what exists for the intellect is not the attributes themselves, which are certainly not "in" the intellect, but their distinction from substance. But a new argument must be added here: the existence of the attributes in substance, which is the key to their identity, is not an indifferent unity, which would result from a simply formal equality; it is a concrete identity, which is an identity in difference. This is why the attributes are necessary to the determination of substance, whose internal causality they express and realize. But how does substance proceed in the attributes, or the attributes in substance? This is what must now be understood.

Let us take up again the division of book I of the *Ethics* proposed by Gueroult. The first eight propositions have as an object the *substantia unius attributi*, which permits one to eliminate the conception of a substrate that is immobile, undifferentiated, and thus in itself unknowable. Thus, it is established from the start that substance only exists in its attributes, which are themselves substantive. But it results also from this reasoning that there are as many substances as there are attributes: as Gueroult remarks, in this initial development substance is written in the plural, as in proposition 5, which demonstrates an essential point for all the rest (two substances could be distinguished only by their attribute).

In propositions 9 to 15, one passes from the plural to the singular: from the *substantia unius attributi*, which is "only" infinite in its kind, to the substance that includes an infinity of attributes, and that can be called absolutely infinite; it includes all the attributes because it cannot lack a single one. This "passage" is summarized in letter 36 to Hudde as follows: "If we assume that something which is only unlimited and perfect of its kind exists by its own sufficiency, *then we must also* admit the existence of a being that is absolutely unlimited and perfect; which being I call God." Thus we are led, as if by the hand, from the idea of the attributes to the idea of substance: if one first knows the perfection of the attributes, one must also know that it cannot be understood outside of the absolute perfection of God who contains all of them. In fact, if one remained at the consideration of the attributes, each taken in itself, one would be naturally led to think of them negatively by opposing them to one another, by apprehending the nature of each of them in the absence of all the others. Yet the infinity of the attributes can be grasped positively only if one connects them to the divine, absolutely infinite, nature, in which they coexist without being opposed. This is why the attributes cannot exist outside of God but are necessarily in him, in which they are affirmed identically as essences infinite in their kind, in a mode of determination that excludes all negativity. At the same time, substance is nothing but the unity of its attributes, which it brings together in its absolute existence.

This reasoning already gave pause to the first readers of the *Ethics*, as is attested by letter 8 from Simon de Vries to Spinoza: "If I should say that each substance has only one attribute, and if I had the idea of two attributes, I could rightly conclude that, where there are two different attributes, there are two different substances. We ask you for a clearer explanation of this too." Yet the problem is here actually unsolvable, to the extent that it poses the diversity of the attributes from a point of view that is first of all numerical: for Simon de Vries "an" attribute is an expression that has no meaning except in relation to the series "one, two, three...an infinity of attributes." This presentation is characteristic, first because in this infinite series it privileges, in order to designate the multiplicity of attributes, a very particular number, which is as if by chance the number two. Yet this choice reveals right away that the question is here envisaged exclusively from the point of view of the finite intellect, which only knows precisely two attributes, thought and extension; as we have already indicated, it is entirely significant that this point of view on the contrary never arises in Spinoza's reasoning, which uses the notion of intellect taken in general.

On the other hand, the breakdown of the attributes according to a numerical succession has for a consequence that the "passage" from substances that are infinite only in their kind to absolutely infinite substance appears as a gradual and continuous progression: everything happens as if the attributes were added to one another in substance, which would be itself composed through this infinite summation. Yet it is entirely remarkable that on the contrary Spinoza presents the process in which substance engenders itself on the basis of its attributes in a completely different way: the latter occurs in a clear rupture, which proceeds without intermediary from one level to another, in such a way that the relationship between the infinite only in its kind and the absolutely infinite first appears as a true contradiction, which will be resolved by force, outside of every attempt at reconciliation.

Let us take up once again the reasoning starting with its beginning: substance is first of all thought in the real diversity of its attributes, as is indicated, for example, by propositions 2 ("Two substances having different attributes have nothing in common with one another") and 5 ("In Nature there cannot be two or more substances of the same nature or attribute"). Next, substance is thought in its absolute unity, insofar as it brings together in it all the attributes by posing itself as identical to them. Here we are dealing with a genuine reversal of perspectives: how should it be interpreted?

One might be tempted to understand this reasoning as a reasoning by absurdity: it is in this sense that the formalist interpretation we have already criticized proceeds. One will say then: in a first moment Spinoza suggests the possibility of really distinct substances, each determined by an attribute, in order to be able next to refute it, by discovering afterward, through an artifice of presentation, the absolute unity of substance that coincides with its unicity. Considered in this way, the reasoning is reduced to a certain way of using proofs: it loses its synthetic nature and its objective meaning. This is why, in accordance with the requirements of the *more geometrico*, which are not simply formal as we have shown, this interpretation must be set aside.

Two moments of argumentation must thus be granted an equal reality: considered from the point of view of the diversity (or infinity) of its attributes, substance is not a fiction, or the representation of a pure possibility, which could only be constructed by a breakdown to the infinite, for such a breakdown has no meaning except from the point of view of the imagination. But it is the same content, an identical reality that appears as diversity, then unity. Yet this content cannot be presented in the harmonious and conciliatory progression of a finished order, unless to make us fall back into the aporia of the immediate foundation denounced by Hegel. It must be presented on the contrary in a contrasted movement, which at the same time raises up these extreme aspects and by the same token demonstrates their solidarity, their community, that is, their inseparability. Also, these two aspects are not successive but simultaneous.

The true meaning of the distinction between substance and the attributes, as it is established by the intellect, then appears: this is what allows substance to be apprehended such as it is, in the real complexity of its nature; that is, what allows us to think its unity up to the end, absolutely. It is because substance includes the infinity of the attributes that it is absolutely infinite. The unity of substance is thus not an arithmetic unity: it does not designate the existence of an individual irreducible to all others by the simplicity of its nature. Substance is not a being, and this is the fundamental condition of its unicity: it is everything that exists and can be understood, which thus has its cause only in itself. Yet this plenitude of being, this absolute affirmation of self, which constitutes substance, cannot be the empty form of the One that would only be One, or that would be, if one can say it, only a One: it is this infinitely diverse reality that includes all the attributes, and that expresses itself in their unity. This reality is not that of a Being that would already enclose this totality, by virtue of an initial gift, but it is at first that of an irresistible movement, through which all the attributes pass and are unified in the substance that appropriates them for itself.

There is only one substance, but it includes an infinity of attributes: its unity is incomprehensible outside of this infinite diversity that intrinsically constitutes it. The result is that substance has multiplicity in itself and not outside of itself, and, from this fact, this multiplicity ceases to be numerical, what Spinoza expresses precisely by saying that it is infinite; in fact, for it, the infinite is not a number to the extent that it cannot be represented by the imagination. One is here poles apart, one sees, from this project of a "philosophical calculation," of this mechanical denumeration of the parts that formally constitute a being, to which Hegel would like to reduce the *more geometrico*.

The result, which Hegel ignored, is that the identity of substance and its attributes is not formal and abstract but real and concrete. The latter develops in a double relation: the one that ties substance to its attributes, without which it would be an empty being in which one could from this fact recognize only a minimum of reality, and not the maximum that belongs to it; the one that ties the attributes to substance, outside of which they would exist negatively, as opposites.

In order to imitate the Hegelian discourse, one could say: the relationship of substance and the attributes is the identity having become that in which the absolute is affirmed as actual. And this process is that of the *causa sui*, or, if one wishes, of substance's return into itself.

The Constitution of Substance in Its Attributes

Until now we have spoken of a self-production or a self-constitution of substance *within* its attributes. We must now specify that the latter has nothing to do with a genesis of substance *on the basis of* its attributes, and eliminate an equivocation that is still found in Gueroult's commentary, which we have followed for the most part until now.

In fact, if all the attributes belong together to substance and constitute its being (*E* IP10S), they do not coexist in it as parts that would adjust themselves to one another in order finally to compose the complete system. If this were so, the attributes would be defined in relation to one another by their reciprocal lack: they could no longer from then on be conceived each through itself, because they would be limited in their own nature by something else. Yet an attribute—for example, extension—could be limited only by itself, which is absurd since it is infinite in its own kind:

> Although...extension negates thought of itself, this in itself is no imperfection in it. But it would argue imperfection in it, if it were to be deprived of extension, as would actually happen if it were limited, similarly if it lacked duration, position, etc.[20]

To think the infinite, whether in the attribute (in a kind) or in substance (absolutely) is to exclude every notion of divisibility: substance is entirely in each of its attributes (since it is identical to them), just as all extension is also in every glass of water, or all thought is in every idea. We have previously said that for Spinoza the infinite is not a number; this is why it escapes every division. Indivisible substance is not the sum of all its attributes.

This requires us to return to one of our previous assertions. We have said that substance did not have the simplicity of a being, given immediately in an irreducible presence excluding from itself every determinate content, but the complex reality of an absolute movement that includes all its determinations. This complexity of substance, which is expressed in the *internal* diversity of its attributes, does not, though, have as its consequence the endowing of it with a composite nature. This is why it must be said that substance is simple just as much as it is complex, in the quite precise sense that it is not divisible into parts:

> [This being] is simple, not composed of parts. For in Nature and in our knowledge the component parts of a thing must be prior to that which is composed of them. This is out of place in that which is by its own nature eternal.[21]

This indication is extremely important, for it excludes every mechanistic presentation of the movement in which substance is produced: the process of the *causa sui*, immanent in substance, is not a temporal genesis, which would operate in a succession of distinct operations, from already given elements, whose combination would produce substance as a result or an outcome. The relation of substance to its attributes is not that of a whole to its parts or of a complex totality to the simple elements that compose it.

From this point of view, certain of the formulations used by Gueroult in order to present the "genesis" of substance are unacceptable, and the use of the texts on which he rests is undoubtedly abusive. For example:

> Undoubtedly, Spinoza conforms, in species, to the prescriptions that he stated in the *De intellectus emendatione*: to reach the simplest ideas (*idea simplicissimae*) in order to reconstruct with them, according to its internal implications, the complex idea that is constituted from them. Consequently, when

it is a question of God, one will discover first the *prima elementa totius natu-rae*, namely, the simple substances with a single attribute, which are *origo et fons naturae*, in order to constitute from them the "total one and infinite be-ing," outside of which nothing is given and which thereby is also *origo et fons naturae*. This reconstruction, which operates according to the norm of the true given idea, leads to the genetic definition of God.[22]

The term that presents a problem is that of *reconstruction*, which here interprets the *more geometrico* in a very particular sense.

Let us remark first that to turn the *more geometrico* into a con-struction or reconstruction of the complex from the simple is to reduce it to a method, that is, finally to an artifice of exposition, which subordinates the necessary progression of the reasoning to the method of an order: here, one that proceeds from parts to whole, or from simple to complex; and we are then not very far from Descartes. But what Spinoza wanted to think through the *more geometrico* was not another method, a new order of exposition, but precisely something other than a method, which submits the presentation of the true to the precondition of an order according to the schema of a necessarily abstract reflection. It is then that one is en-gaged in difficulties whose reason is simply formal; for example, asking oneself if substance comes before the attributes, or the attributes before substance; or else if the attributes are more or less "simple" than substance: from a synthetic point of view, these questions simply have no meaning.

On the other hand, the idea of a construction of substance pre-supposes that the latter would be not only constituted but still composed of elements that would be its attributes. This presupposition is particularly obvious in Guer-oult's translation of the expression *substantia unius attributi* (*E* IP8D), as "substance having a single attribute." Yet this notion is the basis of his entire explanation of the whole beginning of the *Ethics*, since it serves for him to designate the simple ele-ment from which substance is "constructed." This translation is impossible, not only because it substitutes *unicus* for *unus*, but also for a foundational reason: it treats the unity that constitutes each attribute as a number, that is, as the term of a series in which all the attributes figure as elements or moments of an infinite pro-gression, of which substance would be the final expression or the result.

Such a conception is absolutely foreign to Spinozism, as Guer-oult himself has magisterially explained: "The numeration [of attributes] has not finished because it has never begun, for the good reason that there is no numera-tion."[23] One does not pass from the attributes, which would be from then on given one by one, to substance by means of a progression to the infinite:

The axiom of the scholium to proposition 10, part I, as I suggested at the end of that scholium, we form from the idea which we have of an absolutely infinite being, and not from the fact that there are, or may be, beings which have three, four, or more attributes.[24]

Between the *substantia unius attributi* and the absolutely infinite substance that possesses all the attributes, there is *nothing*, no intermediary that would subordinate this passage to the rules of a mechanical composition. This is why it is preferable to present this passage as a reversal, or as the development of a contradiction, the very one that identifies in substance its absolute unity and the infinite multiplicity of its essences.

If the attributes were added to one another, or were composed among themselves in order to engender substance, they would cease to be irreducible, and it is their identity to substance, that is, their substantial nature, which would by this fact be compromised. Then the attributes would no longer be essences infinite in their own kind and thus not able to be limited by anything, but would be degrees of reality, necessarily unequal, and positioned in relation to one another within the framework of a progressive hierarchy that would integrate them all together into the absolute. But Spinoza is as far removed from this Leibnizian conception of order as he is from Descartes's conception.

A very important consequence results from this. We have just seen that the attributes, even if they are really distinct — precisely because they are really distinct — are not like beings that could be enumerated, even in a perspective going to infinity, for this would be to reduce their distinction to a modal distinction, that is, in a certain way to reflect the infinite from the point of view of the finite. Yet that which is true of the attributes is a fortiori true of the substance that contains them all: one can no more count substance than one can count its attributes, at least if one renounces the point of view of the imagination. This is why the thesis of its *unicity* is so difficult to understand: it does not at all refer in fact to the existence of a unique being, of a substance that would exist with a single copy, to the exclusion of all other possibilities:

> Nothing can be called one or single unless some other thing has first been conceived which (as has been said) agrees with it. But since the existence of God is his essence itself, and since we can form no general idea of his essence, it is certain that he who calls God one or single has no true idea of God, or is speaking of him improperly.[25]

This is why, if Spinoza writes "that God is unique, that is... that in Nature there is only one substance [*non nisi unam substantiam dari*], and that it is absolutely infi-

nite,"[26] it must certainly be understood that this notion *non nisi una*, strictly negative, has no causal significance and thus cannot arise in the definition of the divine
nature: absolute substance is unique, in fact, but it is only a consequence, not even
of its own reality, but of our power to imagine, which forges fiction, not only of
two, three, or any number of substances, but more generally of substances existing
in a determinate number, among which "one" is never the first. To say that there is
a single substance is to speak with the imagination, which can only consider the absolute negatively, from nothingness, that is, from the part of the possible of which it
is the envelope. By himself, God is not "one," any more than he is two or three, or
that he is beautiful or ugly. Contrary to a tenacious tradition, it must be said that
Spinoza was no more a monist than he was a dualist, or a representative of any
other number that one wants to assign to this fiction, a number all the better for the
ignorant or for slaves.

The Order and Connection of "Things"

The attributes are not "less" than substance. Nor are some "less" than others; this is
what is expressed by the thesis of their reciprocal irreducibility. The attributes are
incomparable, and this is why they are identical in substance that necessarily possesses all of them, which it could not do if one introduced any inequality among
them. No form of being is superior to another: there is thus no reason for it to belong to God in preference to another or in exclusion of another. It is thus that God is
simultaneously, and in an identical way, a "thinking thing" and an "extended thing,"[27]
but also all the other things that we cannot apprehend by virtue of the limitation of
our intellect. On this point, let us refer to the book by Gilles Deleuze, which offers
a definitive critique of the notion of *eminence* and shows that this notion is completely
foreign to Spinozism. Eminence is in some sense the classical concept of "supersession." Yet Spinoza always reasons formally (*formaliter*), that is, not to the exclusion
of all content, but outside of every perspective of eminence (*eminenter*), for the latter reintroduces into knowledge the presupposition of a possibility that is a fiction.
The imagination proceeds, on the contrary, by such easy transpositions or amplifi-
cations: if a triangle could speak, it would say of God that he is triangular *eminently*
(see letter 56 to Hugo Boxel). God is not in reality at the summit or the end of a
progressive hierarchy of forms, all of whose properties he would bring together by
"superseding" them.

This is why Spinoza is not content to resolve the question posed
by Cartesian dualism; he completely reverses its problematic. In the interpretation
of Spinozism proposed by Hegel we have seen that everything happens as if sub-

stance were principally expressed in two attributes whose absolute unity it constitutes, these very attributes that we perceive, and to which Descartes attributed the
status of independent substances. Then all the other attributes appear in relation to
the latter as possibilities, pure fictions, and they can be conceived rigorously only in
terms of the model of the two "real" attributes that we actually know. Yet it is precisely such a conception that the synthetic reasoning followed by Spinoza renders
impossible: according to the latter, every attribute must be "conceived through itself," that is, in its own infinity, which confers a substantial nature on it, and not on
the basis of its relation with any other attribute. To understand the nature of the attributes is precisely to rule out considering them term by term, so as to compare
them.

When Spinoza says that the attributes are "infinite only in their
kind," an expression we have already encountered, he does not mean that their infinity is in some sense limited and incomplete. Such a conception characterizes, on
the contrary, the point of view of the imagination. In the first dialogue that follows
chapter 2 of the *Short Treatise* Lust declares, "I see that thinking substance has nothing in common with extended substance and that the one limits the other." This
sentence brings together three affirmations that are actually interdependent: (1) the
irreducibility of the attributes is presented as the separation among substances; (2)
these substances exist vis-à-vis one another in relation of limitation; (3) this opposition is a relation with two terms, which is thought on the basis of the distinction
between thought and extension. But these three assertions, and the logic that asso-
ciates them, are undone by reason, for the latter considers things from the point of
view of their necessity: (1) the attributes are identical within the substance that includes all of them; (2) they are therefore not opposed to one another in a necessarily
unequal relationship; and (3) their nature cannot be grasped outside of the fact that
they are an infinity, which forbids that one apply to them an attempt at numeration.

The key to the new reasoning that Spinoza introduces into philosophy is the thesis of the identity of the attributes in the substance within which
they are unified while remaining really distinct. This unity is expressed in a well-
known proposition: "The order and connection of ideas is the same as the order and
connection of things."[28] This proposition is often interpreted as if it formulated a
relationship of agreement, an accord, between everything that depends on thought
and on extension. Such an interpretation is inadmissible. In fact, if in this statement
the word "ideas" does indeed designate the modes of the attribute of thought, the
word "things" (*res*) absolutely does not—in a restrictive way—designate the modes
of the attribute of extension but the modes of any attribute at all, *including thought*

itself: ideas are just as much "things" as any other affection of substance. The proposition thus means that everything is included under an attribute, that is, in any form of being, is identical to what is included under all other attributes, in precisely the same way that it is identical to itself: by returning onto itself, without escaping its own order, thought discovers everything contained within substance, insofar as the latter is expressed in the infinity of all its attributes; it is already toward this conclusion that we had led the theory of *adequatio*. Now this can be said of all the attributes, which are identical to all the others, not in a relationship of comparison, of correspondence, of agreement, or homology, which would imply their reciprocal exteriority, but in their intrinsic nature, which unifies them from the outset within the substance that constitutes them and that they constitute.

From then on, there is no room to posit an identity among two, three, four... an infinity of series or attributes, whose order and connection would be recognized as in agreement. One must understand—which is impossible if one restricts oneself to the point of view of the imagination—that it is *one and the same order, one and the same connection* carried out in all the attributes, and that identically constitutes them in their being: substance is precisely nothing but this unique necessity that is expressed simultaneously in an infinity of forms. There is thus no mystery to the fact that one finds in every kind of being that which also belongs by definition to all other kinds of being: for this, there is no need for the intervention of a prior combination or harmony. We see then how ridiculous it is to present Spinozist "monism" as a supersession of Cartesian "dualism": the mode of thought put to work by Spinoza produces its effects on an entirely different terrain, in which these old questions of philosophy are simply invalidated.

From this displacement of problems results another consequence: our knowledge itself is not limited, any more than attributes limit one another in a term-by-term relationship, which would necessarily be a relationship of subordination, by the fact that it apprehends only two attributes of substance. By grasping only one, according to its own order and connection, it would include substance as it is in its absolute necessity, that is, in the causal chain that constitutes its being. To know the nature of an attribute in its intrinsic infinity is by the same token to know the nature of all the other attributes. This is why, Spinoza says, although we perceive only two attributes of substance, we are nonetheless not *deprived* of the knowledge of all the others, to the extent that we understand that they necessarily exist according to an order and a connection that are the very ones that we know. Thus, within the limits even prescribed to a finite intellect, we can know everything, that is, think the absolute within the form of necessity.

Everything makes sense, then, within the theoretical apparatus put into place by Spinoza: the infinity of the attributes, conceived independently from every numerical series, is the condition for us to escape the traditional dilemmas of philosophy. From the point of view of the absolute, there is no longer the confrontation of incomparable and unequal kinds of being; there is therefore no longer the necessity of justifying their coexistence or their agreement through the compromise of an external, and obviously arbitrary and irrational, guarantee: the causality of substance is at the same time the condition and object of an absolute knowledge, which poses only intrinsically necessary relations, and whose immanent development discovers its forms in itself, outside of every intervention of a free will, whether the latter be situated under the responsibility of a finite subject or an infinite Subject.

Hegel's Error Regarding the Attributes

In order to measure the way traversed, let us return now to one of the texts that Hegel devotes to the question of the attributes:

> Spinoza further determines attribute as *infinite*, and infinite, too, in the sense of an *infinite plurality*. However in what follows only *two* appear, thought and extension, and it is not shown by what necessity the infinite plurality reduces itself to opposition, that, namely, of thought and extension. These two attributes are therefore adopted *empirically*. Thought and being represent the absolute in a determination; the absolute itself is their absolute unity and they themselves are only unessential forms; the order of things is the same as that of figurate conceptions or thoughts, and the one absolute is contemplated only by external reflection, by a mode, under these two determinations, once as a totality of conceptions, and again as a totality of things and their mutations. Just as it is this external reflection which makes that distinction, so too does it lead the difference back into absolute identity and therein submerges it. But this entire movement proceeds outside the absolute. True, the absolute is itself also *thought*, and so far this movement is only in the absolute; but as remarked, it is in the absolute only as unity with extension, and therefore not as this movement which is essentially also the movement of opposition.[29]

The interest of this page — and this is why it must be cited in its entirety — is that it presents together a certain number of assertions that, applied to their declared object, Spinoza's philosophy, prove to be equally erroneous. From then on it is likely that the contempt that Hegel heaps on Spinoza's philosophy depends on the "logic" that has engendered them, a "logic" entirely external to the letter and spirit of Spinozism.

First of all, Hegel reduces the attributes to external forms of reflection, which have lost all real interdependence with the substance from which they have apparently emerged: there is from then on no rational justification for the movement through which substance "passes" into its attributes. This interpretation presupposes, we have sufficiently shown, that the relationship of substance to its attributes is hierarchical and chronological: substance, which then appears as an immediate foundation, is before its attributes, and it is more than they are. But the concept of attribute, such as Spinoza himself has established it, precisely excludes the possibility of such a subordination, which has meaning only from a perspective of eminence.

Next, for Hegel the thesis according to which substance is expressed in an infinity of attributes has no real meaning; this is why he only recalls it for memory, as a simply formal consideration. In fact, if one restricts oneself to content, the unity of substance is always reflected across the relationship of two attributes, which are thought and being; but this content cannot be rationally justified, it is only recognized empirically. Hegel writes elsewhere:

> Spinoza places substance at the head of his system and defines it as the un of thinking and extension, without demonstrating how he arrives at this c tinction and how he succeeds in tracing it back to the unity of substance.

Hegel's error consists here in posing the real distinction of the attributes as a term-by-term relationship, embodied in the difference between two attributes situated side-by-side: from such a perspective it is inevitable that this distinction would appear arbitrary and that it be simply juxtaposed to the unity of substance, given elsewhere. But we have seen that, in Spinoza's demonstration, the existence of an infinity of attributes allowed this difficulty to be avoided from the beginning: the reciprocal irreducibility of the attributes is then perfectly consistent with their identity within substance, whose nature they express in all possible kinds, outside of every empirical restriction.

As a result, the identity of order that intrinsically constitutes substance is reduced by Hegel to a formal correspondence between two external series, the order of things (extension) and the order of representations (thinking): between these two groups there can only be an arbitrary and external community, in the sense of the agreement decreed by God, in Cartesian philosophy, between nature and reason. Yet, from the fact that, in the letter of Spinoza's system, this identity of order in no way allows itself to be reduced to the identity between two separate orders, this entire problematic of agreement between thought and being, which presupposes their separation, is avoided from the start.

On the other hand, the separation of thought from the real, which is according to Hegel the condition of their ultimate reunion within the absolute, devalues thought. Even if it places it in a relation of equality with extension, to the precise extent that it relates thought to the absolute only through the intermediary of its relation to extension, this reasoning puts thought in a position of inferiority in relation to the absolute: "it is in the absolute only as unity with extension," which means that it cannot by itself, by its own movement, be equal to the absolute. Hegel says again:

> True, substance is the absolute unity of *thought* and being or extension; therefore it contains thought itself, but only in its *unity* with extension, that is, not as *separating* itself from extension, hence in general not as a determinative and formative activity, nor as a movement which returns onto and begins from itself.[31]

Thought cannot realize in itself its relation to the absolute, since it must proceed through extension in order to be discovered as the moment of a unity that occurs only within substance. Yet we have said enough not to need to insist again that, in Spinoza, the infinite diversity of the attributes implies that they are at the same time irreducible and equal within substance. Thus, the difference between thought and extension, or any relation between any attributes, does not have as a consequence their subordination to substance, as that which is divided to that which is united, but on the contrary the identification of them absolutely in it. That which is infinite only in its kind is no less infinite than that which is absolutely infinite. This is true for thought as for any other attribute in general.

Finally, the distinction between the attributes, reflected across the distinction between thought and extension, is interpreted by Hegel as a form of opposition: the coexistence of these external forms is also their confrontation, since they concurrently represent the one substance by dividing it. From this fact, the unity of substance is itself only the resolution, the supersession of this conflict, the reunion into the absolute of terms that, in themselves, are separate and antagonistic: it is a unity of opposites, a necessarily abstract unity, which formally reconstitutes, by means of the intellect, a totality that has been previously artificially decomposed into its elements. We are going to see that this transposition of Spinoza's system into terms that are obviously not its own, a transposition that implicitly causes the intervention of the dialectic in the Hegelian sense, with its notions of opposition and contradiction, is at the very foundation of the divergence that separates the two philosophies.

It is by developing this question for itself that we shall manage to shed light on the reasons, that is, the stakes of this entire discussion. For it does not suffice for us to observe that Hegel is "deceived" in his reading of Spinoza, and that he has completely missed the true meaning of Spinoza's system. We must also and first of all understand why, defying the evidence, he wanted at all costs to make this philosophy say exactly the opposite of what it establishes, in a way that leaves no room for equivocation. As if his discourse were at this point as intolerable as it is necessary, whereas it is impossible to eliminate it by a simple refutation, to suppress it completely, by substituting for it the fiction of an inverse and ridiculous discourse.

The fact is that this final debate turns entirely around a single phrase and its interpretation: *omnis determinatio est negatio*.

Translated by Ted Stolze

Notes

1. *E* IDef6Exp.
2. Hegel (1976, 113).
3. Hegel (1976, 537).
4. *E* ID4.
5. Hegel (1983, 256–57), translation modified.
6. Hegel (1983, 259–60), translation modified.
7. *Ep* 2 to Oldenburg.
8. As Doz (1976) has done.
9. *Ep* 10 to Simon de Vries.
10. Gueroult (1968, 109).
11. *E* ID6.
12. *Ep* 60 to Tschirnhaus.
13. *PPC* P7S.
14. An error that Deleuze (1990, 52) himself commits.
15. *Ep* 2 to Oldenburg.
16. *Ep* 4 to Oldenburg.
17. *E* IP19D.
18. *E* IP6C.
19. *Ep* 4 to Oldenburg.

20. *Ep* 36 to Hudde. See also *Ep* 4 to Oldenburg.

21. *Ep* 35.

22. Gueroult (1968, 169).

23. Gueroult (1968, 150).

24. *Ep* 64 to Schuller.

25. *Ep* 50 to Jelles.

26. *E* IP14C1.

27. *E* IIPP1–2.

28. *E* IIP7.

29. Hegel (1976, 537–38).

30. Hegel (1991, 227).

31. Hegel (1976, 536–37).

S I X

Fortune and the Theory of History

Pierre-François Moreau

"IF HUMAN beings could govern all their affairs according to a fixed plan, or if fortune were always favorable to them, they would be bound by no superstition."[1] The first sentence of the *Tractatus Theologico-Politicus* throws us straightaway into the experience of the human condition; and the first condition of this experience — a condition simultaneously constitutive of its structures and first, or almost first, in its perception — is its temporal variability. A little later Spinoza will specify the framework of this variability: episodes of prosperity, episodes of adversity, returns of fortune. If we can speak of pessimism, in a certain sense, or of disillusioned observations, we must hasten to add that this pessimism or this absence of illusion concerns only a given situation's form (its stability) and not its content (unhappiness is no more certain than happiness). The dimension of experience designated by this term "fortune" includes three characteristics, which in fact are formal:

> it is variable in time;
>
> it is repetitive (in the life of an individual, and from one individual to another — as is everything that is recorded under the category "experience");
>
> it is independent of us: each moment is imposed on us without our having chosen it; fortune is the expression of the fact that we cannot

govern our affairs according to a plan fixed once and for all. In other words, our affairs are not our own: the first figure of history is historical chance, insofar as it weighs on us and prevents us from completely harmonizing our plans and our action.

A second condition of experience appears in the same text: this historical variability, far from being insignificant, on the contrary produces what is essential in human behavior. If fortune did not exist, there would be no superstition; nor would there be superstition if this fortune were always favorable. But it is of the essence of fortune not always to be something. However, this initial subordinate clause introduces a lure of hope, an ultimate possibility, not realized to date, of change: if one day there are constituted — little matter how for the moment — certain conditions of life that reduce the effects of the variability of fortune, then superstition will also lessen. We can say that an entire section of the *TTP* and, later, of the *Tractatus Politicus*, is a development of this subordinate clause.

Finally, the third condition of experience: one of the strongest proofs of the irrationality of human beings is that they look for reason where it is not to be found. They look for intention in chance, and, since they know well that this intention is not theirs, they presume that it is another's. They hope to find a content under its form and thus misrecognize it. In other words, one of the aspects of their domination by fortune is that they refuse, when they experience it, to stick to bare fortune. They try to explain the things that escape them (that escape both their mastery and their understanding) by looking for a historical intention;[2] they thus have a spontaneous tendency to anthropomorphize history, just as they anthropomorphize nature. By reading this preface of the *TTP* closely, we can account for the fact that it is perfectly parallel to such texts as the appendix of the first part of the *Ethics*, which explains the finalist illusion regarding natural things. For the same reason that there is a finalism "in space," there is a finalism "in time"; it is no less necessary, since it is rooted simultaneously in experience and in the spontaneous interpretation of experience. It takes the elementary form of belief in signs and omens (the equivalents for history of what miracles are for nature), but these forms and simple imaginary materials can be combined to the point of constituting a theory of Election or Providence.

This theory of fortune plays a key role in Spinoza's system and especially in the areas of the system that rework and rethink the classical tradition of the reading of human life. We shall retain three aspects here: the critical heritage of classical rhetoric, the description of the structures of experience, and the materials for a theory of history.[3]

▌

The *TTP* does not presuppose for the reader the knowledge of the system. However, Spinoza indeed proceeds in the *TTP* through rational demonstrations, but these demonstrations rest on a space of common rationality, which he can legitimately presume to be acquired for cultivated readers of his time. This space is double: it is constituted, on the one hand, by reflections on life and society, which every one of us can himself make or else inherit from a tradition that is anonymous by dint of being repeated, and, on the other hand, by a common culture rather easily identifiable, Latin instead of Greek, based on historical and literary examples instead of the knowledge of great philosophical systems, but in which a kind of common wisdom supplies the means to theorize the lessons of the book of the world. A rhetorical culture not because it would only include orators, but because poets and historians, for example, are quite easily enlisted in a rhetorical schema.[4] In Spinoza's case: Terence, Tacitus, and Quintus Curtius, to be precise.

Now the preface of the *TTP* rests on one of these authors in particular in order to confirm what it advances concerning the relations between the reversal of fortune/fear and hope/superstition. Two explicit references to Quintus Curtius allow us to establish that Alexander fell into superstition only when he conceived of fears regarding fortune (one page later, a third citation to the same author will mark the connections between superstition and the government of the multitude.)[5] We can thus expect to find this common theory of fortune in the *History of Alexander.* It is worth recalling that in the seventeenth century, among authors who were attached to a critical or skeptical tradition, Quintus Curtius enjoyed a reputation as an enemy of superstition, and all the more so as he treated a subject matter that clearly suited it.[6] So it is not surprising that Spinoza had chosen him as a mediator between his readers and himself in order to introduce his theses prephilosophically: he was certain to encounter at least vague agreement as a basis for discussion. It remains to be seen what is covered by these arguments and this lexicon and the choices the philosophical treatment, strictly speaking, proceeds to operate on them.

Let us limit ourselves to book V, the first one cited here. It recounts the events following the battle of Arbela: the surrender of Babylon and the taking of Susia and, on the Persian side, the escape of Darius, the betrayal of the

Bactrician leaders, and finally the series of intrigues that led to the arrest and death of the Great King (the final chapters, which recount the assassination itself, are missing). What is remarkable is that the term "fortune," if it often appears in the text, much more often indicates what happens to the Persians than to the Greeks—when it is not directly placed in Darius's mouth. In paragraph 4, which Spinoza cites, it is not said explicitly that Alexander doubts fortune, but the previous lines (the end of paragraph 3) clearly emphasize the opposition between two historical sequences: one (in the past) in which everything seemed permitted to Alexander ("invincible before that day, he had risked nothing without success" [*invictus ante eam diem fuerat, nihil frustra ausus*]), the other (in the present), in which he seems to come up against obstacles, in which his happiness, until now constant, seems caught in a trap ("now his good fortune was caught" [*tunc haesitabat deprehensa felicitas*]). And it is then that, having had to move back thirty stadia before finding a guide who will allow him to get around and encircle enemy troops, he begins to consult divines through the spirit of superstition. Therefore, if there is no word, there are indeed the characteristics associated with the idea of fortune; there is not even missing the current idea that the excess of reversal enrages its victim: for Alexander's army is not simply checked, it has been cornered in a narrow pass in which his soldiers have had to die without even being able to exchange blows, the most miserable situation for courageous men.[7] To the insolence of happiness past thus responds the supplement of unhappiness that renders one powerless at the moment of reversal. This idea of opposed excesses is tied to the theme of the *ludibria fortunae*, the ironies or mockeries by which the human imagination is struck.[8]

Let us now move on to Darius. Having been defeated, it is normal that he speaks ill of fortune more than the victor does, at the beginning, and at the end of the book he can be seen to compare his past greatness and that of his ancestors with his present ordeals. But another manner of speaking appears: he speaks of his fortune and says to his companions, "You have preferred to follow my fortune rather than the victor's."[9] Fortune is then no longer the abstract distribution of goods and evils; it designates the series of goods and evils attached to everyone— even the predictable series—to such an extent that it could be translated as "fate" or "destiny" and no longer "chance."[10] Here it is no longer variability but, on the contrary, individual constancy that is thrown into relief. The extreme of this constancy is the intention that destines a human being for an end: at this stage Fortune has but to receive a name in order to be regarded as a person, who must be treated gently for fear of irritating it. Thus, in the previous book, the mother of the Great King, receiving news—what is more, false news—of the victory, "remained in the same attitude as before. Not a word escaped her; neither her color nor her expression changed; she sat unmoved—fearing, I suppose, by premature rejoicing to irritate Fortune."[11]

The common notion of *fortuna* presented to the reader by Quintus Curtius thus has three levels:

> the variability of human affairs; the fear and superstition into which, one must observe, reversals throw human beings; their relative forgetting when prosperity returns;

> the series of what happens to an individual; the idea that this series constitutes his destiny;

> finally, the personalization of the intention that is beneath these heights and depths, a personalization at least rhetorical under the historian's pen, but one he does not hesitate to attribute to his characters as real belief.

Can we claim that here we have the complete semantic field of what the term evokes in a seventeenth-century reader? No doubt yet a fourth meaning must be added, which can be read in Machiavelli, and which is not very far removed from what is designated today by "conjuncture": fortune as *occasio* (an "occasion") and no longer simply *casus* (an "occurrence"). More a possibility of being active with regard to history than the observed fact that one undergoes it. It is in any case on this circle of meanings that Spinoza is going to begin his analysis of experience.

II

When Spinoza analyzes the data of human experience, he refers indissociably to what everyone can see in himself, to what he can observe in others, to what he inherits that is already constituted in a classical culture, as much through maxims as through exempla. This is a type of writing to which, in fact, he has recourse rather often (at the beginning of the *Treatise on the Emendation of the Intellect*, in letters, in scholia and appendices in the *Ethics*, and so on), which has other constraints than geometrical deduction, and which plays a different role, just as necessary, but which approaches the reader differently.

What does he say at this level, in this regard, concerning fortune? Two epistemologically essential things:

> "that I estimate that no one ignores it" (thesis A);

> "while believing that most ignore it themselves" (thesis B).[12]

One can say that these two theses frame Spinoza's entire usage of experience. As opposed to geometry, experience is always already known. When one begins to discuss with someone, perhaps he has never heard spoken the mathematical laws (or laws constructed on the model of mathematics) that are going to be demonstrated to him; there is no problem if he knows and accepts the rule of the game. On the other hand, he is bound to have heard, and himself reflected on, what experience teaches (in this case, the laws of fortune; but other possibilities are that a lover returns to a flirt in spite of his pledges, that a drunk or gossip speaks in spite of his will, that no one is so vigilant that he does not sometimes sleep, that if young people are not watched closely they are attracted by fashion and foreign forms of prestige, that loyalty often leads counselors to their loss...). And this knowledge is not an illusion; for Spinoza experience does not deceive. However, people are deceived ("Although deceived a hundred times..." [*Quamvis centies fallat...*]).[13] Why? On the one hand, because they add to experience all kinds of ideologies or mythologies that are the artificial interpretations and prolongation of it. On the other hand, because they do not draw out its lessons and, especially, they do not apply to their own case what they see in others, or else they do not apply in adversity the maxims they employ in a period of calm; the conditions of experience ensure that experience is opaque to its own lessons. Whence the following paradox: everyone ignores none of these lessons except that he is himself ignorant. When Spinoza says that during days of prosperity everyone is full of wisdom, he is hardly being ironic: the propositions in which this wisdom is formulated (those of neo-Stoicism, to identify the ideas' source) are perhaps correct, but they do not take account of the deep-rootedness of human situations and are thus simple "dictates" (*dictamina*), which will be hard to apply in situations, by no means impossible to predict, in which reason is overwhelmed.

Consequently, how should the lessons of experience be treated in this double context of ignorant knowledge? By sorting out what is the lesson, properly speaking (*experientia docet...*), from mythology, we shall then observe that Spinoza's use of the term "fortune" reduces it as much as possible to its formal aspects, to be enumerated shortly; Spinoza makes no reference to individual fortune and even less to its personalization. Equally, by modifying the common theory in order to integrate into it openly the aspects that make it opaque, the preface thus insists on the universal character of the reactions of fear and hope and on the apparent exceptions that constitute stable periods. We might say that the common theory of fortune isolates two kinds of periods and, in its most cultivated forms, characterizes them by the presence or absence of an ideology (superstition) and of its affective rootedness (fear and hope); and that Spinoza adds to it a critical theory of fortune that marks two ideologies and not just one: superstition in troubled periods, the illusion of remaining safe from it in moments of assurance. The inaugural knowledge of the *TTP*, the minimum necessary in order to discuss rationally but not geometrically with the reader, lies in the application of the second of these theories to the first.

Is this all there is? Not if one turns toward the system in the order of its reasons. For one will find there a third theory, in which fortune is this time at the end, not at the beginning, of the reasoning: one can demonstrate, from books I and II of the *Ethics*, that our life necessarily escapes us, that we are submitted to physical and psychological laws we do not master, that we confront, through our body, an order of external encounters, certain of which harm us and certain of which are useful to us. But this theory is not present in the *TTP*, although it is by no means contradicted: what Spinoza elsewhere demonstrates from the premises of the system, here he either shows from the true kernel of the always-already-known or else recalls from the rhetorical culture that has recorded, formulated, and condensed it long before.

III

If the third theory is now applied to the second, it has to be said that in the last analysis there is no historical contingency. The system demonstrates the full necessity of what follows in every human life. But there is a contingency for us; there is the unexpected, and precisely where we least want it. Fortune designates the risky consequences of this absence of chance. The necessary laws that govern natural things, including human actions, do not mark an intention; but our ignorance of these laws, and our inability to deduce singular events from them, ensures that, on the one hand, we live under the form of a temporal and repetitive chance and that, on the other hand, we are tempted to assign them to a Will or an Irony that surpasses us—so as to believe that we have grasped what in fact we cannot grasp. It is at this point that the natural tendency to sacralize History is rooted.[14]

By constructing his critical theory of fortune, Spinoza extracts from the current theory what it has that is positive (which is a negation: that of certainty regarding singular events); he removes from it what would enable a theological elaboration to take hold. Must we then think that the last word of Spinoza's philosophy of history is negative? That he is content to secularize sacred history and reject or dissolve the various philosophies of Providence? The meditation on fortune then leads to reaffirming simply the vanity and meaninglessness of human affairs: all empires perish, and human nature, being eternal, eternally engenders the same effects; thus we never escape from a cyclical history made up of barbarism, civilization, and decadence.[15]

Perhaps this is not so simple: the theory asserts the existence of an eternal anthropological basis of history, but perhaps we do not yet know all its possible effects. From human nature a small number of fixed traits can be extracted that sufficiently explain the space of variations within which arise the success and catastrophes of individuals and societies. There exists, then, despite the variety of individuals, and the irreducible nature of everyone's *ingenium*, a possible description of the human species and its forms of behavior that corresponds to constant motives.

But we always know these motives under an already socialized form. There do not exist individuals really living in the state of nature and, on the other hand, nature does not create peoples; laws and customs create peoples. Therefore, even if individual psychology is at the supposed basis of history, the latter next unfolds within a framework in which the effects of this psychology are always inter-linked with the knowledge of customs and laws, which shape human beings from their earliest childhood.

What then are the effects of fortune? Are they immutable? They are to the extent that fortune is immutably variable. They are even if this variability includes, by an accident that is not impossible, a long period of individual stability; for, as we have seen, perhaps then the individual will be temporarily removed from superstition, but he will not sink roots, perpetually reproduced by the ideological apparatuses put into place during the periods of fear and insecurity. But what will happen if, through a succession of circumstances initially due to chance, an entire society comes to enjoy security? Then not only will superstition recede, but we shall see, in the long run, established institutions capable of reducing it even more, or of developing the civilization and commerce that will reduce it. We shall thus es-cape, in part at least, the ineluctable interplay of fear, hope, and their consequences — not on the basis of a mysterious disappearance of human nature, or of a redemption of corruption, but, on the contrary, through the same interplay of the same neces-sary laws in other conditions. The production of these conditions is indeed origi-nally the work of the same contingency-for-us; they are next reproduced by the ef-fects they have engendered: civilization, reason, and even the philosophical gaze on society that leads in seventeenth-century Holland to the struggle for freedom of conscience.

At this point we can conclude: the critical theory of fortune elaborated in the *TTP* is also a way collectively to escape the *aléas* of fortune. It forms part of the strategy that will permit us, without ignoring the cycles of history, to escape cyclical history.

Translated by Ted Stolze

Notes

1. G III/5.

2. "For if, when they are turned round in fear, they see something happen which offers them previous good or bad memories; they think it portends a happy or unhappy outcome" (ibid.).

3. On other aspects of this problem of fortune, which will not be tackled here, we must refer to Mignini's (1984) remarkable article.

4. On these questions we can only refer to the works of Fokke Akkerman and Theo Zweerman.

5. Quintus Curtius, *History of Alexander* V/4, VII/7, IV/10.

6. Pierre Bayle notes in his article on Quintus Curtius, "The author has even had the wisdom to go out looking for the reproach of credulity that he had to fear," and he cites Françoisde La Mothe Le Vayer (*Jugement des principaux historiens*): "In order to show quite clearly with what circumspection this historian has always treated the things that could be challenged, I would offer here the words with which he accompanies the narration of the dog which allows its limbs to be cut piece by piece in the Kingdom of Sophites, rather than let go and release its grip on a lion: 'As for myself,' he says, 'I report more things than I believe; for I cannot bring myself to vouch for that about which I am in doubt, nor to suppress what I have heard' [*Equidem plura transcribo quam credo. Nam nec affirmare sustineo quibus dubito, nec subducere quae accepi*]." [La Mothe Le Vayer's reference is to the *History of Alexander* IX/1. Trans.]

7. "And this was not the most wretched fate for brave men to bear, but that they were being slain unavenged, like wild beasts caught in a pit. Therefore their wrath turned to frenzy [*Nec id miserrimum fortibus viris erat, sed quod inulti, quod ferarum ritu, velut in fovea deprehensi caederentur. Ita igitur in rabiem versa*]" (V/3).

8. For example, IV/16, V/12 (Darius bound with chains of gold).

9. V/8.

10. It would be necessary also to take into account fortune in the sense of "bad fortune, misfortune," for example, in the case of the Greeks tortured by the Persians (V/5).

11. *Praecoqui gaudio verita irritare fortunam* (IV/15).

12. *Atque haec neminem ignorare estimo, quamvis plerosque se ipsos ignorare credam* (G III/5).

13. Ibid.

14. It is to limit this tendency that the equivalences stated in *TTP* III are in fact devoted, especially the one that defines fortune as "God's direction insofar as he directs human affairs by external and unforeseen causes" and this direction itself by the "fixed and immutable

order of Nature, in other words, the chain of natural things" (G III/45–6).

15. On these questions, and, in particular, on the importance accorded by Spinoza in the very age in which he wrote, see the recent works of Tosel and Balibar; on the theory of history, see Matheron (1971).

S E V E N

The Empty Synagogue

Gabriel Albiac

Imperium in Imperio

Spinoza at Jena

WHEN IN 1809 F. W. Schelling writes that "the real and vital conception of freedom is that it is a possibility of good and evil,"[1] opening the way to the development of a metaphysics of darkness of Boehmian inspiration, the Spinozist nightmare is a terror always lying in wait in the background of German romanticism. It is Spinoza who again inspires, at the distance of a century and a half, the controlled disintegration of the categories of good and evil, and with them the disintegration of the ethical subject.

At the time of their meeting on July 11, 1780, Lessing had said to Jacobi: "Aren't people always saying nowadays that Spinoza is dead as a dog?"[2] And Jacobi, the pious Jacobi, always on the lookout for heterodoxy wherever it could be pointed out, the *Schwärmer*, the zealot who obtains the expulsion of Fichte from his chair after the Quarrel of Atheism and about whom the romantics of Jena are going to ironize cruelly, this Jacobi knows very well what is the cause of the hatred (for him, well deserved) that the work of this Dutch Jew inevitably inspires. Perhaps it is a question of a rabid dog instead of a dead dog:

> If there are only efficient causes and no final ones, then the thinking faculty can, in all of nature, do nothing but observe; its sole function is to accom-

pany the mechanism of efficient powers. The conversation we are now having is merely a concern of our bodies and the whole content of this conversation is reduced to its elements: extension, movement, degree of velocity, along with our concepts of them, and the concepts of those concepts. The inventor of the clock did not, strictly speaking, invent it; he only watched its formation out of the blindly evolving energies. Raphael did the same when he was sketching out the School of Athens as did Lessing when he was writing his *Nathan*. The same applies to all philosophies, arts, forms of government, wars at sea and on land: in short, to everything possible. For even affects and passions do not cause anything at all: they are merely perceptions and ideas; or better, they *come encumbered with* perceptions and ideas. We only *believe* that we act out of anger, love, magnanimity, or reasonable resolve. Pure illusion! Ultimately, what moves us in all those cases is a *Something* which *knows nothing* of all that and, *to that extent*, is totally bereft of sensation and idea. But sensation and idea are purely concepts of extension, movement, degrees of velocity, etc. Now if anyone can accept such a view, I would not know how to refute his opinion. But if a person cannot accept it, he would have to be Spinoza's exact opposite.[3]

The response of the old master Lessing to Jacobi's furious argumentation (furious but well informed) could no longer be stately, courteous, and coldly definitive: "I notice that you would like very much to have your will free. I covet no free will."[4]

"Free will" (which can also be called "arbitrary will"), says Lessing, as a good expert on Spinoza. And in no way freedom *tout court*. It is not a question of a vain literary clause. We are at the heart of the question: the determination of what makes the two expressions not the nuances of the same category but in all rigor two antithetical concepts, mutually excluding one another, in a permanent play of skirmishes that places the whole philosophical front on the verge of war.

How would the very young Schelling, a reader consumed with the *Ethics* from 1795, not have understood it well, when at twenty-one years of age he believed he had left behind him "the desert and desolation" in order to strive toward the imminent philosophical "paradise"[5] in which arrives "the time of announcing to the best part of humanity the freedom of spirit and not to admit that it mourns the loss of its chains"?[6] Here is the Schelling who has known how to understand, from the beginning, that there is no other Spinozist problem (and that there is no other romantic problem, whence his fascination) than that of freedom. And it is only on the basis of the *Ethics* that it becomes obvious that "the highest dignity of philosophy consists precisely in the fact that it waits for all of human freedom."[7]

Really Schelling—and, with him, all the members of Schlegel's romantic inner circle at Jena—refuses to be the "exact opposite of Spinoza" hoped and prayed for by Jacobi. He knows that since the seventeenth century it is only from the point of view of Spinoza that it is possible philosophically to pose the problem of freedom. "Philosophically": this is the entire stake of this group. Spinoza or *Nichtphilosophie*, Hegel writes in his time. Everyone has had the same suspicion. And they have, though, experienced fear at the moment of passing to the threshold of Spinoza's development. The *Ethics* terrifies these German philosophers of the last decade of the eighteenth century who seek theoretically to sublimate the revolutionary experience of freedom. They are no longer so naive or *Schwärmer*, or simply ignorant, to proclaim, as Jacobi did, a "free will" whose conceptual inconsistency they know (for the will and volition in general, mercilessly, are an imaginary fabrication). Their problem from then on is another consistency: it engages the entire project of *emendatio philosophica* of life that is the great idealism. Its terms can only be the following: "either no subject but an absolute object, or else no object but an absolute subject. How can this dispute be settled?"[8]

It is thus on a disjunction that the nineteenth century in philosophy opens, a disjunction that Fichte's lectures in 1794 at the University of Jena proclaim for the next two centuries: transcendental materialism or idealism? Just as our century closes on a disjunction: Spinoza or Hegel?[9] On this point Marx is only the privileged witness—and the vehicle—of this battle, which continues today.

But in 1809 Schelling, already in full possession of his precocious intellectual maturity, wanted to break, once and for all, with the obsessive fascination for Spinoza. And this is why he wrote a treatise on freedom, regarded by Heidegger[10] as the closure of classical idealism, and which in reality is nothing but a treatise on evil, essentially marked by the Boehmian mysticism of darkness. Schelling is not deceived—how could he be—he, the best expert on Spinoza at the turn of the eighteenth and nineteenth centuries? There is no other way. The only line of retreat passes through an unassailable—but perhaps also essentially sterile—idealism: Schelling, so prolific until 1809, afterward publishes practically nothing; he dies in 1854, in other words, twenty-three years after Hegel, a silent witness of the collapse of his world and of the threatening rise of storms over Europe.

"The real and vital conception of freedom is that it is a possibility of good and evil,"[11] Schelling thus wrote. Nothing more conventional in appearance, nothing that is less apt to rouse our attention. But this formula is situated right at the end of the long introduction that opens the *Philosophical Inquiries into the Nature of Human Freedom*, a detailed exposition of the "only system of freedom" existing in philosophy: Spinoza's. But Schelling's explicit intention is indeed to open, with his own definition of freedom, the only alternative way to the impossible materialism of the thinker of Amsterdam: that of those the German idealist qualifies as "philosophers of nature" (*Naturphilosophen*) (already claimed by Franz von Baader).[12]

Everything appears clear, despite the complexity of the text, if we pay attention to the main point, commented on at length by Heidegger: Schelling's treatise has nothing, absolutely nothing, to do with the question of free will. Freedom is not presented in the treatise as a property of man; it is on the contrary man who is considered in it as a good characteristic of freedom; freedom is only the essence that contains man and through which man passes and, as such, is a determination of being in general, in that which is most characteristic of man only to the extent that he attains freedom.[13] Here, then, is an ontological conception of freedom, an authentic metaphysics of freedom, during the Enlightenment, at great variance from the very boring discourse of anthropology. As the exact opposite of Jacobi the defender of free will, Schelling's territory, once again, is that of Spinoza. "Freedom has always been our only problem,"[14] wrote the young Hegel to the still-younger Schelling, in the midst of the years of revolutionary fascination. "Freedom," not the "free will" of the religions of salvation and the anthropologists — their secular inheritors. Freedom as the only ontologically established principle. "The time has come for the higher distinction, or, rather, for the real contrast, to be made manifest, the contrast between Necessity and Freedom, in which alone the innermost center of philosophy comes to view."[15]

Here begin all the problems of the great idealist speculation, there where the phantom of Spinoza lies in wait at every corner of the discourse. Yet the first pages of the *Philosophical Inquiries into the Nature of Human Freedom* are attacked by those who, like Jacobi himself during the Quarrel of Atheism, had defended the radical incompatibility of freedom and reason, in order to pass from it to the radical proposition of a systematic ontology of freedom from which nothing would be excluded. But all this is only the preparation before confronting the true problem: such a systematic ontology (or at least one of its aspects) already exists: it is Spinoza's system that Schelling presents, anachronistically, as a complete pantheism.[16]

The reader will be astonished perhaps that, having arrived at this point, Schelling presents a scrupulous defense of the irreducibility of the Spinozist theses against the banal accusations of fatalism that allege the absence of autonomy of the will in Spinoza. In fact, if the *Philosophical Inquiries into the Nature of Human*

Freedom proceed in this way, it is in order to avoid every sterile diversion or polemic, which would cause us to drift onto the terrain of the worst readings of Spinoza's text... and it is in order better to choose, just like that, the true field of battle. In fact:

> The most drastic expression in Spinoza is probably the statement: The individual being is Substance itself viewed in one of its modes, that is, in one of its consequences... To proceed, if the denial of freedom, not of individuality, should now be declared to be the essential characteristic of pantheism, then a multitude of systems would come under this heading which are otherwise essentially differentiated from it. For the true conception of freedom was lacking in all modern systems... until the discovery of Idealism.... Dependence does not determine the nature of the dependent, and merely declares that the dependent entity, whatever else it may be, can only be as a consequence of that upon which it is dependent; it does not declare what this dependent entity is or is not.... Immanence in God is so little a contradiction of freedom that freedom alone, and insofar as it is free, exists in God, whereas all that lacks freedom, and insofar as it lacks freedom, is necessarily outside God.[17]

Whence Schelling's surprising conclusion, when he finishes his critique of Jacobi by accepting straightforwardly "the terrible truth: all philosophy, absolutely all, which is based on pure reason alone, is, or will become, Spinozism."[18]

Upon reaching these lines, amazement is almost inevitable. After fifteen years of vain attempts to refute Spinozism, is Schelling then disposed to capitulate to this philosophy that is "the only purely rational philosophy"? Does he then prefer the wager over the destruction of reason that was Jacobi's? The two options are clearly unthinkable for Schelling, barring a philosophical suicide. And, in the final analysis, nothing will be able to save him from this suicide, but the hour has not yet come: for the last time no doubt, and setting out with an extreme fury, Schelling struggles to win the battle of reason. It is suitable in his eyes to displace the problematical knot in its totality. Spinozism

> is not fatalism because it lets things be conceived in God; for... pantheism does not make formal freedom, at least, impossible. Spinoza must then be a fatalist for another reason, entirely independent of this. The error of his system is by no means due to the fact that he posits all *things in God*, but due to the fact that they are *things* — to the abstract conception of the world and its creatures, indeed of eternal Substance itself, which is also a thing for him.[19]

Does one then understand better the function played by this renewed definition of freedom as a "faculty of good and evil"? It is necessary, it seems to me, to specify only the following:

> the banally anthropological sense that the expression "faculty of good and evil" preserves in all the traditions of a spiritualist tendency (in which its use is common) is here strictly refined: he wouldn't know how to use the definition of free will, and he refers to an exclusively ontological sphere;

> the categories of "good" and "evil," put into play here, cannot therefore in any case refer specifically to the human being; it is a question of the fundamental principles of a metaphysics, and they manifest at a stroke the Being of the existing being (*to ti en einai*, the *quidditas*), whence Schelling's specification: "Only after recognizing evil in its universal character is it possible to comprehend good and evil in man too."[20]

> in the Treatise of 1809, the introduction has for a specific objective the avoidance of the reification (that is, the nonsubjectivation) of Spinoza's totality, God, substance, or Nature, in agreement with the dilemma (*kein Subjekt/kein Objekt*) presented in the letters of 1795.

It seems to me that it is equally easy to understand what Schelling's central theoretical problem becomes. If good and evil are not categories limited to the sphere of human behavior, but fundamental principles of every existing being, what becomes of God? Must evil also be the fundamental principle (*Grund*) of the divine being? This is a truly diabolical question, since "either real evil is admitted, in which case it is unavoidable to include evil itself in infinite Substance or in the primal Will, and thus totally disrupt the conception of an all-perfect Being; or the reality of evil must in some way or other be denied, in which case the real conception of freedom disappears at the same time,"[21] such as Schelling's idealism requires.

We won't enter here into the original and very elaborate exposition Schelling devotes to the metaphysically decisive question: how is it possible, given the existence of evil, to justify God?[22] Let us simply note that for a mystic like Boehme, "the basis of evil must therefore not only be founded on something inherently positive, but rather on the highest positive being which nature contains,"[23] by means of which evil is introduced into the proper *Grund*, the ontological foundation of divinity. It is the recourse to such a doctrine that permits an alternative to the deontologization of good and evil that Spinoza had made the basis of his own philosophy of freedom to be presented here. However, such a model carries a cost that Schelling, from 1809, is scrupulously going to pay: philosophical silence, the explicit abandonment of the only framework of philosophy. It is a wager. As such, it is respectable — intellectually respectable. An important reactionary thinker of the previous century pointed it out with perspicacity:

> Henceforth in these systems as in all those produced by pagan naturalism, what becomes of Evil? ... Paganism has made God (and thereby the soul) principally consist in a natural existence, submitted to the necessity that dominates all of nature. ... If, then, there is evil, it is nothing but a physical imperfection, which is inevitable and fatal, as much as impossible to explain.[24]

"Henceforth in these systems as in all those produced by pagan naturalism," writes Ravaisson. Very well. But philosophy is precisely a pagan — essentially a pagan — discipline. There is no "Christian philosophy" any more than there is an "Oriental" or "Jewish" philosophy. And the fact that the originally pagan — more the Greek — essence of philosophy had been carried to our time from the Middle Ages, under the form of Christian representations, in no way allows one to say — as Heidegger has splendidly shown[25] — that philosophy must become "Christian" at a given moment. Philosophy is not to know of salvation, and it cannot coexist with it. It is to this "final shore" (*erlanger Vorträge*)[26] — to use his own words — that the "fear of Spinoza" (*metus Spinozae*) leads Schelling: up to the intolerable in a consequent idealist optics, up to a metaphysics of freedom based on the suppression of all values. Or, what amounts to the same, a deliberately materialist metaphysics of freedom. Let us now try ourselves to venture into the wild jungle into which idealism would not know how to enter.

Of Gallows and Writing Cases

"If human beings were born free, they would form no concept of good and evil so long as they remained free."[27] Cards on the table. The concepts of good and evil are for Spinoza the instruments of the production of a slave subjectivity. There is no freedom that is not situated beyond good and evil. Miguel (or Daniel Levi) de Barrios, in his *Libre alvedrío*, not even hesitating to quote Thomas Aquinas in support of his conception of volition, testifies to the horror that such an impiety inspires in him. Against it he proclaims a definition of free will as being, "according to Origen, a/faculty of reason/which discerns good and evil/chooses between the two."[28] Barrios's horror was shared by all his contemporaries, coming from the most diverse horizons.

The first echos of scandal appear on the public (or semipublic) scene at the beginning of the year 1665. This is perhaps the only time that Baruch de Spinoza, in his lengthy correspondence, was not sufficiently faithful to his key-word "caution" (*caute*). In fact, in the course of an exchange of letters between December 1664 and June 1665, carried away by the drunkenness that is produced by complacency in an apparently shared friendship, he perhaps believed "it is from a free decision of the mind that he speaks the things he later, when sober, wishes he had not said."[29]

From Dordrecht, December 12, 1664, William de Blyenbergh, a merchant who presents himself as "someone who is unknown...who, driven only by a desire for pure truth in this short and transitory life, strives to plant his feet firmly in knowledge, as far as the human intellect allows, someone who, in his search for truth, has no other end than the truth, who seeks to acquire, by science, neither honor nor riches, but only truth,"[30] addresses himself to the "unknown friend" Baruch de Spinoza. He submits to him, between some measured but warm praises, "certain difficulties" having arisen after the repeated reading of the *Principles of Descartes' Philosophy* (and their appendix *Metaphysical Thoughts* [*Cogitata Metaphysica*]) published in 1663. The letter, whose calculated courtesy seems at first to have captivated the philosopher, particularly insists on a major difficulty:

> So it follows that God is the cause not only of the soul's substance, but also of the soul's motion or striving, which we call will, as you maintain throughout.
>
> From this assertion it also seems to follow necessarily, either that there is no evil in the soul's motion or will, or else that God himself does that evil immediately. For the things we call evil also happen through the soul, and consequently through such an immediate influence and concurrence of God.

Then he seeks an example by referring to the "concrete case" of Adam's acting, when he transgresses the divine prohibition. Thus, "either Adam's forbidden act is no evil in itself, insofar as God not only moved his will, but also moved it in such a way, or else God himself seems to do what we call evil."

For that of a shopkeeper, a simple amateur of speculative activity, William de Blyenbergh's theological perspicacity is rather remarkable. In light of the three following letters, most commentators hold, however, that the first was touched up by a professional of the theological profession, at least on the technical and formal plane. There exists no way to be sure of this. Whoever wrote the letter of December 12, he makes a proof of great penetration, since he reaches the heart of a system that has not yet been exposed publicly, except under the extraordinarily elliptical form of a critique of Cartesian philosophy. No doubt one discovered in it the thesis according to which

> no thing is said to be either good or bad considered alone, but only in respect to another [thing], to which it is advantageous in acquiring what it loves, or the contrary. So each thing can be said at the same time to be both good and evil in different respects. . . . However, those who eagerly seek some metaphysical good, needing no qualification, labor under a false prejudice, for they confuse a distinction of reason with a real or modal distinction.[31]

But probably the merchant of Dordrecht ignored the existence of the first detailed exposition of this problem, sketched in the *Short Treatise*.[32]

Dated January 3, 1665, Spinoza's response, which designates himself as philosopher and, as such, among "those who are above the law," cannot be of a friendlier tone in his invitation: "to bring us to a closer acquaintance and genuine friendship" based on "the love of truth."[33] This friendliness pushes him, not without imprudence, to advance the themes and theses that overhang all the great theoretical abysses of the *Ethics*. First of all, the genealogy of Blyenbergh's interpretative error: "it appears that by evil you understand the will itself," which invalidates the whole question: "as I too would grant, if it were so." Then comes the formulation of the rejection of the entity of good and evil, illustrated by the very example chosen by his correspondent:

> As an example, I too take Adam's decision, or determinate will, to eat the forbidden fruit. That decision, or determinate will, considered only in itself, involves as much perfection as it expresses of essence. . . . Therefore, we will be able to find no imperfection in Adam's decision, if we consider it in itself, without comparing it with others which are more perfect, or show a more perfect state.

For the current reader things would be clear. Regarding the example invalidated by the "case of Adam" that his correspondent imposes on him, Spinoza uses a model of argumentation that the *Ethics* will push to the limit of theoretical rigor: every development of power—whether chewing a mouthful or raising one's arm forcefully in order to beat—can only be considered as the expression of the perfection of the subject who exercises it (that is, of a tendency to persevere, not to disappear):

> The action of beating, insofar as it is considered physically, and insofar as we attend only to the fact that the man raises his arm, closes his fist, and moves his whole arm forcefully up and down, is a virtue, which is conceived from the structure of the human body.[34]

Every evaluation in itself appears useless to him. And if we continue to qualify things as "good" or "bad" in general, this is only the effect of a *habitus* that is spontaneous and philosophically deprived of meaning.

Such is the first exchange of letters between the merchant and the philosopher. Such are the incredibly important questions that are tackled in this exchange. Such is this tone of cordiality. But it is at this precise point that the idyll is going to be abruptly interrupted.

Horrified — sincerely or not, no matter — by the tranquility with which Baruch de Spinoza throws into the garbage the key and most tenacious categories of religious traditions, Blyenbergh, before coming to "criticize many things"[35] in his correspondent's missive, deems it necessary to open his letter with a solemn declaration of principles:

> You should know that I have two general rules according to which I always try to philosophize: the clear and distinct conception of my intellect and the revealed word, or will, of God. According to the one I strive to be a lover of truth, according to the other, a Christian philosopher. Whenever it happens, after a long investigation, that my natural knowledge either seems to contradict this word, or is not easily reconciled with it, this word has so much authority with me that I suspect the conceptions I imagine to be clear, rather than put them above and against the truth I think I find prescribed to me in that book. And no wonder, since I want to persist steadfastly in the belief that that word is the word of God, i.e., that it has proceeded from the highest and most perfect God, who contains many more perfections than I can conceive, and who perhaps has willed to predicate of himself and of his works more perfections than I, with my finite intellect, can conceive today.

Christianity and Cartesianism! It is as if he had spoken of rope in the house of a hanged man! Spinoza had to reread this letter several times to believe his eyes. To deal him the blow of these confessional philosophies! The twenty-some pages that follow these verbose repetitions on a problem that the first letter posed with a degree of clarity could only have accentuated Spinoza's astonishment. As a result, the latter manifests an irritation that his dry response does not seek to dissimulate:

> When I read your first letter, I thought our opinions nearly agreed. But from the second, which I received on the 21st of this month, I see that I was quite mistaken, and that we disagree not only about the things ultimately to be derived from first principles, but also about the first principles themselves. So I hardly believe that we can instruct one another with our letters. For I see that no demonstration, however solid it may be according to the laws of

demonstration, has weight with you unless it agrees with that explanation which you, or theologians known to you, attribute to sacred Scripture.[36]

However, he does not give up clarifying his position on the theme of evil. Perhaps because, despite the crudity of Blyenbergh's point of view, Spinoza becomes aware of the difficulty and the central nature of the question, he is going to agree to return in this third letter (which would have been the last) to the deontologization already pointed out in his first response. He does it this time by relying on a beautiful reflection on blindness:

> I say, therefore, that privation is, not the act of depriving, but only the pure and simple lack, which in itself is nothing. Indeed, it is only a being of reason, or mode of thinking, which we form when we compare things with one another. We say, for example, that a blind man is deprived of sight because we can easily imagine him as seeing, whether this imagination arises from the fact that we compare him with others who see, or his present state with his past, when he used to see. And when we consider this man in this way, by comparing his nature with that of others or with his own past nature, then we affirm that seeing belongs to his nature, and for that reason we say that he is deprived of it. But when we consider God's decree,[37] and his nature, we can no more affirm of that man than of a stone, that he is deprived of vision. For at that time vision no more pertains to that man without contradiction than it does to the stone, since nothing more pertains to that man, and is his, than what the divine intellect and will attribute to him.[38] Hence, God is no more the cause of his not seeing than of the stone's not seeing, which is a pure negation.
>
> Similarly, when we attend to the nature of a man who is led by an appetite for sensual pleasure, we compare his present appetite with that which is in the pious, or with that which he had at another time. We affirm that this man has been deprived of a better appetite, because we judge that then an appetite for virtue belongs to him. We cannot do this if we attend to the nature of the divine decree and intellect; for in that regard, the better appetite no more pertains to that man's nature at that time than it does to the nature of the Devil, or of a stone.[39]

With two more reprises William Blyenbergh is going to irk Spinoza by suggesting that the latter's positions forbid establishing the distinction between virtue and crime.[40] But the philosopher has wasted enough time. To the blissful questioning of the shopkeeper, he responds with a jest close to an insult:

Finally, your third question presupposes a contradiction. It is as if someone were to ask: if it agreed better with the nature of someone to hang himself, would there be reasons why he should not hang himself? But suppose it were possible that there should be such a nature. Then I say...that if anyone sees that he can live better on the gallows than at his table, he would act very foolishly if he did not go hang himself. One who saw clearly that in fact he would enjoy a better and more perfect life or essence by being a knave than by following virtue would also be a fool if he were not knave. For acts of knavery would be virtue in relation to such a perverted human nature.[41]

One more letter and the correspondence is interrupted. In 1674 William Blyenbergh publishes his fanatical refutation of the *Tractatus Theologico-Politicus* (*De waerheyt van de christelijke Godst-dienst*) and in 1682 his refutation of the *Ethics*.

Creatures of Desire

We cannot lose sight of the dates of the "correspondence on evil." In 1665 the *Nação* is ripe for the explosion of the Sabbataï Tsevi affair; some months later the definitive crisis will occur. The Lurian conception of evil, the *qelippah*, which is for the Kabbalah the obverse of the *En-Sof*, was to play in this event, we have said, the role of a crystallizer of the new doctrine. The reign of husks and shells (the literal meaning of *qelippah*) traditionally used by the kabbalists to designate the universe "of evil and the demonic powers"[42] had drifted, since Isaac de Luria, toward an interiorization of the demonic principle at the very root of the *En-Sof* (the hidden God who is indefinite and foreign to every creation, which Jacob Boehme will call *Grund*, the foundation of God the Creator) so that the world in its complexity can reach existence:

> Know therefore that the supernal space is like a field, and the ten points [that is, *sefiroth*] are sown in it. And even as the grains [of seed] grow each according to its virtue, so also these points grow each according to its virtue; and as the grains do not attain to growth and perfection if they remain in their original manner of being—for only in their decomposition is their growth—so it is also with these points.... Only by their breaking could the divine configurations [*parsufim*] be perfected.[43]

As elliptical as the text is (this is the rule of Kabbalah), one thing, in any event, appears indisputable: the idea of the necessity of a wrenching that, setting out from the essential latent negativity of the divine, provokes the scattering whose splinters are the world. This world of disorder and multiplicity—sometimes compared with that of the various colors issued from the composition of white light—"had to fall from the high summit to the depth of the pit so as to be smashed and dashed to pieces, like the wheat which is separated into flour and bran by grinding. Moreover by their fall the unclean forces are separated from holiness."[44]

By assigning to the world of the "childishness and madness"[45] of the kabbalists the ontologization of evil, its substantivization, in 1665 Baruch de Spinoza examines a tradition purely rooted in the spiritual subsoil of his Marrano compatriots in Amsterdam. Without this rooting, nothing of what was going to be produced in the following months would have any explanation. But the explosion of Sabbatian madness, which we have seen extended into the community as a trail of powder, could only reveal the urgency of the theoretical and religious problem posed by Luria's mysticism, by leading it to its limits.

By developing the most radical aspects of his conception of the *qelippah*, Nathan de Gaza—a prophet who has appeared to us as the true organizer of the Sabbatian corpus—has wagered on the descent to hell, with all its consequences: that is, the necessity of receiving (through the intermediary of the Messiah) the sparks of divine power (of the plenitude of being) that burn in the *qelippot*. The messianism of absolute moral transgression that Sabbataï proclaims presupposes an absolute substantialization of evil according to Luria's doctrine. Without it, the duty of recuperation of divinity without the darkness of the abysses would lose all meaning. As Gershom Scholem remarks:

> At this point, Sabbatian doctrine introduces a dialectical twist into the Lurianic idea. According to the new, Sabbatian version, it was not enough to extract the sparks of holiness from the realm of impurity. In order to accomplish its mission, the power of holiness—as incarnate in the messiah—has to descend into impurity, and good has to assume the form of evil. This mission is fraught with danger, as it appears to strengthen the power of evil before its final defeat. During Sabbatai's lifetime the doctrinal position was that by entering the realm of the *qelippah*, good had become evil *in appearance* only. But there were more radical possibilities waiting to be explored: only the complete transformation of good into evil would exhaust the full potential of the latter and thereby explode it, as it were, from within. This dialectical liquidation of evil requires not only the disguise of good in the form of evil but total identification with it.... The messiah descended into the realm of the *qelippah* in order to destroy it from within.[46]

As a philosopher, Spinoza seems to make a rigorously opposed idea his task: the destruction of evil can only be the fruit of absolute exteriorization (which, in the final analysis, is reduced to noting that "evil" is a word of four letters, as much a slave to the imagination as any other word). And, with it, the destruction of the "good" (a word equally of four letters in this case, and as much a slave to the imaginary genealogies that precede it). And this philosophical destruction really has nothing dialectical about it—this should be clear. Neither good nor evil refer, in Spinoza, to any play of the *Aufhebung*, of the "negation of the negation." Of them there remains nothing in their negation: they are simply reduced to extraverbal (imaginary) nothingness, nothing more. Fine. But what in this case is their intraverbal being?

Evil is not (except as a word); nor is good. To what reality do they allude, while eluding it? Beginning with the *Short Treatise* Spinoza thinks that he has clear ideas on this subject, anticipating Nietzsche on much of these aspects: beyond good and evil, as a unique way of speaking of what is bad and what is good:

> To say briefly now what good and evil are in themselves, we begin as follows:
>
> Some things are in our intellect and not in Nature; so these are only our own work, and they help us to understand things distinctly. Among these we include all relations, which have reference to different things. These we call *beings of reason*.
>
> So the question now is whether good and evil should be regarded as *beings of reason*. For one never says that something is good except in respect to something else that is not so good, or not so useful to us as something else. So one says that a man is bad only in respect to one who is better, or that an apple is bad only in respect to another that is good, or better. None of this could possibly be said if there were not something better, or good, in respect to which [the bad] is so called.
>
> Therefore, if one says that something is good, that is nothing but saying that it agrees well with the universal Idea which we have of such things. But... things must agree with their particular Ideas, whose being must be a perfect essence, and not with universal ones, because then they would not exist.
>
> As for confirming what we have just said, the thing is clear to us, but to conclude what we have said we shall add the following proofs.
>
> All things which exist in Nature are either things or actions. Now good and evil are neither things nor actions. Therefore, good and evil do not exist in Nature.
>
> For if good and evil were things or actions, they would have to have their definitions. But good and evil, say, Peter's goodness and Judas's evil, have no definitions apart from the [particular] essence[s] of Judas and Peter,

for these [essences] alone [are] in Nature, and without them [the goodness of Peter and the evil of Judas] cannot be defined. Therefore, as above, it follows that good and evil are not things or actions which are in Nature.[47]

Without pushing the reflection too far, one spots the weak points of the argumentation in the *Short Treatise*: the purely relative categories of "good" and "evil," thanks to which the possibility of escaping the substantial good and evil of traditional thought appears to open up, are not yet provided with a theoretical content that is sufficiently clear. It must be recognized that they will not be clear before the definitive editing of the *Ethics*: that is, to take up Gilles Deleuze's beautiful formula, when Spinoza understands good and evil as "the two senses of the variation of the power of acting: the decrease of this power (sadness) is bad; its increase (joy) is good."[48]

The main point of Spinoza's position can be followed throughout book IV of the *Ethics*. His point of departure seems no longer to want to leave any doubt regarding the position adopted:

> As far as good and evil are concerned, they also indicate nothing positive in things, considered in themselves, nor are they anything other than modes of thinking, or notions we form because we compare things to one another. For one and the same thing can, at the same time, be good, and bad, and also indifferent.[49]

If, in spite of this, one continues to want to make use of the vocables *bonum* and *malum*, faced with the necessity of constructing an ideal fiction of the human paradigm or model of life (*exemplar*), their meaning will no longer have anything in common with their hypostatized employment and usage until now. Thus, one will understand "in what follows . . . by good [*bonum*] what we know certainly is a means by which we may approach nearer and nearer to the model of human nature that we set before us. By evil [*malum*], what we certainly know prevents us from becoming like that model."[50]

It is clear, here, that the model, the *exemplar* (a term that in scholastic Latin translates the Greek *paradeigma*), far from returning to the Platonic conception of the ontological priority of the *eidos* over its imperfect imitations, presents all the features of a convention, of a name. However, something remains in suspense: what must be the criterion according to which the convention, the fiction of the model, must be constructed, in order to allow us to classify human beings into "more or less perfect, insofar as they approach more or less to this model"?[51] In any case, such a criterion could not refer to the reproduction of a formal essence, which, we have seen, only exists as a name.

For the main thing to note is that when I say that someone passes from a lesser to a greater perfection, and the opposite, I do not understand that he is changed from one essence, or form, to another. For example, a horse is destroyed as much if it is changed into a human being as if it is changed into an insect. Rather, we conceive that his power of acting, insofar as it is understood through his nature, is increased or diminished.[52]

However, definitions I and II of book IV, seemingly not concrete, present the good and the bad in terms of the effect of positive or negative usefulness (that which is useful to us is good, and that which excludes us from the useful is bad). They are clarified by what, in propositions 38 and 39, is specified regarding usefulness and goodness, in the concrete case of the body: what is useful to us is what renders us capable of "affecting" other beings "in a great many ways," and the good is what preserves this capacity to act. If adequation to the *exemplar* is expressed by the search for usefulness, and usefulness is expressed in a genesis from the capacity of simultaneously acting and preserving itself, an ethics of action can only be reduced in the final analysis, from reduction to reduction, to the articulation of "power" (*potentia*) and "joy" (*laetitia*), by which the good ends up being summarized in Spinoza: "The knowledge of good and evil is nothing but an affect of joy or sadness, insofar as we are conscious of it."[53]

But, if there is no good and bad except according to the increase or the decrease of the power of the subject of this goodness or badness, and if virtue (in the most Machiavellian sense of the word: the sole materialist meaning, all things considered, of *virtus* is force) is reduced to usefulness, to the point that "the more each one strives, and is able, to seek his own usefulness, that is, to preserve his being, the more he is endowed with virtue; conversely, insofar as each one neglects his own usefulness, that is, neglects his power to preserve his being, he lacks power"[54]— what role is there to attribute in this case to the persistence of the usage of notions of good and bad? The question is neither otiose nor byzantine, if one takes account of the fundamental principle of Spinoza's materialism, according to which there is nothing that is not necessary, considering the recourse to chance as one of the "asylums of ignorance" that his system violently rejects. As material (more precisely, as natural) as any other being, every word possesses in its existence a necessity, whose rigorous genealogy must be established by philosophy. To say that good and evil are imaginary products is not to resolve any problem—it is only to pose it. But it is certainly to pose it by setting out from a point of view of unaccustomed radicality: the one that buries the "knowledge of evil" in the pits of "inadequate knowledge," and identifies it concretely with "sadness itself, insofar as we are conscious of it."[55]

Let us take up again the example of the arm that beats—or the example of the mother one murders, in another shocking passage of Spinoza's correspondence. This arm, by deploying the motor capacities of the body in order to realize its action, is perfect by beating, just as the gesture that eliminates the mother is perfectly binding. Various representations in terms of values can be symbolically connected with this "virtue which is conceived from the fabric of the human body," a virtue of beating or of killing. No desire born from them, that is, no desire born from a passional sphere "would be from some usefulness, if human beings could be guided by reason." In the specific condition of servitude of human beings, every action is carried passionately—which amounts to saying that every action is also passion, passivity:

> Therefore, if a man moved by anger or hate is determined to close his fist or move his arm, that...happens because one and the same action can be joined to any images of things whatever. And so we can be determined to one and the same action both from those images of things which we conceive confusedly and from those images of things we conceive clearly and distinctly.[56]

In summary: clarity and distinction are useless, at least in matters of ethics, that is, of action. Letter 23 to Blyenbergh considers, by provocation, "for example, Nero's matricide, insofar as it comprehends something positive," namely the capacity of habitually beating a human female of given age and condition, until death follows. This "was not knavery. For Orestes, too, performed the [same] external action, and with the [same] intention of killing his mother. Nevertheless, he is not blamed, or at least, not as severely as Nero is. What, then, was Nero's knavery? Nothing but this: he showed by that act that he was ungrateful, without compassion, and disobedient," all things equally deprived of essence, and therefore simple beings of the imagination, according to the terminology of the *Ethics*.

The knavery, in fact, is only an imaginary thing. The good and the bad are only designations, displaced symbolically, in order to project in terms of value the experience of the power and powerlessness that leaves in me some recallable traces of "joy" (*laetitia*) and sadness.[57] For "cheerfulness cannot be excessive, but is always good; melancholy, on the other hand, is always evil."[58]

So be it. But the characteristic dynamic of joy, in its specific ethical universality, here produces an irremediable ambiguity, a final highly sophistical trap: if, in fact, the correct knowledge of reality (and of ourselves who belong to reality) is the only solid guarantee of *laetitia* and that which keeps us in ignorance[59] (thus bad in itself) is the only guarantee of sadness, what happens when, faced with the inaccessibility of the joy that we desire, our consciousness chooses to fall back into self-mystification and the tranquil plunge into consoling ignorance, against the suffering entailed by becoming conscious of frustration?

It is clear that frustration in itself is only the fruit of an inadequate knowledge that, because it tries to escape the laws of natural necessity, projects onto the world, as if they were real, its phantasmagoria (as necessary in their genesis as the laws they pretend to elude). But Spinoza—and this is the crucial point of his incalculable advance over all forms of "rationalism"—takes great care not to fall into a naive acquiescence before the intellectualist mythology of the rational elimination of the mystifying elements. There exists no knowledge that could displace an affective state...unless to become itself an affect. Thus, "no affect can be restrained by the true knowledge of good and evil insofar as it is true, but only insofar as it is considered as an affect."[60] And if, as we have seen, "nothing forbids our pleasure except a savage and sad superstition,"[61] the task of the philosopher could with difficulty be content to be only a simple (and just as sad) condemnation of the imaginary paradises and other opiates that render sustainable, at least on the level of dreams, our intolerable universe of abjections, of servitudes. Not to condemn, not to denigrate. To understand. To establish the why, the how. Why, but especially how "we strive to further the occurrence of whatever we imagine will lead to joy, and to avert or destroy what we imagine is contrary to it, or will lead to sadness."[62]

"What we imagine": the whole theoretical problem is found in these three words. How are images produced in me? Concretely, according to what paths of determination? This should be the only relevant series of interrogations to understand forms of human behavior. However, here is what does not allow the practical stakes of the question to be revealed: "Most of those who have written about the affects, and the human way of living, seem to treat, not of natural things, which follow the common laws of Nature, but of things which are outside Nature."[63] Such is the prejudice that deforms everything and bars access to a precise analytic of subjective behaviors. If we do not manage to get rid of these, we will be forced to remain attached to the world of childish, religious superstitions—or their secular humanist, no less stupid, variants. In the heart of this pleasant asylum turn those who "conceive a human being in Nature as a dominion within a dominion. For they believe that a human being disturbs, rather than follows, the order of Nature, that one has absolute power over one's actions, and that one is determined only by oneself."[64] And for this very reason, for want of causal explanations, they promulgate whining clerical decrees, by "attributing the cause of human impotence and inconstancy, not to the common power of Nature, but to I know not what vice of human nature, which they therefore bewail, or laugh at, or disdain, or (as usually happens) curse. And he who knows how to censure more eloquently and cunningly the weakness of the human mind is held to be godly."[65]

Seldom did Spinoza wage a battle harder than the one he led, throughout his life, against the expectation of the final hour for the sinner's soul, thirsty for holy water, that is, against the attitude of

> those who prefer to curse or laugh at human affects and actions, rather than understand them. To them it will doubtless seem strange that I should undertake to treat human vices and absurdities in the geometric style, and that I should wish to demonstrate by certain reasoning things which are contrary to season, and which they proclaim to be empty, absurd, and horrible.[66]

For once Spinoza allows himself to be arrogant with those who throughout the centuries have overburdened human beings with the chains that torment them and demean them to the most bestial of conditions, that of the submissive stupidity that adores its servitude: he directs a veritable slap at their foolish faces:

> But my reason is this: nothing happens in Nature which can be attributed to any defect in it, for Nature is always the same, and its virtue and power of acting are everywhere one and the same, that is, the laws and rules of Nature, according to which all things happen, and change from one form to another, are always and everywhere the same. So the way of understanding the nature of anything, of whatever kind, must also be the same, namely, through the universal laws and rules of Nature.
>
> The affects, therefore, of hate, anger, envy, and the like, considered in themselves, follow with the same necessity and force of Nature as the other singular things. And therefore they acknowledge certain causes, through which they are understood, and have certain properties, as worthy of our knowledge as the properties of any other thing, by the mere contemplation of which we are pleased.[67]

The conclusion imposes itself: it is only within the framework of a general theory of Nature that there will be room to understand all things (human or other) that it contains. Thus, natural things among natural things, "I shall consider human actions and appetites just as if it were a question of lines, planes, and bodies,"[68] and the affects and passions

> as properties which belong to it in the same way as heat, cold, storm, thunder, and the like belong to the nature of the atmosphere. Inconvenient though

they be, such things are necessary properties; they have definite causes through which we try to understand their nature, and a true understanding of them gives the mind as much satisfaction as the apprehension of things pleasing to the senses.[69]

Therefore, Nature first of all. And only all that which is in it.

And this is why the *Ethics* begins as it does: the ethics is a physics, which is a metaphysics. Which means "Nature." And it is from here that one must set out.

Nature (which Spinoza indifferently calls "God" or "substance") is "the immanent, not the transitive, cause of all things."[70] Setting out from a premise of this scale, the whole part is played out, and the revolution that the *Ethics* undertakes is off and running, never to stop. The terms (*causa immanens/causa transiens*) proceed from the Suárzian tradition, very likely by way of the manual of Adrian Heereboord, who defines them as follows: "The immanent cause is the one that produces its effect in itself, so that the intellect is called cause of its concepts; the transitive cause is the one that produces its effect outside of itself" (*Causa immanens est quae producit effectum in se ipsa, sic dicitur intellectus suorum conceptum. Causa transiens est quae producit effectum extra se*).[71] The use that Spinoza makes of them must rob them of their brilliance.

The transitive cause constituted, in fact, for the Scholastics, the finished variant of the Aristotelian final cause. In fact, as a good Thomist, Suárez writes that "to the concept of (efficient) cause belongs that it is essentially diverse from its effect and that the effect depends on the cause."[72] Such is, all things considered, for the great Scholastic, the aspect of the definition of the efficient cause that endows it with its extrinsic nature (in opposition to the formal and material causes, which are both intrinsic) and that at the same time requires the careful separation of the being proper to it and the being its effects owe to it:

> For matter and form, strictly speaking, are not causes through action, but through a formal and intrinsic union, and the end, as such, is a cause only through metaphorical license; on the other hand, the efficient cause is a cause through the characteristic action that emanates from it. Thus, this cause does not cause its effect by conferring on it its own formal and characteristic being, but another which emanates from it through action, through which it is differentiated from the material and formal causes: the latter cause an effect in that they confer on it their own entity to them, this is why they are called intrinsic causes; on the other hand, the efficient cause is extrinsic, that is, it does not transmit to the effect its own and (so to speak) in-

dividual being, but another which really derives and emanates from it through action.[73]

And the problem becomes even more acute (and the barrier of the extrinsic nature all the more insurmountable) when we tend toward this supreme type of efficient cause — first and transitive par excellence — which is God.[74] The God of the Scholastic and Christian tradition, of course, but also the God of every monotheistic religion, which Cajetan characterized as follows: "Everything which has existence (*esse*) distinct from its quiddity is produced efficiently by the First Cause; every being other than the First Cause has existence (*esse*) distinct from its quiddity; therefore, every being other than the First Cause is produced efficiently by the First Cause."[75]

Every concept of transcendence, but equally every hope of salvation in the hereafter that could be sustained only by surmounting the barrier of transcendence, hangs on the tenuous thread that, in the Judeo-Christian tradition, makes God a transitive (and in a certain way immanent) cause. This God, in his absolutely free will, chooses the world in a deliberate and arbitrary way, this world here, for "God truly, properly, and without metaphor, wills and loves what he freely wills, loves, and what he could have not loved." There is more: insofar as willing, God appears to go excessively further than the human being who wills moderately, since "the divine will, in order that it not be an informing form or acting act, but a very pure act, we must think that it constitutes God as willing in a more elevated way, and that he attains his secondary objects, without in the same action there being produced any change or real addition."[76]

Proposition 18 of the first part of the *Ethics* ("God is the immanent, not the transitive, cause of all things") rejects these positions without palliatives or solutions of compromise. The demonstration that accompanies this proposition destroys, as if there were any need, every attempt at negotiation, by recalling and explaining the destructive premises that cement it:

> Everything that is, is in God, and must be conceived through God (by P15),[77] and so (by P16C1)[78] God is the cause of things, which are in him. That is the first thing [thing to be proven]. And then outside God there can be no substance (by P14),[79] that is (by D3),[80] thing which is in itself outside God. That was the second. God, therefore, is the immanent, not the transitive cause of all things, q.e.d.[81]

We have already had the occasion to emphasize what the Spinozist monism of substance owes to certain aspects of Cartesianism, specifically those that Descartes will himself submit to self-criticism in the *Principles* in 1664, and the abyss that separates Spinozism from every form of monotheism. However, it is worthwhile confronting here a problem posed in 1901 by Karppe,[82] brilliantly explained by Dunin-Borkowski,[83] and periodically taken up again by all specialists on Spinoza.[84]

The central thesis of "everything is in God" (or in Nature) that is articulated around propositions 5 ("In Nature there cannot be two or more substances of the same nature or attribute") and 11 ("God, or a substance consisting of infinite attributes, each of which expresses eternal and infinite essence, necessarily exists"), through the formula according to which "in Nature there is only one substance, and that it is absolutely infinite"[85] — could this thesis that, we propose, opens up the horizon of contemporary materialism pass for the pure and simple transposition of some well-known Kabbalistic theses?

Dunin-Borkowski thought he could follow its trail (correctly, it seems to me) in certain passages of the *Door of Heaven*, the great kabbalistic manifesto in Castilian of don Alonso (alias Abraham Cohen) de Herrera. From the first chapters of this work, the erudite Jesuit extracted some key texts that say that "everything is one in God," "there do not exist two substances of a single attribute," "there exists only one substance with an infinity of properties," "substance is determined according to a plurality of infinite essences, which are only its modifications."[86]

I am not going to enter here into the question, which I do not believe that I have any way of settling, of knowing whether or not Baruch de Spinoza had material access to Herrera's text either in its original manuscript version written in Castilian,[87] at the time of his apprenticeship in the vicinity of the synagogue, or later in the summarized version that Isaac Aboab translated into Hebrew and had published in Amsterdam in 1650.[88] The Latin translation[89] that Wachter used, and through him Leibniz, was published a year after Spinoza's death. Nothing prevents believing that Spinoza had read this text. Let us remark that by reading the Herrerian thesis, the young philosopher would have found only the synthetic expression of theoretico-theological perspectives, which would have become familiar to him anyway during his rabbinic formation.

The *Door of Heaven* and the *House of God* (the two manuscripts that constitute the kabbalistic oeuvre of the famous descendent of don Gonzalo de Córdoba) are probably the greatest heights of Zohar of explicitly neo-Platonic filiation that the Kabbalah had produced in the seventeenth century. And certain formulas of monistic appearance, such as those that have been quoted, can only evoke for us those passages in which Spinoza praises certain Hebrews who have seen "as if through a cloud" certain interesting elements in order to have done with the Cartesian dualism of thought and extension ("...when they maintained that God, God's intellect, and the things understood by him are one and the same")[90] and refers us finally to the text, the perennial source of all Jewish spirituality: the incredible book of splendor, the *Zohar*.

> Everything is bound and united in a same whole..., to the point that it is easy to see that everything is one, that everything is the Ancient (God), and that there is no distinction between the whole and Him.
>
> Everything is one and everything is Him, everything is one thing without distinction or separation.
>
> The ancient Holy exists enveloped in a figure of the One. He is One and Everything is One, and all the lights that shine from Him are One, and enter into the One.... The Ancient of ancients envelops every thing, he is Everything.
>
> God is the beginning and the end of all the degrees of creation; all these degrees carry his mark and his nature and one cannot denumerate them except through the One. He is one despite the numerous forms that he has on Him, it is on Him that superior and inferior things are suspended....
>
> Master of the world, you are one, you are not according to the numbers, you are the sublime of sublimes, the mysterious of the mysterious.... You have produced ten forms that we call Sefiroth, you are enveloped in them yourself, and since you are in them, their harmony remains stable. The one who represents them as separate acts as if he destroyed your unity.[91]

The weight of this inspiration, of this myticism of the Whole coming from the *Zohar*—equally established, although with less precision and richness, in the *Bahir*—was enormous from the time of the Renaissance. And not only in Jewish milieus. A frequent formula in Fray Luis de Granada (who, of course, dealt with the Inquisition) resonates with this echo:

> What is God? Soul or reason of the universe? What is God? Everything that we see: for in everything we see his wisdom and his assistance: and in this way we confess his greatness: which is so great that one cannot think of one greater. And so only he is all things, the one who inside and outside has nourished this great work which is his. What difference is there between the divine nature and our own? The difference among others, is that the best part of ours is the mind; whereas he is all mind, all reason, and all understanding.[92]

However, Karppe himself, after having collected the texts of the *Zohar*, after having insisted on their pantheistic resonance and even having sensed in them the outline of some "constitutive elements of Spinoza's doctrine," offers us the key that destroys every attempt to limit the metaphorical approach of the texts: "every pantheistic doctrine consistent with itself implies that gradual development occurs by virtue of an internal necessity and consequently is eternal; on the contrary, the *Zohar* situates this development within time and makes it depend on the will of the first being."[93]

Without pausing on the anachronistic use that Karppe makes of the word "pantheism," or on the inexactitude that consists in attributing to Spinoza a model of "gradual development" or of "emanative cause" (we have shown that it is precisely the rejection of these models that separates him even from the most radical of the neo-Platonists of the Renaissance, including Giordano Bruno), it nonetheless remains that really the question of the divine will is an absolute break and a point of no return. If "God or Nature acts from the same necessity from which he exists...,"[94] as the author of the *Ethics* has defended with intransigence, nothing appears weaker than the thesis of those

> others [who] think that God is a free cause because he can (so they think) bring it about that the things which we have said follow from his nature (i.e., which are in his power) do not happen or are not produced by him. But this is the same as if they were to say that God can bring it about that it would not follow from the nature of a triangle that its three angles are equal to two right angles; or that from a given cause the effect would not follow — which is absurd.... neither intellect nor will pertain to God's nature.[95]

And that in all rigor, for "the will cannot be called a free cause, but only a necessary one," since "the will, like the intellect, is only a certain mode of thinking. And so ... each volition can neither exist nor be determined to produce an effect unless it is determined by another cause, and this cause by another, and so on, to infinity."[96]

The God-Nature who "acts from the laws of his nature alone, and is compelled by no one,"[97] since he is everything (*hen kai pan*: one and all, to take up again Lessing's time-honored — perhaps unfortunately — formula), condenses precisely in it what definition 7 of book I explains: "That thing is called free which exists from the necessity of its nature alone, and is determined to act by itself alone."[98] This free substance, because unique and infinitely powerful, "does not produce" — cannot in any way produce — "any effect by freedom of the will."[99] And this for the pure and simple reason that to speak of free will or arbitrary will is a contradiction in terms: it is the absurd hypothesis of an autonomous heteronomy. Freedom is an autonomous necessity that only obeys the proper self-determination of its own power.

This is why—the exact opposite of Juan de Prado, whom Orobio reproaches for having maintained that "God can do everything that is not repugnant, but that by himself he has not done everything that he can" and that "sometimes through the contingent course of events [the nature of things] is perverted and some strange and admirable effects, entirely extraordinary, result from him, such as the diversity of monsters, remarkable floods, the falling of meteors and comets in the atmosphere,"[100] the exact opposite of every recourse to contingency and chance—Spinoza's Nature,[101] this substance that has neither arbiter nor aspiration (i.e., a will), is the only essentially free reality, precisely because "in Nature there is nothing contingent, but all things have been determined from the necessity of the divine nature to exist and produce an effect in a certain way."[102] And this absolute empire (which is an absolute empire over itself), by which is defined the necessary and essential freedom of Substance-God-Nature, carries a name in which is expressed all its being: absolute autonomy, absolute freedom, strictly speaking, are only partial denominations of an absolute power, of an infinite power.

In it is expressed the quintessence of book I of the *Ethics*: the unique and infinite substance we have called Nature, God, can now be designated, almost pointed out, in a concrete way: it is power. "God's power is his essence itself."[103]

One is amazed in discovering here, once more, an echo of the commentary of Fray Luis de Granada on pseudo-Dionysius, when he writes that "Saint Dionysius situates three things in the Creator just as in his creatures (which are being, power, and working), among which there exists such an order of proportion, such is the being such is the power, such is the power such are the works. Thus, by the works we know the power, and by the power the being."[104]

Thus, in Spinoza's system the freedom of the infinite power is necessary, faced with the heteronomous servitude of free will. There is a loss of illusions of the will for this human being as a thing-among-the-things of substance: "Those, therefore, who believe that they either speak or are silent, or do anything from a free decision of the mind, dream with open eyes."[105] To dream with open eyes: we are here, again, at the point from which we have set out, but, nonetheless, in such conditions, after this long journey through substance, that we can strive for the concrete analysis of this concrete thing that is our delirious subject—necessarily delirious.

The introduction of necessity in the treatment of the "anomalies" of subjective behavior changes the point of entry and modifies the stake: such anomalies do not exist; the subject is necessarily as it is, and as it happens in everything, the recourse to contingency or unforeseeability in the explanation of one of its avatars is only an admission, hardly masked by grandiloquence, of our ignorance. It is not "contingence" but the name we give "to a defect of our knowledge," which is produced when we find ourselves faced with a thing whose "essence involves a contradiction, or if we do know very well that its essence does not involve a contradiction, and nevertheless can affirm nothing certainly about its existence, because the order of causes is hidden from us."[106]

Alongside da Costa who sees in the world of religious manipulations of consciousness the fruit—of a barely conceivable viciousness—of the most arbitrary priestly infamy, alongside Juan de Prado who overcame it with good humor as sources of sinecure for his ministers, Baruch de Spinoza is on the way to understanding definitively how the necessity that without exception governs every representative consequence of consciousness (mystifying or not) is as solid, necessary, and anonymous as the necessity that leads the raindrop that falls at this precise moment on the corolla of this rose.

But if "a human being is necessarily always subject to passions, . . . follows and obeys the common order of Nature, and accommodates himself to it as much as the nature of things requires,"[107] how can one define the ontic singularity of this thing among things that we call the human being? Or else—a question no doubt prior—how can one define what it is to be a thing? First of all, it is clear that it is not to be substance. Things—all things—are in substance; they cannot therefore be substantive. The recourse to an analogy in order to account for what Aristotle metaphorically calls physical substance is here inflexibly rejected—a question that Spinoza wound up posing for himself, by deliberately trying to reinvent twenty-two centuries of metaphysics.

What is it to be an entity (an existent)? *To exist* or *to be-there*, he responds. To struggle for impossible permanence, to persevere against the polymorphous *occursus* of the infinite wealth of the rest of existents. "Each thing, as far as it can by its own power, strives to persevere in its being" (*Unaquaeque res, quantum in se est, in suo esse perseverare conatur*).[108] *Strives*, Spinoza says: *conatur*. The topos—of idealist, and especially Hegelian, origin—on the passive or static nature of the Spinozist ontology has weighed a lot more on commentators on the *Ethics*, for a century, so we can be content to speak in detail of the *conatur*. Insofar as it is the being characteristic of things, the *perseverare* at question throughout Spinoza's oeuvre is anything but the admission of an already crystallized state.

The computerized lexicon of the *Ethics* by Guéret-Robinet-Tombeur here provides some very useful information: on sixteen occurrences of the infinitive *perseverare*, fifteen are governed by the main verb *conor* (thirteen under the form *conatur* and two under the form *conamur*). In only one case is it untied from this overdetermination, in a minor context that touches on our theme only marginally: at the end of the preface to book IV, when Spinoza mentions the impossibility of establishing ontological hierarchies according to the more or less lengthy duration of the *perseverare*. And *conor* is, without equivocation, a verb of action that indicates a tendency toward activity ("being disposed to," "trying to," "striving to"). The determination that it requires over the *perseverare* is absolute.

"To be an existent" is (and is uniquely) to strive to persevere: to be confronted actively with the permanent risk, to the continual expectation of annihilation. To be is to be subtracted actively from nothingness. Neither an eleatism of the *perseverare*, nor a dialectics of the *conor*. A logic of the *occursus*, a logic of war:

> For singular things are modes by which God's attributes are expressed in a certain and determinate way..., that is..., things that express, in a certain and determinate way, God's power, by which God is and acts. And no thing has anything in itself by which it can be destroyed, or which takes its existence away.... On the contrary, it is opposed to everything which can take its existence away.... Therefore, as far as it can, and it lies in itself, it strives to persevere in its being, q.e.d.[109]

The *Ethics* designates *the specifically human mode of applying this effort (conatus)* as "desire" (*cupiditas*). And desire is said to be "the very essence of the human being,"[110] ontologically prior even over *laetitia*, since "no one can desire to be blessed, to act well and to live well, unless at the same time he desires to be, to act, and to live, that is, to actually exist."[111]

Here begins a new series of problems. For one must be clear: only substance can have essence, or what is called essence, as much in good Aristotelian tradition as in all Spinozist rigor, expressed without equivocation by definition 4 of book I of the *Ethics* ("By attribute I understand what the intellect perceives of a substance, as constituting its essence"). Undoubtedly, the sliding of its use outside of the substantial sphere, for example, its application to the thing called a human being, can only introduce important elements of confusion: the latter, precisely, have given hold to what important contemporary commentators qualify as a "Spinozist anthropology." We have already denounced this genuine contradiction in terms as the most improper of acts of hermeneutical arbitrariness that could be inflicted on Spinoza's text.

The definition of desire as the "essence of the human being, insofar as it is conceived to be determined, from any given affection of it, to do something"[112] first fulfills a polemical function against the Aristotelian tradition, which relates desire to the sphere of imperfection, of the incomplete, of unformed matter ("matter is the subject of desire, just as a female desires a male and the ugly desires the beautiful").[113] Whence this consequence: what is important about this definition lies in the clear insistence on desire's active dimension, its essential connection with the capacity to do something, and something without which the very *esse* of human beings would come undone: the preservation of their own existence. That is, prior to, and independent of, the fact that we possess or do not possess adequate knowledge: in order to be able to know, it is necessary to be and not cease to be. "Both insofar as the mind has clear and distinct ideas, and insofar as it has confused ideas, it strives, for an indefinite duration, to persevere in its being and it is conscious of this striving it has"[114]—this is a consciousness independent (and prior on the ontological plane) in relation to what its knowledge is (adequate or inadequate), since "we neither strive for, nor will, neither want, nor desire anything because we judge it to be good; on the contrary, we judge something to be good because we strive for it, will it, want it, and desire it."[115]

Thus, the reference to the "essence" of a mode (a human being or some other) can never be considered, in the manner of the Aristotelian *to ti en einai* or the Scholastic *quidditas*, as a principle of substantial individuation, whereas Suarez defends it by writing that "the very essence and the form of the totality is the same thing as the nature of each being."[116]

As Gilles Deleuze has correctly indicated, in Spinoza

> the modal essences are simple and eternal. But they nevertheless have, with respect to the attribute and to each other, another type of distinction that is purely intrinsic. The essences are neither logical possibilities nor geometric structures; they are parts of power, that is, degrees of physical intensity. They have no parts but are themselves parts, parts of power, like intensive quantities that are composed of smaller quantities. They are all compatible with one another without limit, because all are included in the production of each one, but each one corresponds to a specific degree of power different from all the others. [117]

The reciprocity of the action of the modes is, in effect, a decisive aspect of Spinoza's definition of power insofar as it is essence. The distance hollowed out in relation to the Cartesian definition of the three autonomous substances (*res cogitans, res extensa,* and *res infinita*) wants to be an abyss. Spinoza, after a lengthy attack against the conception of substance in Descartes, writes:

> My intent here was only to give a reason why I did not say that anything without which a thing can neither be nor be conceived pertains to its essence — namely, because singular things can neither be nor be conceived without God, and nevertheless, God does not pertain to their essence. But I have said that what necessarily constitutes the essence of a thing is that which, if it is given, the thing is posited, and if it is taken away, the thing is taken away, that is, the essence, is what the thing can neither be nor be conceived without, and vice versa, what can neither be nor be conceived without the thing.[118]

And inversely, reciprocity — carried to the extreme limit at which every being is refused essence independent of the thing — thus constitutes the key to the Spinozist position on the problem of the relation between "essence" and "thing." Such a treatment deprives essence of every possibility, not only of preexistence, but even of formal survival on the margin of the concrete thing. One will thus call essence the relational reciprocity of powers characteristic of the infinity of things that are found in the world, in Nature. We are not in the presence of underlying entities that would configure real being as its true *ontos on,* its real reality, but in the presence of a theory of physical beings whose simple configuration operates essentially in struggle, since they exist only in tangled intersections of the power deployed in order of battle. The real existence of power, placing itself in the face of every alterity, precedes, then, every essence and constructs it. "The striving by which each thing strives to persevere in its being is nothing but the actual essence of the thing."[119]

I would like one to appreciate how strong this formulation is; how much it abolishes every possibility of endowing any essence of the modes with the least autonomy or ontological independence (I do not even speak of primacy). Essence is the *conatus*; and the *conatus,* the effort, is nothing but the conflictual relation of beings with one another on this infinite terrain of encounters (i.e., of impacts) that is Nature. And this conscious *conatus* that is the human *cupiditas* cannot, truly at all, escape the empire of such a rule.

In fact, "it is impossible that a human being should not be a part of Nature, and that he should be able to undergo no changes except those which can be understood through his own nature alone, and of which he is the adequate cause."[120] Quite the contrary: the tension in the play of multiplicity, the appetite not to dissolve into its whirlpool, but to preserve its integrity of collisions in confrontations, reveals to us a human reality appreciably different from a placid self-determination: "the power of the human being, therefore, insofar as it is explained through his actual existence, is part of God or Nature's infinite power, that is . . . , of its essence."[121] A part, therefore, is indeed that: one part with (against) other parts. "Next, if it were possible that a human being could undergo no changes except those which can be understood through the human being's nature alone, it would follow . . . that he could not perish, but that necessarily he would always exist."[122]

Not only the limitation but conflict itself: otiose death (about which no free human being must waste time thinking) also has the same source, the essential network of conflictual relations that, as for the rest, define the human being in the world. There is no way out. Every attempt to save human beings from their essential destiny of things among things, of things in conflictual relation with things, is condemned by the theory in advance to the most lamentable failure:

> Therefore, if it were possible for a human being to undergo no changes except those which could be understood through the person's nature alone, so that . . . he would necessarily always exist, this would have to follow from God's infinite power; and consequently . . . the order of the whole of Nature, insofar as it is conceived under the attributes of extension and thought, would have to be deduced from the necessity of the divine nature, insofar as it is considered to be affected with the idea of some human being. And so . . . it would follow that the human being would be infinite. But this . . . is absurd.
>
> Therefore, it is impossible that a human being should undergo no other changes except those of which he is himself the adequate cause, q.e.d.[123]

Quod in Nigras Lethargi Mergitur Undas

Here we are now before the final key to the *Ethics* and all Spinozism, this philosophical revolution without return, which, after having emptied beings of every underlying essentiality, situates us in the face of the materialist horizon of our modernity: against the logic of essences — which had been, until then, that of metaphysics — a logic of powers in conflict, a logic of war.

In sum, the only essential principle of every concrete reality, *potentia*, the essence characteristic of an infinite and unique substance, cannot know in its deployment any resistance that limits its autonomy: its logic is that of a development that, insofar as it is purely self-defined, produces in complete freedom the very conditions of self-knowledge (*amor Dei intellectualis*) without any restriction or interference. But when we are obliged to pass from the plane of substance to that of its modes—fragments of power that collide with one another, brush up against one another, are arranged, sometimes composed, often delivered from mortal battles—the freedom of some is always the result of an overabundance of power that is exercised by the submission of the other's power. Yet there are neither rules nor "laws" to reduce the conflicts or limit their effects, "the right of each one is defined by his virtue, or power."[124] Thus, nothing and no one (thing, person, or institution) can aspire to normalize the conditions of conflict on the road to a permanent equilibrium. Nothing and no one can any more, in this war of all against all (of everything against everything), rest on confidence in his own domination: this would be the worst of stupidities, for "there is no singular thing in Nature than which there is not another more powerful and stronger. Whatever one is given, there is another more powerful by which the first can be destroyed."[125] This is an axiom. We live on the lookout. Our anxiety is that of John Ford's old gunslinger who knows that one day, each day closer, a quicker gunman will come into town.

The constant possibility, the continuous risk of annihilation, permanently revolves around the essential *conatus*, characteristic of all beings: there is no life without risk, no being without wagering. Such is the space that I would qualify—despite conventions—as the tragic Spinoza: the one who, in all lucidity, notes the impossibility of resting on what, in fact, is unthinkable: a static substantiality. Life as threat, as despairing lookout and expectation, is the only metaphysical incentive of Spinoza's morals. Because one must live, be, remain in one way or another, at any cost. But "the force by which a human being perseveres in existing is limited, and infinitely surpassed by the power of external causes."[126]

And on us, fragmentary powers aspiring to infinity, despite all our subjective effort to lose ourselves in the phantasmagoric illusion of "making" the world in our image, "to enjoy a false appearance of freedom,"[127] reality imposes: we are the product of this world, and it is not our product, we its creatures so frail and despairing. Our frantic passion is to struggle to devour the world; but finally "the force and growth of any passion, and its perseverance in existing, are not defined by the power by which we strive to persevere in existing, but by the power of an external cause compared with our own."[128]

Not only does the exterior undo us; it literally forms us. And when necessary, the exterior will annihilate us. Gilles Deleuze's commentary reveals this with a great beauty:

> If death is inevitable, this is not at all because death is internal to the exist-
> ing mode; on the contrary, it is because the existing mode is necessarily
> open to the exterior, because it necessarily experiences passions, because it
> necessarily encounters other existing modes capable of endangering one of
> its vital relations, because the extensive parts belonging to it under its com-
> plex relation do not cease to be determined and affected from without.[129]

In the final analysis, from the permanent lookout for an infinite and unavoidable risk,
what can make ethical the physical universe of necessary events? Death: the necessary metaphysical bridge between physics and ethics. "I who had based all my desires/
under a species of eternity/I am going to lay down in the sun my shadow in July."[130]

Thus annihilation lies in wait. Already inscribed in the human
impossible nature, because "insofar as human beings are torn by affects which are
passions" (and they necessarily are), "they can be different in nature."[131] Consequently, nothing authorizes their composition in harmonic terms to be thought a
priori, to the extent that human beings dominated by their passions are "contrary to
one another."[132] That is, that they are, since nothing of what is possible cannot be,
in Spinoza's universe. It is the lookout in relation, always conflictual, with this inevitable hell that is the other, what Spinoza saw with no less precision than Jean-
Paul Sartre. Hell, since its power ceaselessly threatens my own power, resists its deployment, confronts it and tries in vain to simulate the outline of an impossible
agreement, on a common territory or burrow. In vain. The only thing that is common to us is our desire of domination over the exterior, and each of us is the exterior of others. One thing in common: mutual war.

It must be known: ethics, in all rigor, is nothing but the battle
for power. And there exists no battle for power, authentic conflict of powers, worthy of this name, whose ultimate stake is other than death. To know the final foundation of our essence as *occursus*, as an implacable clash of powers, is to know, in the
last analysis, that only the horizon of death situates our relative autonomy, our fragile
dose of freedom: the one that corresponds to a permanent duel with hostile powers
that, from all sides, surround me and in the face of which, confronted with their capacity to annihilate me, to reduce me to nothingness, I am finally powerful and free,
and throwing myself into the eye of the cyclone of a fray that will finish—I know—
by getting the better of me.

"Death is less harmful to us, the greater the . . . clear and distinct
knowledge"[133] in our mind. A recognition of death's paradoxical splendor: confronted with the unbearable host of those who are feeble-minded, slaves of a morn-

ing drowned in the depths of hope, of the immortality that is only a poor metonymy of memory, the philosopher's today (there is no day after), the hero's today, is only the experience of a dice throw, as equals, with death, the nothingness (which is everything) on the mat. Only my power will have managed to exist "from the necessity of (my) nature alone"[134]—such is freedom—when the future (my future is the future), this last refuge of renouncing alterity, will have been suppressed. A limit-experience that language and the imagination exorcise, as always, through verbalization. Through the words that rhetorize death, by turning it into images, the experience of the hero is broken into little glasses and cigars, on the nightstand of the old combatant: a bullfight in a bedroom. Death, the final horizon of a limited power that tries to enjoy, to live, as life is worth being lived: below its possibilities—thus Hector lives his sole moment of free and powerful life when, snatched from the trap of Athena, he throws himself into the encounter of the infinitely superior power of the invincible Achilles, in order to find in it his own death. The freedom of being against God, against Nature, substance of inconceivable power, against the conjugated force of everything and all: end without finality, such is death. It is not spoken. It is. It is not spoken, it is not thought. To name it is to drown it in ridicule and chatter. "A free human being thinks of nothing less than of death."[135] A free human being dies his death—without an image.

Of course, one can always resort to the little death, to the simulacrum of sickly life that accepts defeat in the face of the law of exteriority and in submission to the pettiness of the daily universal order. Resigned surrender, repentance, renouncement—"voluntary" or not—of one's own power: "no reason compels me to maintain that the body does not die unless it is changed into a corpse. And, indeed, experience seems to urge a different conclusion. Sometimes a human being undergoes such changes that I should hardly have said he was the same human being."[136]

"Such changes": those of human beings, those of peoples. Aboab, Morteira, Menasseh, the entire *Nação*, the New Synagogue, combination and key, not yet built at the time of the sordid exclusion. Uriel, he too, no doubt, was only free and powerful in the evening of 1640, when the bullet had shot from the barrel... and Doctor Juan de Prado, who in another life could not have outlived his horse. "Such changes": language, however, even in Amsterdam, almost outside the world, perseveres. It alone. When there remains nothing of the identity of the people that in its force was forged... "Such changes": language, perpetual, always. "May Adonai erase it." Language is memory:

I have heard stories, for example, of a Spanish poet who suffered an illness; though he recovered, he was left so oblivious to his past life that he did not believe the tales and tragedies he had written were his own. He could surely have been taken for a grown-up infant if he had also forgotten his native language.[137]

Translated by Ted Stolze

Notes

1. Schelling (1936, 26).

2. Vallée (1988, 93).

3. Vallée (1988, 89).

4. Ibid.

5. Schelling (1950, letter I).

6. Schelling (1950, letter II).

7. Schelling (1950, letter V).

8. Schelling (1950, letter IV).

9. Macherey (1979).

10. During a 1936 seminar. See Heidegger (1985).

11. Schelling (1936, 26).

12. Von Baader (1963, V, 263): "If the spirit of speculation in modern times were oriented toward this theologian [Jacob Boehme] and similar medieval minds, instead of toward Spinoza and those similar to him, the philosophy of religion would go much better."

13. Heidegger (1985).

14. A letter from Hegel to Schelling dated 1794.

15. Schelling (1936, 3).

16. I say "anachronistically," since, as one knows, the term "pantheism" had not been put into play before John Toland's work.

17. Schelling (1936, 16–20).

18. Schelling (1936, 21).

19. Schelling (1936, 22).

20. Schelling (1936, 58).

21. Schelling (1936, 26).

22. Schelling (1936, 73–74).

23. Schelling (1936, 44–45).

24. Ravaisson (1953, 33–36).

25. Heidegger (1958).

26. For a precise analysis of this text, see Albiac (1979).

27. *E* IVP68.

28. De Barrios (1680).

29. *E* IIIP2S.

30. *Ep* 18.

31. *CM* I/6.

32. *KV* I/10.

33. *Ep* 19.

34. *E* IVP59S.

35. *Ep* 20.

36. *Ep* 21.

37. In this correspondence Spinoza uses a "conventional" terminology, which obviously has no place in his own theoretical system.

38. See the previous note.

39. It is worth emphasizing, if only briefly, the implacable rejection by Spinoza of every form of anthropological essentialism. This rejection is particularly obvious in the passage from *E* IIP40S1 (parallel in his definition of the human being to the text cited on blindness); he ironizes regarding universal "notions [that] are not formed by all in the same way, but vary from one to another, in accordance with what the body has more often been affected by, and what the mind imagines or recollects more easily. For example, those who have more often regarded human stature with wonder will understand by the word *human being* an animal of erect stature. But those who have been accustomed to consider something else, will form another common image of human beings — e.g., that the human being is an animal capable of laughter, or a featherless biped, or a rational animal. And similarly concerning the others — each will form universal images of things according to the disposition of his body." Starting from a perspective in which the human being is nothing but an imaginary representation, every space for a supposed "philosophical anthropology" disappears, and its ambition to be theoretical is suppressed in a critical . way. It is not that there exists no "Spinozist anthropology"; it is that there exists, from Spinoza's perspective, no anthropology that is not delirious. On this theme, see Matheron's (1978) excellent article, reprinted in Matheron (1986).

40. *Ep* 22.

41. *Ep* 23.

42. Scholem (1973, 33).

43. Scholem (1973, 35).

44. Scholem (1973, 36).

45. "I have also read, and am acquainted with, a number of kabbalistic triflers whose madness has never

ceased to amaze me" (*Legi etiam et in super novi nugatores aliquos kabbalistas, quorum insaniam nunquam mirari satis potui*) (*TTP* IX).

46. Scholem (1973, 801–2).

47. *KV* I/10.

48. Deleuze (1988, 71).

49. *E* IVPref.

50. Ibid.

51. Ibid.

52. Ibid.

53. *E* IVP8.

54. *E* IVP20.

55. *E* IVP64D.

56. *E* IVP59S.

57. "Joy is the passage of a human being from a lesser to a greater perfection"; "Sadness is the passage of a human being from a greater to a lesser perfection" (*E* IIIDef. Aff. 2, 3).

58. *E* IVP42.

59. *E* IVP27.

60. *E* IVP14.

61. *E* IVP45S.

62. *E* IIIP28.

63. *E* IIIPref.

64. Ibid.

65. Ibid. See the nearly identical formulas of the *TP* I.

66. Ibid.

67. Ibid.

68. Ibid.

69. *TP* I/4.

70. *E* IP18.

71. Heereboord, *Hermeneia* I/17; quoted in Gueroult (1968, 246).

72. Francisco Suárez, *Disp. Met.* XII/ii/10.

73. Ibid., XVII/ii/6.

74. "It must be remembered that one can demonstrate with evidence that the being that is necessary in itself is the source or efficient cause of the other beings" (Ibid., XIX/ii/4).

75. Cajetan (1964, 209).

76. Suárez, *Disp. Met.* XXX/ix/35.

77. *E* IP15: "Whatever is, is in God, and nothing can be or be conceived without God."

78. *E* IP16C1: "God is the efficient cause of all things which can fall under an infinite intellect."

79. *E* IP14: "Except God, no substance can be or be conceived."

80. *E* ID3: "By substance I understand what is in itself and is conceived through itself."

81. *E* IP18D.

82. Karppe (1901).

83. Dunin-Borkowski (1910).

84. For the current state of the question, see Brann (1977).

85. *E* IP14C1.

86. See Dunin-Borkowski (1910, 184–90, 550).

87. *Puerta del cielo.*

88. Herrera (1650; 1655).

89. Herrera (1678).

90. *E* IIP7S.

91. Karppe (1901, 404–8).

92. Karppe (1901, 2).

93. Karppe (1901, 409–10).

94. *E* IVPref.

95. *E* IP17S.

96. *E* IP32, D.

97. *E* IP17.

98. *E* ID7.

99. *E* IP32C1.

100. Orobio de Castro (MS, 75).

101. Who, it must not be forgotten, wrote these words, which appear to consummate a formal rupture of his theoretical agreement with this old friend: "No truly sound reason can persuade us to believe that God did not will to create all the things which are in his intellect, with that same perfection with which he understands them" (*E* IP33S2).

102. *E* IP29.

103. *E* IP34.

104. Granada (1992, vol. 1, chap. 35, 143).

105. *E* IIIP2S.

106. *E* IP33S1.

107. *E* IVP4C.

108. *E* IIIP6.

109. *E IIIP6D.*

110. *E* IIIDef. Aff. 1: "Desire is the very essence of the human being, insofar as it is conceived to be determined, from any given affection of it, to do something."

111. *E* IVP21.

112. *E* IIIDef. Aff. 1

113. Aristotle, *Physics* 19 to 20–5.

114. *E* IIIP9.

115. *E* IIIP9S.

116. Suárez, *Disp. Met.* XV/xi/4.

117. Deleuze (1988, 65).

118. *E* IIP10S2.

119. *E* IIIP7.

120. *E* IVP4.

121. Ibid.

122. Ibid.

123. Ibid.

124. *E* IVP37.

125. *E* IVAx.

126. *E* IVP3.

127. *E* VP10S.

128. *E* IVP5.

129. Deleuze (1988, 100).

130. Gimferrer (1968).

131. *E* IVP36D.

132. Ibid.

133. *E* VP38S.

134. *E* ID7.

135. *E* IVP67.

136. *E* IVP39.

137. Ibid.

E   I   G   H   T

Superstition and Reading

André Tosel

Superstition, Skepticism, Orthodoxy

ONE COULD show that superstition, in its fundamental connection with practical powerlessness, by reproducing itself produces new effects that are, on the "theoretical" plane, so many transformed forms of knowledge *ex auditu* and *ex signis*, situated under the sign of exteriority. Alexandre Matheron has been able to show that the entire vision of the world of ancient and medieval man is this transformed form. The preface of book IV of the *Ethics* produces the genealogy of the cosmology of kinds and essences starting with the hypostasis of a spontaneous axiology that is anchored in our illusion of being the center of the world and our search for the useful:

> After human beings persuaded themselves that everything that happens, happens on their account, they had to judge that what is most important in each thing is what is most useful to them, and to rate as most excellent all those things by which they were most pleased. Hence, they had to form these notions, by which they explained natural things: *good, evil, order, confusion, warm, cold, beauty, ugliness*. And because they thought themselves free, those notions have arisen: *praise* and *blame, sin* and *merit*.[1] (G II/81)

To rational theo-cosmology, that science fiction, is linked a normative anthropology whose kernel is a moral vision of the world: the world of objective values is presented as created by the God-Person, for ourselves, creatures of this world. In this enchanted world of values, we present ourselves as the realization of a model or of a norm of human nature created by God, "ruler of Nature and humanity" (*rector naturae et humanitatis*). We apply to ourselves the schema of the fabrication by which we have imagined ourselves to account for the things of the world, as the approximation of substantial forms:

> Human beings are accustomed to forming universal ideas of natural things as much as they do of artificial ones. They regard these universal ideas as models of things, and believe that Nature (which they think does nothing except for the sake of some end) looks to them, and sets them before itself as models.[2] (G II/206)

There exists, then, a model, a metaphysical idea of human nature, precisely that of man, as a free creature, the only one to be endowed with the power to recognize his creator, to love him, to conform to his will; hence, to be able to sin, to choose against his creator, to lack his own essence. If nature can sin by not always following the norm of kinds and species (the status of the abnormal and the corresponding problem of the justification of the divine in the face of cosmological disorder), man is able not to conform to the law that requires him to recognize God as Creator and Judge. He is capable of *not* obeying his essence, the search for the Good.

The form of life and thought illustrated by superstition turns around the idea of a nature of Man, drawn from the uncertain experience of desire, rooted in fear and hope. Singular individuals realize their form or essence more or less perfectly, this realization being confined to their freedom, a freedom understood as intrinsically sinful. Anthropology thus permits the closure of theo-cosmology in a system of Providence: inside the cosmos created according to the system of archetypes contemplated by the divine intellect to the culminating point of this hierarchy of beings ordered according to their degree of perfection in which every being is in search of its specific form, Man sits enthroned as the being whose own perfection is freedom and spirit. Man's eminence is the counterpart of extreme responsibility, since he can lack his own perfection by sinning before God, by not recognizing him as the transcendent Creator and Judge.[3]

Yet this moral vision of the world, this normative anthropology, is of a piece with an institutional form of life. The preface of the *Tractatus Theologico-Politicus* identifies the spontaneous politics of superstition. Superstition enjoys its golden age in a society dominated by the figure of despotic power. The latter is, in fact, tied to a cultural, ecclesiastical authority, which establishes political power as the organ of the divine will, as the representative on earth of the *rector naturae*. For their part, subjects associate with all their desires the reference to this divine will; and if they were dispersed into a multiplicity of functions, each claiming divinity, they would end up by the logic of their confrontations necessitating the intervention of an earthly "Savior" who will justify his victory by reference to his God, having become God of the Entire Nation.[4] Whatever the degrees of despotism assumed by such a power, the limit-horizon is the "Turkish State" in which "simple discussion passes for sacrilege."

At any rate, superstition ultimately implies the double differentiation of an ecclesiastical elite that is supposed to know the divine will that it teaches to the "vulgar" and of a despotic political power in conflictual solidarity with this elite, which legitimizes or consecrates it. The constitution of a dominant church is simultaneous with the emergence of a transcendent state of subjects, monarchy, whose "great secret, its prop and stay, is to keep human beings in a state of deception, and with the specious title of religion to cloak the fear by which they must be held in check, so that they will fight for their servitude as if for salvation."[5] There is no more effective means to govern the crowd, the masses, than superstition.

This institutionalization of superstition into a theoretico-political, eccelestico-monarchical bloc reinforces the intellectual terrorism characteristic of superstition by giving to theologico-political authorities the power of life and death over the development of the sciences and philosophy and over the development of ethical and political research. Hatred of thought becomes the regulator of human life:

> Hence it happens that one who seeks the true cause of miracles, and is eager, like an educated man, to understand natural things, not to wonder at them, like a fool, is generally considered and denounced as an impious heretic by those whom the people honor as interpreters of nature and the Gods. For they know that if ignorance is taken away, then foolish wonder, the only means they have of arguing and defending their authority, is also taken away.[6] (G II/81)

Because superstition identifies thought and obedience, it thus constitutes the theory of its renunciation of theory. Insofar as the "intellect" (*intellectus*) is an "intellect of faith" (*intellectus fidei*), it thus requires a "sacrifice of the intellect" (*sacrificium intellectus*). At the foundation of superstition lies the fear of God, that is, refuge in ignorance and simultaneously the fear of thought. Faith as prejudice requires the contempt of reason. Belief in God is thus belief in the corrupted nature of "filthy reason" (according to Luther's expression). By rejecting knowledge, superstition rejects the knowledge of itself. Having done this, it defends itself as a form of life that cannot envision its own supersession and that sacralizes itself, thus compounding its misunderstood servitude. The subjective theory of superstition, which is servitude for philosophy, is a love of servitude. A treatise on, and against, superstition, then, cannot be read by the superstitious. If the knowledge of superstition must take into account superstition as a rejection of knowledge, a resistance to theory, the theory finds itself confronted with this resistance. It must circumvent the censorship that superstition requires in the minds it dominates, which is materialized in the institutions in which it exercises its power. In all rigor, the superstitious cannot understand the knowledge that concerns them, for this knowledge has as its objective their destruction as superstitious: "I do not invite the vulgar to read this work, nor all those who are victims of the same affect" (G III/12).[7]

By whom will the *TTP* be read, then? What can be done with this difference in nature between science and superstition? Only an indirect path is possible in order to thwart the skeptical hatred of thought.

How to Write under the Persecution of Superstition

If superstition is totalitarian, it remains capable of degrees. The imagination is not deprived of the affirmative power characteristic of every idea, provided that it is a question of an idea that is true, of a true idea. Even at its lowest degree our search for what is useful to us remains affirmative. It is never completely deprived of some true ideas, even if the latter are in conflict with the dominant mass of false ideas and fictions. These true ideas are clear and distinct ideas that we form and that include all the reasons of the knowledge of their object.

If the *Ethics* deduces true knowledge and its genesis, the *TTP* seeks to form this knowledge practically from some true ideas that are already present, in minds that are also credulous and dominated by the ontotheological conception of the world. The *TTP* presupposes the existence of minds animated by the desire to know. It is addressed to "philosophical readers," capable of allowing the force of the true to act within them against the forces of the prejudices of the vulgar. It presupposes minds that, without possessing the developed system of the true, already make an effort "to philosophize freely and reject that reason be the servant of theology."[8]

The *TTP* is addressed, then, neither to the superstitious nor to philosophers but to friends of philosophy, to philosophers in formation, who experience dissatisfaction before the intellectual terrorism of superstition and who have already detached themselves from it to the extent that they experience the desire "to think for themselves." The *TTP* is addressed to those who "dare to think" (*aude sapere*). The *TTP*, as Leo Strauss has accurately seen, is a book written for potential philosophers, out of love for them, out of love for philosophy. Only such philosophers can form the process of a definitive escape out of superstition and help others to escape it. The *TTP* rests on the internal contradictions of the first mode of life, on that which in it persists as a search for the useful and *in*sists as a formative power of true ideas.

By doing this, the *TTP* modifies the tradition in which it is inscribed, the tradition for which the major problem is that of the relations between philosophers and nonphilosophers, in the midst of the city dominated by the institutions of revealed religion and where the latter has more the characteristics of a Law than a Faith. The *TTP* is a book written for and in a situation in which philosophers are still persecuted, in which they can only write and be read by thwarting the censorship that strikes philosophy, in which writing itself must thwart the conjuncture of persecution characteristic of an intellectual, moral, and political order that forbids all free search for what is true, all *Theoria*.

On the basis of some studies by Leo Strauss it becomes possible to renew our understanding of this text.[9] As a Jew by birth, Spinoza was first initiated into Judeo-Arabic philosophy, a philosophy tied to an organization of the city and knowledge different from the Christian tradition, which Spinoza also inherits insofar as he is Dutch living in a reformed Christian land. The Judeo-Arabic question is situated, in fact, in relation to revelation.[10] But as opposed to the Christian tradition as such, it is understood not as a simple faith but first as a "Law" (*Thora*): more than as a dogma formalizing certain existential attitudes, it appears as a totalizing social order, which governs not only actions but also thoughts and opinions. If medieval Christianity tried to impose such a spiritual and temporal unity, it never managed to do so to the same degree. The struggles of priesthood and empire were not stopped at Canossa, and very quickly political power in the West developed its own autonomy.

On the contrary, theocracy had better luck in Islamic society and in the Jewish subsocieties of the Diaspora. In this situation philosophical reflection—which sought something other than simple commentary on sacred texts—encountered a particular difficulty. For orthodox theologians, revelation signifies a perfect life and political order. The freest minds, which took up again for themselves the philosophical intention of knowledge, were then confronted with the task of thinking about the intelligibility of this revelation. They set about to justify rationally religious life at the same time as philosophical life as such. In this tradition philosophy is always tormented by an internal tension: the philosopher—who also remains a pious theologian—cannot repress the requirement characteristic of the philosophical mode of life, which is life according to comprehension. He must acknowledge life according to the divine law and life according to knowledge, since the latter represents the fulfillment of human perfection. To resolve this contradiction, the philosopher projects the possibility of the philosophical life into the Prophet-Legislator, whose first task also is to reveal and establish the moral and political order as a religious order. This prophet-legislator—Mohammed, Moses—is presumed by the philosopher to have realized the philosophical life in himself: he is put forward as the supreme philosopher, and his authority permits his disciples to lead the philosophical life in the city in which the Law securely reigns.

The Platonic philosophy of the "Republic" and the "Laws" permits this problem to be resolved: the Philosopher-Legislator is identified with the Philosopher-King. The philosopher can thus deal with philosophy, but he deals with it as a philosopher. The philosophical treatise on prophecy turns the latter into a knowledge concerning the order of the city; it is a treatise on political philosophy, which is compatible with the revealed law. Within the Judeo-Arabic tradition this is a "philosophical" tendency illustrated by Maimonides.

As Leo Strauss again remarks, this is not the only tendency within this tradition. There are philosophers who develop with more intransigence the idea of the philosophical life, of a perfect life, based on the science of being and including the royal art of politics. In this case, the philosopher is distinguished from the Legislator-Prophet-King: he does not need this triple figure in order to find and produce the happiness that life according to thought procures. Philosophy finds a theoretical dignity that distinguishes it from Religion and Law. Religious speculation about beings and their relation to revelation does not replace the science of being that defines the highest human perfection. Before the latter, religious speculation retains an irreducible inferiority.

This quite heterodox tendency then encounters its constitutive difficulty. The philosopher must maintain himself in the city without arousing the suspicion of the theologico-political authorities or being accused of transgressing the Law. At the same time he must develop his own search for knowledge, which for him is what is essential. The philosopher is then condemned to live according to two regimes, to speak two languages. He must split himself in two and formulate the theory of this theologico-political constraint, which obliges him to employ a ruse. The free philosopher thus maintains the orthodox language of his confession, and, moreover, he uses it to make it speak his own heretical views. Philosophical speech and the philosophical text henceforth move into the midst of persecution; they must integrate this condition into their very texture.

Confronted with the orthodox resistances that cannot tolerate the sufficiency of the philosophical life, threatened by a persecution that can proceed even to suppress the possibility of philosophical life itself, the philosopher must thwart the censorship of the authorities and overcome the internal censorship of those of his readers who, while by being able to become his disciples, are initially faithful. The historical form of resolution of this contradiction that the heretical philosopher invents is not original. It is the resumption itself of the traditional form of speculation within the regime of the theologico-political Law; it is the resumption of the commentary on sacred texts and on the commentators on these texts themselves.

By exposing the founding Word and others' interpretations, the author appears as one interpreter among others in the infinite tradition of commentators; he presents his own commentary. He can then defend as a philosopher—for example, under the form of a hypothesis—what as a man and believer he is supposed to loathe and also what, as a citizen conscious of the impossibility of overturning the community, he rejects.

The philosopher must transmit his knowledge to reliable disciples. He must, therefore, compromise with the social order; he must even adjust this social order so as to make it acceptable both to the ignorant vulgar and to philosophy. The philosopher works out a political compromise by accepting the mode of life of the theologico-political community to which he belongs and by forming a "party" of disciples, which constitutes the kernel of a new community in the midst of the superstitious city. The philosopher has for a task to transform received opinions, which are those of apprentice-philosophers, by relying on their desire for a superior life, and to form from these opinions some approximations of truth. For want of an impossible conquest of the believing masses, members of the other city, the philosopher organizes his own city, the one he secretly governs. He practices a double teaching—esoteric and exoteric—within the same practice of commentary on texts. Exoteric teaching is the form under which the philosophy is made visible in the theologico-political community.

Spinoza, by virtue of the community to which he belonged, knew the vicissitudes of philosophy in the Jewish city; and although recent, the community of Amsterdam maintained the internal organization that tradition bequeathed it. It had martyrs of free thought, and Spinoza was raised in the proximity of sensational theologico-political affairs. Before him were excommunicated Menasseh ben Israel and Uriel da Costa, who criticized the theory of the immortality of the soul.[11] But, even after being excommunicated, Spinoza lived in a city that was still Christian, dominated by an orthodox Calvinist church, and full of numerous sects, all of which appealed to the Reformation and challenged the orthodoxy of Calvinism. Knowing both the Jewish tradition — for example, Maimonides, Crescas, Alphakar — and the Christian Scholastic tradition — Spinoza made use of texts by Saint Thomas and the contemporary Scholastic theologians Heereboord and Burgensdijk, as well as works of Reformation theologians, for example, Calvin and Voetius. Spinoza thus had to confront and analyze two publics. Although he did not fool the synagogue — which earned him an excommunication that the rabbis would have otherwise wanted to avoid — he spent the rest of his life close to reformed Christians, who were tormented by the emergence of free thought, of the new science, and all the problems of the time.

At the crossroads of two kinds of censorship and persecution, Spinoza knew in any event the art of writing suitable for a time of persecution, even if in a society of ship owners, bankers, and friends of the sciences the intolerance was relative. Precisely because the antisuperstitious forces were developed and with them the new science, the struggle entered a decisive phase. For the first time, perhaps, philosophy had to be introduced with the hope of stabilizing the philosophical life once and for all. Before publishing the theoretical, genetic, and causal exposition of the forms of life — an exposition that is itself inside the superior form of life — the philosophical circle, which is not yet the "party of philosophers," must be consolidated. The conditions for the hegemony of the new form of life must be ensured practically by multiplying the bearers of this mode of life, by developing into philosophers all those who experience the desire to seek the true. This is a practical work of metamorphosis as much as it is the morphology of a morphogenesis.

The Art of Writing: The Said, the "Said-Between"/Prohibited.

Levels of Reading and the Operation of the *Sive*

The following is the effect of censorship on the art of writing: the heretic or dissident cannot *not* be established in the language of the dominant tradition, experience it, and speak it. This is the only way to maintain contact with his public. The philosopher-reader, extremely desirous that he participate in the true science, remains a prisoner of the community's prejudices. The philosopher cannot and must not break up this community of language. The *TTP* is situated on the terrain of Judeo-Christian ontotheology; it introduces no new words and verbally accepts all the concepts of the tradition. Therefore, it proceeds to transform this common language into the true language. This operation of transformation, this reforming treatment must take account of the danger constituted at every moment by the offensive return of prejudice, of superstition, its skeptical effect and its anti-intellectual terrorism.

From then on one must carry out this operation of transformation by degrees, by lessening the impact to a minimum. The orthodox theses of rational theology—whether those of Maimonides or of reformed Christianity—are mentioned and repeated at length; they form the majority fabric under which by allusions, by voluntary silences, another fabric must be introduced. Spinoza criticizes traditional theses, then, by carrying out a strategy that must introduce new ideas, while neutralizing the recurrent pressures of skepticism and fideism. For this is the stumbling block: censorship is based on the fideism of believers. If readers are hardly friends of thought, they are nonetheless capable of spotting critical intention. At any moment they can unmask the author and denounce him.

This threat is all the more serious given that between the philosopher of the seventeenth century, who lives in a decisive age, in a free republic, and the philosopher of the eighteenth century, who still lives in the middle of an entirely religious city, there are huge differences. The sage of the seventeenth century does not try to find a way around censorship in order to be content to reproduce in his person and in those of his disciples the freedom to think, in order to ensure the possibility of the philosophical life in the midst of the uncultivated masses from whom he expects nothing. He struggles to the death with censorship because his time is one that opens up the possibility of having it out once and for all with prejudice. There is thus even greater urgency.

In a city in which the *conatus* finds an opportunity to develop its positive kernel outside of speculative constructions and to initiate a mode of realization that liberates its productive force, its capacity to act, the struggle for philosophy has an entirely different impact. The community of disciples can finally hope to escape from secrecy; it can hope to constitute itself openly into a party of reason; it can finally be regarded as educative of the blind masses. In the latter, in fact, the ferments of a new life, the urgency of a new mode of the reproduction of life, are acting. The journey that an elite, a minority, an avante-garde has first had to bring about the philosopher can from now on envisage as the future path of humanity.

The relation of the philosophical community to the mass of ignorants, to the *vulgus*, is modified, just as the possibility of a development of the *conatus* opens up.

The Method for Interpretation of Holy Scripture:
Critical History and the Theory of Forms of Life

How is this book written out of love of philosophy and philosophers to be read? This question is not external to the economy of the *TTP*, since the latter poses in all its depth the question of reading—and does so regarding the book of books, the Bible, the text to which all believers refer. Can or must the indications given in the *TTP* on the method of interpretation of Scripture be applied to the *TTP* itself? Leo Strauss also knew how to pose the decisive question. Spinoza begins by suspending the validity of the religious thesis affirming divine inspiration as the author of the holy books. This operation of neutralization consists in opposing the truth of exegetical practice to its self-consciousness. In fact, the commentary of a text supposedly written under the direction of the Holy Spirit is a human practice that governs the delirium of superstition. Every interpreter claims to be the addressee of the book, its elected, its privileged interpreter. Under these conditions the practice of the commentary and the editing of supposedly holy texts winds up in the proliferation of contradictory disputes concerning "true beatitude":

> We see that nearly all human beings parade their own ideas as God's Word, their chief aim being to compel others to think as they do, while using religion as a pretext. We see, I say, that the chief concern of theologians on the whole has been to extort from Holy Scripture their own arbitrarily invented ideas, for which they claim divine authority.[12] (G III/97)

The frenzy of interpretation, the will to impose one's own interpretation as legitimate, accompanies and contradicts the reference to life according to Scripture, which is reputed to exclude conflicts. The conduct of seduction characteristic of superstition is determined "in a blind and reckless desire to interpret Scripture." The theoretical disqualification of theological speculation based on Scripture is irreversible:

> It is therefore not surprising that, to make Scripture appear more wonderful and awe-inspiring, they endeavor to explicate it in such a way that it seems diametrically opposed both to reason and to Nature. So they imagine that the most profound mysteries lie hidden in the Bible, and they exhaust themselves in unravelling these absurdities while ignoring other things of value. They ascribe to the Holy Spirit whatever their wild fancies have invented, and devote their utmost strength and enthusiasm to defending it.[13] (G III/98)

All speculative theology that is based on biblical theology is thus rejected. And with it everything in the Bible itself seems to authorize it. Which is to say that the Bible is right away posed as a composite Book, mixing teachings that one can qualify, subject to more data, as divine, and as irrational beliefs imposed by the passions of the soul as a regime of the *conatus*.

Spinoza confirms this judgment by implementing the new method of interpretation of Scripture. He specifies that for him Scripture leaves a residue that is unintelligible to the understanding. In a double sense. First and foremost, the Bible literally teaches "things that cannot be deduced from the natural light,"[14] for example, that "God is a fire," "God is jealous," that is, "submitted to passive affections of the soul." In this case, the unintelligibility is relative and only consists of irrationality: it is open to a refutative critique and a demonstration accounting for the true and false.

On the other hand, after applying the method of interpretation, there remain texts that simply cannot be made intelligible, whose falsity cannot be shown, and that remain forever truncated. In this case, the unintelligibility is absolute, it is not caused by a false meaning but by a literal "non-sense" that nothing can dissipate. In the first case, it was a question simply of the error of human beings who, pushed by passion, forge inventions and "despise Nature and reason." In the second case, it is a question of human "negligence" at the time of the editing and transmission of the texts they have themselves written and that have been altered by "time which devours everything."

One should not confuse the unintelligibility opposed "to the truth of things" and the unintelligibility resulting from the human impossibility of establishing the "meaning of a discourse,"[15] for not all meaningful discourses are true. Thus, to establish meaningful discourse — whether absurd or irrational — one must first apply oneself to make allowance in Scripture for definitively inaccessible texts, and next in a second moment to carry out for the established text a discrimination of the false and true. Meaning is not exhausted in the order of the true: the excess of meaning that is at the same time its lack of truth is precisely the paradox of writing. Spinoza's method of interpretation is based on taking this paradox into account:

> For the point at issue is merely the meaning of the texts, not their truth. I would go further: in seeking the meaning of Scripture we should take every precaution against the undue influence, not only of our own prejudices, but of our faculty of reason insofar as that is based on the principles of natural cognition.[16] (G III/100)

Above all, Scripture must be interpreted by means of Scripture; the literal meaning must be followed and restored. The meaning of Scripture is first and foremost literal:

> In order to avoid confusion between true meaning and truth of fact, the former must be sought simply from linguistic usage, or from a process of reasoning that looks to no other basis than Scripture.[17] (G III/100)

What do we find in Scripture? Essentially some theses whose intelligibility should not be prejudged and that do not have for an end the development of knowledge, of "things which cannot be deduced from principles known by the natural light," that is, not really theses at all but narratives bearing on the history of a people, "histories," mixtures that are first indissociable from legends, extraordinary events, chronicles arranged for the greater glory of a people or a community of faith, prophecies, revelations, everything "adapted to opinions and to the judgments of human beings dominated by the imagination."[18]

This mixture contains in particular moral teachings that can indeed be established rationally and demonstrated by "common notions,"[19] but which are presented in the Sacred Texts in a nondemonstrative form, accessible to the great mass of people.

More precisely, Spinoza's method is governed by its object, which is present first as an unintelligible text. The method assumes the initial form of a *Historia Scripturae*. Of a "historical investigation," a "critical history" of Scripture, or else a "critical examination of the data of history," a historical knowledge of Scripture. One will note that this method indissociably ties the concept of history to the methods of critical establishment of texts. It is Richard Simon who, as a good reader of the *TTP*, in 1678 would call this method by its definitive name: critical history.

Spinoza defines this critical history in terms—and this is the novelty—that are not opposed to the "method of interpretation of Nature." Spinoza consciously does not inscribe himself along the path that will be the one taken by the new hermeneutics and that, in the modern world since Schleiermacher and Dilthey, opposes the science of Nature and the science of mind, physical explanation and meaningful comprehension. Here it is not the comprehension of meaning that is subordinated to the explication of the true, but the reverse. In Spinoza understanding or interpretation remains a philological activity that consists of a first moment of bringing together the data of observation in order, in a second moment, to attain "an exact historical knowledge." Interpretation is first a matter of ensuring in the case of an unintelligible text what the authors have said, of the way in which they understood what they said in the age in which it was said, without asking if the authors possessed an explicit knowledge of what they seemed to understand. Next, it is a matter of explaining, that is, of identifying, authors' assertions, of specifying their implications, of subjecting them to the test of the examination of their logical consistency, of understanding them in relation to a form of life.

At this level one can speak of error, one can show how error is tied to the genesis of a desire, of the useful. At the limit, explanation consists of understanding the author better than he understands himself. From the beginning, Spinoza unifies the interpretation of Scripture and the interpretation of Nature within a single method of resolution of intelligible problems:

> Now to put it briefly, I hold that the method of interpreting Scripture is no different from the method of interpreting Nature, and is in fact in complete accord with it. For the method of interpreting Nature consists essentially in composing a detailed study of Nature from which, as being the source of our assured data, we can deduce the definitions of the things of Nature. Now in exactly the same way the task of Scriptural interpretation requires us to make a straightforward study of Scripture, and from this, as the source of our fixed data and principles, to deduce by logical inference the meaning of the authors of Scripture.[20] (G III/98)

This text, often cited and commented on,[21] obliges us to make some previous assertions more precise. Strictly speaking, the critical or historical method constitutes only the first aspect of a much larger method, which has for an analogue, in the interpretation of Nature, the stage of observation or "natural history." The second aspect or moment is the one that biblical thought infers — therefore its different levels, without this time excluding the reference to the true — just as for Nature comes the moment for the "definition of natural things."

Spinoza thus establishes a parallel between the Bible and Nature, but this analogy does not lend itself to operations of a spiritualist kind. It is not Nature that becomes a text or book; it is instead texts and the Bible that become Nature, that is, natural objects open to a natural interpretation. It is no longer a question of an analogy but of an explanation. And, inversely, the text of Nature does not refer to a transcendent and analogous meaning that would be reserved behind or below its literal statement. The meaning of this text develops according to univocal statements. It is nothing but the order of this statement. Likewise the naturalness of the text excludes every dependence on an order of signification that would require submission to a Master Meaning, to a meaning that might make Law. Meaning exists or insists in the "definition" of biblical subjects from the sole data provided by critical history. Considerations of perfection, of the sacred, do not arise in the construction of the definitions of natural things from data defined by Nature itself. Nor do they arise when it is a question of references to sacred values in the knowledge of the Bible: the latter must be derived from data provided by the Bible itself. Knowledge of the function and genesis of the sacred and the divine is itself neither sacred nor divine. Knowledge of the entire Bible must result exclusively from the entire Bible, as one thing among other things:

> All knowledge of Scripture must be sought from Scripture alone.... There-fore, just as definitions of the things of Nature must be inferred from the various operations of Nature, in the same way definitions must be elicited from the various biblical narratives as they touch on a particular subject. This, then, is the universal rule for the interpretation of Scripture, to as-cribe no teaching to Scripture that is not clearly established from studying it closely.[22] (G III/99)

The comparison between Nature and Scripture must be read in the sense of a con-tinuation from the latter to the former. It is not Nature that is a book written by a God-Word interpellating his creature. It is Scripture that is a natural reality that must be described from its constitutive data and defined genetically from its forma-tive elements. The Holy Spirit would thus not know how to be present to the hu-man authors of Scripture. Whether it is a question of Catholic theory (inerrancy of the Holy Spirit to the editor of the Sacred Books, controlled and actualized by an interpretative Master who makes himself sacred) or the reformed thesis (*Scriptura sola*, which is also *Sola fide*), Spinoza rejects religious hermeneutics. The "reformer" gives way to the "historian," criticism to the philosopher-scientist, who explains the datum and constructs it by its causes.[23] There is a primacy of *explicare* and *determinare*.[24]

The Content of Historical Critique

What is the content of this historical critique? Spinoza distinguishes three indisso-ciable parts to it:

1. Knowledge of the language of Scripture, in this case, Hebrew.

2. Gathering the statements present in each text, and regrouping these statements according to each significant theme, prior to any judg-ment of truth.

3. Knowledge of "the particular circumstances" surrounding the edit-ing of each Holy Book; the life of all the authors and redactors; the cultural traits, intentions, interests, and objectives pursued; the real

vicissitudes of the reception of the books by successive publics; their modifications or alterations; and finally, their constitution into a Canon—all this deserves study.

This third point also requires that one study with authors "the times and nations in which and for which the texts were written," in order not to confuse eternal teachings with others valuable for one time only and intended for a small number of human beings.[25]

Historia is not a chronology of the periods of any given odyssey; it unifies genesis and structure. The destruction of the hermeneutical relation to history enables us to escape sacred history; it is the prerequisite for every scientific determination of history. The idea of a history governed by an absolute teleology, by a providence, is thus rejected. Sacred history is a delirous history, that of a Word heard, guaranteed by signs, transmitted to credulous listeners, and always destined to be betrayed. The critique of superstition reveals the connection between superstition and Scripture. It is simultaneously a theory of Scripture, a critique of the Myth of the Book, since it leads us back to the knowledge of the occasions, states, and nations for which the Book was written.

For Spinoza the myth of the Book, the myth of reading a book as a submission to its appeal would not know how to be purified by a theology of the word or by an ontology of meaning. Spinoza carefully handles another relation with existence and history that exceeds the teleological framework. He refers to a natural science of the modes of life; the Bible is treated as a natural thing, as an effect and aspect of a form of life. The causal knowledge of the Bible does not belong to the form of life in which the Bible effectively intervenes.

The critical method of Scripture rests on the distinction between life governed by the Bible and the true knowledge of that life, which belongs to another form of life. From this point of view every attempt to harmonize the *TTP* and religious faith is doomed to failure: in particular, the Christian meaning of existence as calling for a decision for or against the divine word has no meaning within the internal economy of Spinoza's method.[26]

This causal history of Scripture belongs, then, to the causal science of Nature. Scripture and its teaching must be explained by their concrete function in determinate circumstances, in their relation to an organization of desire dominated by imagination and passivity. More precisely—and in the restricted sense of the word—history is the first moment of causal explanation. It starts from the data that are the texts transmitted by the tradition; it infers authors' thought through a legitimate way of reasoning. History is assured first by the most universal and fundamental elements of biblical thought, by the contents of thought clearly and distinctly affirmed in common by all authors as valuable for all time and addressed to all human beings.

History must then "descend" to derivative, less universal themes, to the more or less contradictory lessons relative to less general objects, and to those specific to individual authors. From the common to the particular according to the model of interpretation of Nature, the passage from observation, from natural history, to the interpretation of Nature as such, that is, to the definition of particular phenomena from "actions of Nature":

> Now in examining natural phenomena we first of all try to discover those features that are most universal and common to the whole of Nature, to wit, motion-and-rest and the rules and laws governing them which Nature always observes and through which she constantly acts; and then we advance gradually from these to other less universal features. In just the same way we must first seek from our study of Scripture that which is most universal and forms the basis and foundation of all Scripture; in short, that which is commended in Scripture by all the prophets as doctrine eternal and most profitable for all humanity.[27] (G III/102)

What will be established as a common teaching will be the existence of a unique, all-powerful God, who must be worshipped, who watches over everything, and who loves all those below who worship him: the God of superstition, but such as he can be associated with practical behavior, certainly passional, but compatible with peace. In fact, "those who worship him are those who love their neighbor." This God has no theoretical dignity: he remains the passional and imaginary God of the prophets. Whereas all assert his existence, all are divided on the way to understand his nature:

> Having acquired a proper understanding of this universal doctrine of Scripture, we must then proceed to other matters which are of less universal import but affect our ordinary daily life, and which flow from the universal doctrine like rivulets from their source. Such are all the specific external actions of true virtue which need a particular occasion for their exercise. If there be found in Scripture anything ambiguous or obscure regarding such matters, it must be explained and decided on the basis of the universal doctrine of Scripture. If any passages are found to be in contradiction with one another, we should consider on what occasion, at what time, and for whom they were written.[28] (G III/103)

This method individualizes as a common foundation of the Bible a kernel that it re-fines, in such a way as to distinguish from this common foundation all the contra-dictory speculative theses concerning God. This common foundation does not re-cover so much a simple idea of God as it does the idea of God insofar as it is linked to determinate practical behaviors. The ideo-practical aspect of faith as a system of behaviors governed by a belief carries it onto the ideological aspect itself. Critical history reconstructs this common foundation and determines it within the properly practical dimension of religious faith itself. Consider the following thesis: instead of being a theory about God, religion is a practical reality that is organized around simple questions concerning human behavior. Here appears another aspect recov-ered by, but distinct from, superstition: the effectiveness of forms of human behav-ior, themselves abstracted from their ideological justification.

Interpretation cuts the text off from its vertical reference to a divine meaning that demands consent and faith; it reinserts it into the causal series that is that of the development of *conatuses* — since every rule of life has only an im-manent meaning. The thesis of the practical content of the biblical teaching is thus posed as an explanatory principle for other teachings of the Book.[29]

To interpret Scripture by means of Scripture amounts to show-ing that the internal texture of the literal meaning requires putting this human mean-ing into perspective under the horizon of deployment of the *conatus* in practice. As a law of enclosing the interpreter within the mirages of a secret, hidden, deep mean-ing, the method refers the text to the dimension of realization of a life confronted with circumstances. Unintelligibility itself is included as a necessary effect, and is produced by a specific form of life confronted with specific circumstances.

The *TTP* is an intelligible text that offers access to unintelligi-ble texts, since it teaches that unintelligibility is always relative to a practical form of life that can be understood from the point of view of another, more comprehen-sive, more intelligent, and stronger form of life.

The Legitimacy of an Application of Critical History to the *TTP*

But why then is the *TTP* not written like the *Ethics*, as an intelligible text unfolding according to this intelligible order between everything that is the geometrical order? Why does the Euclid of philosophy introduce his philosophy by means of a non-Euclidean treatise? If the *TTP* is an intelligible text that states the rules for reading unintelligible texts, can these rules themselves be applied to the *TTP*? Does one have the right and obligation to situate the *TTP* in time, to explain it in relation to its nation and its age? Is intelligibility related to historicity? Or does the latter only affect the unintelligible? At the very moment that Spinoza constructs the possibility of a relationship with a desacralized history and grasps history by a causal method, doesn't he exclude himself and his work from their relationship to history? The opposition made between intelligible and eternal texts and unintelligible and historical texts seems to lead to this difficulty.

In fact, at the limit, an intelligible text possesses an eternal intelligibility; it has value for all times and places. It can be understood by reason of the deployment alone of its internal order of truth, having abstracted from taking into consideration the language in which it is written, the particular goal of its author, and the nation to which it belongs. The true idea of an intelligible text in its own process effaces the circumstances that then become external to its own empirical genesis. The eternal intelligibility of the true refers back to the history of errors and unintelligibility; the true has no history. From this point of view the true excludes the history of its own advent:

> Euclid, whose writings are concerned only with things exceedingly simple and perfectly intelligible, is easily made clear by anyone in any language; for in order to grasp his thought and to be assured of his true meaning there is no need to have a thorough knowledge of the language in which he wrote. A superficial and rudimentary knowledge is enough. Nor need we enquire into the author's life, pursuits, and character, the language in which he wrote, and for whom and when, nor what happened to his book, nor its different readings, nor how it came to be accepted and by what council. And what we here say of Euclid can be said of all who have written of matters which of their very nature are capable of intellectual apprehension.[30] (G III/111)

At the limit, a truly Euclidean philosophical work carries necessity along with it, in any case the possibility of effacing even the name of its author. The order of the true is anonymous; in its own exposition it alters the conditions of its production, the historicity of its author and its discovery. It is inscribed within the order of absolute necessity, foreign to the *aléas* of "time which destroys everything." It develops *sub specie aeternitatis*.

An intelligible text concerning intelligible objects such as Euclid's *Elements* or the *Ethics* itself seems self-explanatory. Only partially intelligible texts require critical history in order to give the reason for their degree of unintelligibility and its forms. They concern "nonperceptible things," that is, those which are incapable of demonstration or moral certainty, "things obscurely expressed, narratives which seem to go beyond the limits of credence."[31] The latter can only be explained on the basis of the author's passional subjectivity, of his public, of the mode of life governing both of them, governing the time and nation under consideration. In an intelligible book concerning intelligible or perceptible things, the reader does not have to start with the data not provided by the book itself; he brings about the true meaning, once again, directly by considering the subject matter itself, by considering things that become truly known by and in the reading of the book itself.

If this is so, it would seem that here is the genuine rule of reading that must be applied to the *TTP*, the rule of self-inclusion and self-explanation. In this case, the critical history of the *TTP* itself recovers the totality of procedures regularly used by modern specialists of the history of philosophy. But these procedures would then be non-Spinozist; they would be superfluous, because outside the internal development of the order of the true. If the *TTP* is an intelligible book, it does not require, it seems, according to Spinoza's declaration, knowledge of the readings, commentaries, and variants that constitute its own interpretative tradition. The *TTP* seems to exclude, in order to be read, the rules of reading it applies to the Bible. It would require simply to be read and reread, so as to be able to correct errors of the first reading. If an author who considers intelligible subjects seems to lose himself in obscure presentations or to contradict himself, he refers to intelligent readers to undertake the reading again, to produce the correct order, to consider for himself the subject considered — badly considered — in order to determine the truth. Regarding intelligible texts, rereading does not amount to a repetition of the difficulty, but to its reformulation so as to produce its solution. In short, we could not then treat the *TTP* as the latter treats the Bible, because the *TTP* is not an unintelligible text.

But can we then read the *TTP* as Spinoza reads Euclid, as he himself writes the *Ethics* and estimates that we can ourselves read it in our turn? No, for there is clearly a difference at the heart of intelligible texts themselves: some expose the order of things themselves and expunge from their internal economy the scoria of their relation to time; they abstract from the empirical circumstances of their formation. Other intelligible texts — which have for an object situations dominated by unintelligibility, the nonperceptible — cannot expose the order of the true by abstracting from its empirical order of production. The exposition and the discovery of the true do not coincide: the exposition of the true requires a logical absorption of temporality into eternity, into the necessity of the thing itself. The discovery of the true requires a circumstantial treatment of the errors such as they are presented here and now, in time, for a certain age, nation, and individual.

The *TTP* makes it its objective from its preface to organize the circumstances of human life according to one's usefulness finally understood. Yet one cannot organize these circumstances without knowing them, and the knowledge of these circumstances proceeds precisely by means of a critical history. It is only considered as a true product that the true excludes from this point of view taking into account the circumstances when it occurs. But Spinoza's theory includes the genesis of the true and false. If one does not confuse the development of the true in its order with the elimination of errors, the development of the true also includes taking into account the circumstances that obstruct it and those which require it. As has been shown by the connection that unites superstition, error, and *conatus*, the *TTP* is fundamentally a theory of history, intervening within history in order to require the reorganization of knowledge and life. In every circumstance care must be taken to ensure access to the self-explanatory development of the true; thus, this self-explanation must be anticipated by means of a temporal introduction, by taking account of the circumstances to be organized and reorganized.

History must be considered such as it unfolds until then, or such as it is presented at the present moment. The *TTP* aims to understand its time, and it does not challenge reality: it seeks to provide an exact knowledge of it, *sincera historia*. Spinoza is convinced that his time and age are determined as a time of the arrival of true science and true life. He understands history not as the past but as the coexistence of a struggle between two possibilities of life and knowledge. In other words, the forces and causes that produce unintelligibility are still active; it is important from then on to apply to the *TTP* itself, an intelligible reading of a relatively unintelligible text, its own criteria of reading concerning unintelligible texts. Unintelligibility always acts in the present as imagination and passion; the genetic and causal knowledge of unintelligibility must be produced for the present. From this point of view, to read the *TTP* as a Spinozist is to understand the circumstances and the nation for which it was itself written. We are therefore justified in applying to the *TTP* the constitutive moments of critical history. This historicism is not, paradoxically, contrary to Spinoza's supposed logicism.

The idea of a critical history of the *TTP* thus seems sustainable. It must take into account the circumstances that in this time and nation have prevented the appearance and deployment of a superior form of life. Spinoza knows that the time in which he is writing will pass away, that his text itself will grow old, that the circumstances that have prevented the formation of a superior form of life can become unintelligible for future readers. Nothing is certain, and the same causes that have led human beings to signify their problems in partially intelligible texts like the Bible continue to act. Everywhere that the mastery of circumstances of life is difficult, the unintelligible is reproduced. The *TTP* is thus conscious of the lasting nature of the reproduction of the unintelligible tied to the reproduction of the life governed by the imagination and passion. The *TTP* thus records in its own text the rules of reading to rescue it from that which threatens to render it itself unintelligible, from the domination of passion and the imagination. Wherever a situation of powerlessness is on the agenda, wherever the unintelligible triumphs, a treatment against powerlessness and the unintelligible must be made possible. One must thus make possible for the future the reading of the *TTP* as a partially intelligible text that contains within it the means to reduce this unintelligibility, since it states what rules of reading should be followed for unintelligible texts.

Translated by Ted Stolze

Notes

1. *E* IApp. See Matheron (1988, 113–26).

2. *E* IVPref.

3. *E* IVPref. "Perfection and imperfection, therefore, are in reality only modes of thinking, that is, notions we are accustomed to feign because we compare individuals of the same species or genus to one another" (G II/207).

4. *TTP* Pref.

5. Ibid. " . . . so that they will fight for their servitude as if for their welfare" (. . . *ut pro servitio, tamquam pro salute pugnent*) (G III/7).

6. *E* IApp.

7. *TTP* Pref. "I know, too, that the vulgar can no more be freed from their superstition than from their fears" (G III/12).

8. *TTP* Pref.

9. It is a question of Leo Strauss's magisterial study, "How to Study Spinoza's *Theologico-Political Treatise*, " in Strauss (1952, 142–201).

10. See Gardet and Anawati (1948) and Gardet (1969).

11. On the heterodox Jewish milieus, see the studies of Revah (1958; 1959; 1959–60). See the contributions of Méchoulan (1970; 1976).

12. *TTP* VII.

13. Ibid.

14. Ibid.

15. Ibid. "Then again, the meanings of many nouns and verbs occurring in the Bible are either completely unknown or subject to dispute" (*Significatio deinde multorum nominum et verborum, quae in Biblis occurunt vel prorsus ignoratur, vel de eadem disputatur*) (G III/106).

16. Ibid.

17. Ibid.

18. Ibid. "It should be observed that Scripture frequently treats of matters that cannot be deduced from principles known by the natural light; for it is chiefly made up of historical narratives and revelation. Now an important feature of the historical narratives is the appearance of miracles; that is . . . stories of unusual occurrences in Nature, adapted to the beliefs and judgments of the historians who recorded them" (*Notandum quod Scriptura de rebus saepissime agit quae ex principis Lumine Naturali notis deduci nequeunt; eius enim maximam partem historiae et revelationes componunt: et historiae miracula potissimum continent, hoc est narrationes rerum insolitarum Naturae opinionibus et judicio historicorum, qui eos scripserunt, accomodatum*) (G III/98–9).

19. Ibid.

20. Ibid.

21. See in particular Zac (1965, 25ff) and Malet (1966, 186–96). Also see Breton (1977, 38–40). The latter work is the only one truly to take seriously the analogy between the interpretation of Nature and the interpretation of Scripture.

22. *TTP* VII. "Therefore all knowledge of Scripture must be sought from Scripture alone. . . . This, then, is the universal rule for the interpretation of Scripture, to ascribe no teaching to Scripture that is not clearly established from studying it closely" (*Tota itaque scripturae cognitio ab ipsa sola peti debet. . . . Regula igitur universalis interpretandi Scripturam est nihil scripturae tamquam eius documentaum tribuere quod ex ipsius historia quam maxime perspectum non habeamus*) (G III/99).

23. The principle of pious hermeneutics retains an irreducible kernel in which is affirmed the thesis that Scripture is the Revealed Word of God, such as the latter states it in the two Testaments. If God is the author of the Holy Books with principle title, as the Catholic tradition still maintains today, the prophets equipped with the charisma of interpretation are only authors with instrumental title. The Church, that is, the Master, authenticates in the inspired writings that which is relative to a given historical situation and that which is the true Word of God that is of value for all times; it is helped by the same Holy Spirit that inspired the sacred authors. This thesis of inerrancy leads to sacralizing the interpreter. See the classical formulation of Saint Thomas Aquinas (*Summa theologiae* II[a] II[ae], question 171,

article 6). It is summarized in the formula: "Whatever is contained in Holy Scripture is true" (*Quicquid in Sacra Scriptura continetur verum est*). The most daring of exegetes was not able to renounce this principle. The most audacious of readers of the *TTP*, in a Catholic country, was Richard Simon: it is he who gave right of the city to the concept of critique. He went further than Spinoza in the "detailed study of versions of the Hebrew text from Moses until our time" (the title of the first part of the *Histoire critique du Vieux Testament*, 1678). But Richard Simon wanted to reconstruct the principle of inerrancy on contact with the new philology. If the rules of critique were established independent of faith, Simon aimed to neutralize the consequences of critique and to reaffirm the tradition. It is here that he parts with the "impious Spinoza." The latter would not know how to write, as Simon did in the preface to the *Histoire critique du Vieux Testament*, 1680 edition: "Scripture is not clear by itself independent of the Tradition. . . . If one does not link the tradition with Scripture one ensures almost nothing certain in Religion. This is no more to abandon interest in the word of God than to associate with it the tradition of the Church, since the one that refers us to the Holy Scriptures has also referred us to the Church in which it has confided the Sacred Deposit" (nonpaginated edition). See Grelot (1965) and Auvray (1968).

24. *TTP* VII.

25. Ibid. "Again, to avoid confusing teachings of eternal significance with those which are of only temporary significance or directed only to the benefit of a few, it is also important to know on what occasion, at what period, and for what nation or age all these teachings were written down" (*Ne documenta aeterna cum iis quae ad tempus tantum vel paucis solummodo ex usu poterant esse confundamus refert etiam scire qua occasione, qua tempore et cui nationi aut saeculo, omnia documenta scripta fuerunt*) (G III/102).

26. It is on this point that we part with the interpretation of Malet (1966), who tends to preserve the rights of a purified, demythologized exegesis, to reconcile Spinoza and Bultmann (1969–70).

27. *TTP* VII.

28. Ibid.

29. This point has been emphasized by Breton (1977, 29–48).

30. *TTP* VII.

31. Ibid.

From the Subject to Collectivities:
The Politics of the Multitude

N I N E

Jus-Pactum-Lex: On The Constitution of the Subject in the *Theologico-Political Treatise*

Etienne Balibar

To Sylvain Zac

I

THE OBVIOUS intrinsic historicity of Spinoza's philosophy impresses on each of the texts (almost all incomplete or aporetic) that constitute it the nature of a unique experience of writing, whose theoretical effects remain irreducible to the uniformity of a "system." Before worrying about the problematic, conflictual meaning in all of them, we must follow each of these experiences of writing in its detours and its own complexity. This is also the best way to experience the originality of Spinoza's undertaking in relation to the ideological currents it intersects while remaining, in the last analysis, irreducible to them—for example, "natural rights theory." From this point of view, the classical problem posed, in the *Theologico-Political Treatise*, by the articulation of the notions of *pact* and *law*, seems to me to deserve a new examination. By following the very movement of the text, without retrospectively projecting onto it a "truth" that in particular the *Political Treatise* would possess (in which Spinoza essentially "abandons" the concept of pact and considerably reduces the meaning of the concept of law), and without prejudging a "strategy of writing" with a double foundation, whose keys would be found in the *Ethics* (and which would prohibit considering as the author's authentic thought the search for a *vera religio* for a determinate time and place), it seems to me possible to highlight perhaps better than has been done until now both the explanatory power of the *TTP* and the reasons for the aporias over which its political problematic stumbles. Such an analysis will also help, I hope, to clarify the profound contradictions of the very idea of *contract* and bourgeois juridical ideology, from which Spinoza tendentially escapes — by trying to turn its constitutive concepts against their dominant usage, without necessarily situating him simply either *within* the contractarian lineage or *outside* it.

Pactum, inscribed by Spinoza in the heart of the *TTP*'s argumentation, is neither a terminological survival, an anticipation, nor a concession, but a central political and theoretical stake. However, compared with the classical figures of the *social contract*, its definition is disconcerting. Far from the beautiful simplicity that can be found in Hobbes or Rousseau, it apparently abounds in breaks in argumentation and in denials.

The key to its interpretation in fact seems to me to reside in the formulations by means of which Spinoza opens chapter 17:

> The picture presented in the last chapter…although it agrees quite with practice, and practice can be made to conform to it more and more closely, must nonetheless remain in many respects no more than theory.
>
> [*Contemplatio praecedentis capitis…, quamvis cum praxi non parum conveniat, et praxis ita institui possit, ut ad eandem magis ac magis accedat, numquam tamen fiet, quin in multis mere theoretica maneat.*] (G III/201)

This formulation, in fact, can only trouble anyone who would have read chapter 16 as an account of "foundations," who would construct the Spinozist variant of a simultaneously physicalist and metajuridical theory of civil society; for these two features, as they are found, for example, in Hobbes (physics of individual *conatus* or powers, metajuridical form of the social contract), in their conjunction, would seem to exclude such a restriction in principle.

From two things one, in fact. Either Spinoza means that the genesis of civil society by means of a collective decision or a convention, whether "tacit or explicit," of individuals to unite themselves into a single body, to live *ex solo rationis dictamine*, and to transfer the totality of their natural right to the sovereign in such a way that it not be held by any law (*nulla lege temeri*) is only a *theoretical* schema, of which *real* societies represent only a more or less faithful approximation. But what is then the chain of real causes? In all probability, a simple process of aggregation of individual powers, which depending on the circumstances leads to different relations of force, with more or less unity of the social body and more or less power for the sovereign. But an approximate pact is no longer a pact. Likewise, an approximately *summa potestas* is no longer a state power, an *imperium*: it is at most a "leadership." ... Or else Spinoza means that, since there are really civil societies that are states, *a certain form* of the pact must necessarily be given (at least as long as a sovereign power is maintained), but only in an *ideal* case does it take the form of an "integral transfer." In this case, in fact, there is a strict equivalence between the mechanism of the transfer and the collective essence of sovereignty (its character of *res publica*). Individuals by hypothesis preserve no right competing with the sovereign, but they do not thereby become slaves, since

> no one transfers his natural right to another so completely that he is never consulted again, but each transfers it to a majority of the entire society of which he is a member. In this way all remain equal, as they were before in the state of nature.

> [*in eo nemo jus suum naturale ita in alterum transfert, ut nulla sibi imposterum consultatio sit, sed in maiorem totius societatis partem, cuius ille unam facit. Atque hac ratione omnes manent, ut antea in statu naturali, aequales.*] (G III/195)

But this case would be only a theoretical "limit." In reality the pact would in fact usually signify instead that individuals become unequal, and that in their submission there is an inevitable part of slavery, of existence *alieni juris*.

One must recognize that in the two hypotheses the thesis according to which the civil state defined by the pact preserves the fundamental equation of right and power and the thesis that sees in the *imperium democraticum* "the most natural state" and the state closest to freedom — the characteristic thesis of the *TTP*'s problematic — enter into contradiction. Or again, what basically amounts to the same thing, the adequation between the form of the pact and the genesis of civil societies from the power of individuals becomes entirely problematic. The preservation of natural right in the *respublica* calls into question the form of a pact, or else the latter must signify — as in Hobbes — a negation of the natural right of individuals.

One can doubt that this is indeed the meaning of the specification brought by Spinoza. That would signify, in fact, a "utopian" configuration of the entire final part of the *TTP*, to be read a little like the following: after having proposed in chapter 16 a "theoretical" concept of civil society (reconciling absolute sovereignty and individual freedom), Spinoza would move on in chapters 16 and 17 to examine the inconveniences resulting from the fact that "practice" deviates from it, before proposing in chapters 19 and 20 a political model inspired "as much as possible" by this theory. This reading would not oblige us only to establish a definitive split between "theory" and "practice," but, to paraphrase our author, it would reverse the causal order of nature, such as it is expressed in the very argument that makes of the search for the utility common to all men a *lex humanae naturae universalis*. Moreover, it would render completely unintelligible (at least turn it into a tactical concession, a rather naive verbal ruse) Spinoza's affirmation that the Republic of the United Provinces is already essentially a *libera respublica* or a democracy. It is more worthwhile, then, to look for something else, and for that it is enough in fact to pay attention to the way in which the author himself develops his argument:

> And this I think that experience itself clearly teaches; for men have never surrendered their right and transferred their power to others so completely that they ceased to be feared by the very rulers who received their right and power, and, although deprived of their natural right, became less dangerous to the state as citizens than its external enemies....Hence we must admit that the individual retains his own right in many of his actions, which therefore depend on nobody's decision but his own. But we cannot form a true idea of how far the right and power of the state extends unless we note that its power is not restricted to the power of coercing men by fear, but includes absolutely every means it has to make men obey its commands; since it is not the motive for obedience which makes a man a subject, but the will to obey....We must not therefore jump to the conclusion that because a man's action arises from his own deliberation he does it by his own right and not by the right of the state; for since his actions always arise from his own deliberation and decision, both when he is bound by love, and when he is forced by fear to avoid evil, there would on that view be no sovereignty at all, and no right over subjects whatsoever....My point is also proved most clearly by the fact that obedience is less a matter of the outward action than of the mind's inner activity, so that the man who wholeheartedly decides to obey all the commands of another is most completely under his rule; and in consequence he who rules in the hearts of his subjects holds sovereignty as much as possible.

> [*Atque hoc ipsam experientiam clarissime docere existimo; nam nunquam homines suo jure ita cesserunt, sumaque potentiam in alium ita transtulerunt, ut ab iss ipsis, qui eorum jus, et potentiam acceperunt, non timerentur, et imperium, non magis propter cives, quanquam suo jure privatos, quam propter hostes periclitaretur....Quare concendendum unumquemque multa sibi sui juris reservare, quae propterea a nullius decreto, sed a suo solo pendent. Attamen, ut recte intelligatur, quosque imperii jus et potestas se extendat, notandum imperii potestatem non in eo praecise contineri, quod homines metu cogere potest, sed absolute in omnibus, quibus efficere potest, ut homines eius mandatis obsequantur: non enim ratio obtemperandi, sed obtemperantia subditum facit....Non igitur ex eo, quod homo proprio consilio*

aliquid facit, illico concludendum eum id ex suo, et non imperii jure agere; nam
quandoquidem tam cum ex amore obligatus, quam cum metu coactus ad malum
evitandum, semper ex proprio consilio, et decreto agit, vel imperium nullum esset,
nec ullum jus in subditos, vel id necessario ad omnia se extendit, quibus effici potest,
ut homines ipsi cedere deliberent. . . . Quod etiam hinc quam clarissime constat, quod
obedientia non tam externam, quam animi internam actionem respiciat; adeoque
ille maxime sub alterius imperio est, qui alteri integro animo ad omnia eius man-
data obtemperare deliberat, et consequitur eum maxime tenere imperium, qui in
subditorum animos regnat.] (G III/201–2)

This development, which Spinoza relates to experience, can immediately be seen
to contain nothing that contradicts or even restrains the meaning of the previous
"theory": it is exactly the same process of constitution of a civil society, and consequently of an *imperium*, which is analyzed here, and which was just presented as the
constitution of a *pact*. However, two points are put into relief that a formal reading
of chapter 16 could have missed: first, every society is constantly threatened with
destabilization by its own members more than by external enemies (or forces); next,
what we could call (with Louis Althusser) the *society effect,* or the production of obedience in the very mind of citizens, is in the last analysis the very impulse of the *imperium.* The two are obviously linked, in a way that applies to every form of state.
In the following paragraphs, Spinoza will again summarize his thought by designat-
ing with a new expression the element in which is played the state's constitution and
preservation: *varium multitudinis ingenium.* Note that chapter 16 spoke of *individua,*
of *popula,* of *societas,* but not (or not yet) of *multitudo.* By speaking here of experience, Spinoza has thus not sought to oppose "theory" and "practice." He has instead proposed to insert clearly at the heart of theory a fundamental practical idea:
it is to the same extent that individuals always preserve an incompressible part of
their "right" that they can completely transfer sovereignty to the state. It is the extent to which the "means" that allow the state to make itself obeyed do not remain
external but penetrate inside the *animus,* the *decretum,* and the *consilium* of subjects
that these subjects continue, however, to affirm their own "right" (or their power).
In short, they continue to *exist* as individuals. The state does not absorb the individuality of its members, but the latter are nothing outside of it. How can we think this
paradox?

      In order to characterize Spinoza's method here, I see no other
possibility than to introduce a notion that is foreign to his terminology, despite the
risks that this carries: the notion of *dialectic.* And dialectic in several senses of the
word:

1. The definition of the "pact" in chapter 16 is still *abstract* (and not "theoretical"): it *poses a problem* and introduces the first elements of its development. Only the concrete analyses that chapter 17 involves will show how this development is brought about and what determinate object corresponds to this concept. The initial definition must, then, if one wants to draw out its precise meaning, be read in a recurrent way, based on its actual application. Until then, it remains in abeyance. In addition, this dialectical movement of concretization is already sketched out at the heart of chapter 16 itself, which in fact does not give *one* but indeed *three* increasingly complex definitions of the pact in succession: first, as a simple *conspiratio in unum*, in view of the common utility; next, as an absolute transfer of the *juria uniuscuiusque* and constitution of the *imperium*, which poses the double problem of force and law and conditions of obedience; finally, as a complete organization of the juridical order, at the heart of which we find the double question of coherence and limits: that of public right and private civil right (do they have the same principle?), that of obedience to God and obedience to the power of the state (do they have the same object?).

2. The definition of the pact, although it describes a process of unification of individual powers under a common law, immediately proposes a series of contradictions. In fact, it does not cease to present *contradictory terms*: the exclusive appetite of individuals and the rational calculation that "dictates" the preference for the form of peace that is civil society; absolute submission to the sovereign and the unconditional affirmation of self-interest (a contradiction whose development is the dialectic of obedience, exposed to all the risks of misrecognition by the individual of his own genuine interest); and finally, the representations of the common good by which individuals are seized by divine law and civil law. Spinoza simply affirms then and there, abstractly, that in practice these contradictions are neither resolved nor transcended but contained within *limits* compatible with social existence itself.

3. Finally, Spinoza's definition can be considered dialectical in the sense that the passage from the abstract to the concrete, as the development of the initial formula's contradictions, arises identically from a *historical* study. This is what chapters 17 and 18 do: one will note then that the *pact* does not have as a function the thinking of an absolute origin of human societies, nor an ideal foundation of the juridical order as such, but the explanation of the *complex of causes* that permits a given state to preserve its own form, and at the same time to make intelligible the apparent anarchy of its political history, the cycle of its internal conflicts, the movements of the reinforcement and weakening of its collective power. By an

incredible torsion in relation to its traditional usage, the pact becomes *the concept of a history*. But this originality only appears if the totality of chapters 16 through 20 is read as the complete development of the concept, and especially if one notes that the successive *pacts* evoked regarding the history of the Hebrews are not *something other than* the pact previously defined, but its concrete application.

Spinozist history presents, for a modern reader, some remarkable characteristics. It does not aim at universality, and yet it is fully theoretical, that is, explanatory. In fact, it aims at historical *singularity*. The pact only exists as specified by its historical circumstances: *there are as many real states as there are forms of pact*. If a general concept is necessary—a genuine *common notion* in the sense of the second kind of knowledge, inscribed in a progression that aims not at the transcendental but at singular essences—it is finally to make possible the variation of conditions and forms, the analysis of differences. This is why Spinoza will be able without contradiction to affirm at the same time that the Hebrew state cannot be taken as a model (*imitari*) and that the study of its history explained by its causes delivers immediately current lessons (*dogmata*).

One perceives better, then, what constitutes the singularity or anomaly of Spinoza's reference to a *state of nature*. What is important is not so much to know if, hypothetically or not, the state of nature chronologically precedes the civil state. It is above all the question of the *exteriority* of the one in relation to the other. In Hobbes the state of nature is the place and the concept of the antagonisms that the social pact must *overcome* once for all (*it must be escaped*), and its intrinsic contradiction is opposed term by term to the noncontradiction of law (*droit*) and the state. For this reason it does not cease to threaten, but from outside, the civil state of peace and law, at minimum, for example, the way that religious discords rekindle civil wars. In Spinoza the thesis according to which the civil state *does not abolish* the state of nature has as its correlate—despite the fears that can be inspired in it by the revolutions and seditions that try to change the form of government—the affirmation that the civil state can never be entirely dissolved. It is not by an external "nature" but by its very social form that every state is permanently threatened *from inside*.

What does the "moment" of the pact mean, then? Precisely that the conflicts inherent in human nature (passional conflicts that one can discern simultaneously in the fluctuations of the individual "mind" [*animus*] and in those of the "temperament of the multitude" [*ingenium multitudinis*]: strictly speaking these are the same) are going to assume a singular form of development, by being fixed on institutional "objects" and collective emotions. It is only with the *tacit or explicit* conclusion of a social pact of a given form (whether it be of Moses' constitution, the formation of the Roman Republic, or the independence of the United Provinces) that the contradictions of human individuality and communication truly become explicit (rather than cease to be). This is why, in the description that Spinoza proposes of it to us, the initial state of nature, which is also that of a savagery that is extremely hypothetical and without great intrinsic importance, remains relatively indeterminate: neither openly peaceful nor irremediably hostile, and above all characterized by powerlessness. It is in the civil state, the only truly real one, that the power of human nature develops, hence, the passions of love and hate, fear and hope, the tension of the tendencies to peace and war, to obedience and rebellion.

The dialectic of social contradictions can then take shape. No doubt they are always explained by general laws of human nature (or "pyschology"). But they are not the contradictions of Man or Humanity as such: in particular, they are not contradictions between the passional *nature* of Man and his rational *destination*. They are, if one can risk this problematic formula, *the contradictions of singular essences themselves*, or of historical essences in their present existence. The history of the Hebrew state shows that *the same causes* (the same institutional structure) explain first its incredible stability (in particular, and we shall return to it, the effect of patriotic cohesion produced by the theocratic conjunction of the civil law and the religious law), followed by its weakening and ruin: "How the state could have been eternal if the just anger of the lawgiver had allowed it to continue in its original form" (*Qua ratione imperium aeternum esse potuerit, si justa legislatoris ira in eodem persistere concessisset*) (G III/220). In other words, the contradiction is immanent in the singular form of the pact, but emerges in complete form only in the course of its history, when the ambivalence of its effects is completely apparent. To study the structure of the pact (or of a given civil society) cannot consist simply in characterizing, or even formalizing, the clauses of an engagement, but rather requires showing what constitutes its relative force, what enables it to endure and also what can destroy it. One understands, then, why in chapter 16, cutting short the illusion of an "obligation" implied in the very statement of a transfer of rights, Spinoza was not afraid to pose contradictorily that every *imperium*, by definition, absolutely *binds* subjects or citizens, although it has no other guarantee than its power, or its existence, and consequently it does not *obligate* them at all. This does not mean that sovereignty can do without guarantees, but that its real history coincides with the emergence of practical guarantees that confer on it the form of obedience produced by its institutions. Yet this *history of obedience*, an authentically concrete element of politics, can be thought of only as a combined history of interest, force, and belief.

II

The pact is indeed necessarily double, or rather *overdetermined*. Let us pay attention to the stages and movement of the argument. In chapter 16 Spinoza began by "founding" the pact, or the constitution of civil society, on the consideration of individuals' power and interest alone. Or rather on the analysis of the limits of this power. It is not enough to say that it is "finite," it is necessary to say that by itself it is practically nonexistent. The idea of the pact corresponds from the beginning with an implicit "calculation" of reason — inasmuch as the latter is identified with the consciousness of what is useful to one under all its forms (to choose the lesser of two evils, to increase one's means of action over external nature and over oneself, to develop knowledge). Spinoza observes that men, in practice, always bring about this "rational" choice (in this sense, reason, if it does not define it, is no longer external to human nature). This is why they "exchange" the limitation of their individual right — up to pure and simple abandonment, that is, up to the fact of existing only in and by means of civil society, of becoming *political animals* — against the means that it obtains for them to overcome this initial limitation.

The *teleological* nature of this argument has often been brought up: if civil society is not the Good in itself, at least it is the best of possible human conditions. But if men "are born ignorant of all things, and before they can learn the true way of living and acquire the habit of virtue . . . a great deal of their life has passed by" (*ignari omnium rerum nascuntur, et antequam veram vivendi rationem noscere possunt et virtutis habitum acquire, magna aetatis pars . . . transit*) (G III/190), must one decide in favor of a *ruse of reason*, which, despite their ignorance and submission to the empire of the appetite, would realize itself through the unconscious impulse of their desire? The construction seems both empiricist and finalist.

However, it is not, we have said, Spinoza's last word. It is instead a question for him of discovering in what conditions, according to what modalities, this still very indeterminate general result is attained. Or if one wishes: of what proximate causes it can be the effect. However, this first movement then leads to a new problem. By the form of the pact, a sovereign collective power is instituted in a completely natural way, immanent in the interplay of human powers. But the question of its effectiveness remains. On the one hand, we see clearly that, without this pact, no particular contract, hence no social life, would hold up against the passions. On the other hand, we see just as clearly that this pact that guarantees all the pacts by itself includes no guarantee. Spinoza's description clearly opposes Hobbes's, from whom he retains neither the idea of a given *speech* that would entail obligation between human subjects ("I trust him") nor the idea of complete alienation for the sake of a third *arbiter*, who would not be "actively involved" in the contract and thus could in return guarantee it indefinitely. Obviously, he considers them fictions that enable us to escape from the definition of right as real power. Which amounts to saying that the causes sought are not on the order of juridical representation but of political practice. Isn't there a circle here? No doubt, but it is the circle of the exercise of power, which can draw its force at every moment only from those it constrains (in a duality of action and reaction), and not the circle of an ideal *guarantee*, which would somehow *precede* itself.

It indeed seems, though, that "after the fact" Spinoza proceeds to introduce a mechanism of guarantee. The end of chapter 16 adds a second pact to the first one:

> For if men were naturally bound by divine right, or if divine right were right by nature, there would have been no need for God to make a contract with men, and to bind them by a pact and an oath. Hence we must admit unreservedly that divine right only came into force when men made an explicit pact to obey God in all things; by so doing they so to speak surrendered their natural freedom and transferred their right to God, just as they do in the civil state.

> [*Si enim homines ex natura jure divino tenerentur, vel si jus divinum ex natura jus esset, superfluum erat, ut Deus cum hominibus contractum iniret, et pacto et juramento eosdem obligaret. Quare absolute concendendum jus divinum ab eo tempore incepisse, a quo homines expresso pacto Deo promiserunt in omnibus obedire, quo sua libertate naturali quasi cesserunt, jusque suum in Deum transtulerunt, sicuti in statu civili fieri diximus.*] (G/198)

Now several specifications impose themselves here. First, there is nothing fictional about this "new" pact (even if it operates in the midst of fictions, which we shall see later)—no more in any case than the previous contract (*sicuti*). Spinoza's formulation must be read *sensu literali*, in the same way as the social pact itself. In fact, these two "pacts" have exactly *the same nature*, and proceed from the *same* development of the power of individuals. Second, if the "civil" pact (or the pact *insofar as* it is "civil") includes no guarantee, neither does the "religious" pact (or the pact *insofar as* it is "religious"). Either regarding sovereigns or regarding subjects, God has at his disposal no absolute constraint (not even the intervention of his prophets). This is why the effectiveness of the religious pact, under a given historical form, itself falls entirely within the field of politics.

There is, however, a formal difference between these two pacts: if the first takes the form of a collective relation between the subjects and sovereign, and immediately constitutes a collectivity (which means that its nature is fundamentally that of an *association*), the second is essentially a relation between each individual and God, and is presented as a personal *submission*. Spinoza proceeds to play with this double difference of form in order to combine the two pacts into the same mechanism, to overdetermine the first by the second: "all are bound to obey its decrees and commands (= the state) on the subject (= religion) in accordance with their promise which God bids them keep" (*omnes ad eiusdem* [= *imperii*] *de eadem* [= *religione*] *decreta et mandata, ex fide ipsi data, quam Deus omnino servari jubet, obtemperare teneri*) (G III/199–200). In other words, if it is true that the religious pact (with God) includes in itself no more force than another (every individual, in this respect, whether he is a subject or sovereign, *cum suo periculo licet* [G III/199]), this pact can nevertheless function as a guarantee in relation to the first, on the condition of finding itself in practice placed under the first pact's control. The circle of causes and effects thus expands. The supplementary force of religious *fides*, submitting individuals to God, "frees" them from slavery in relation to the *imperium* (that is, from the pure relation of forces) at the very moment when, by turning the damage caused to others into a violation of right (*injuria*) and a sin, it subjects them internally to the ends of civil society. *Nothing more* than the initial necessity has thus intervened with this overdetermination, except that the terrain of analysis has been displaced. The rationality of the social pact is no longer presented as an ideal end or as an enigmatic fact but as the combined effect of utility and religious imagination.

To analyze the interplay of this combination in history is the object of chapter 17. One would not understand its reasoning if one did not see that Spinoza here is constantly inspired by Machiavelli. The key formula: *religionem in rempublicam* (or *in imperium*) *introducere*, especially used in chapters 5, 17, and 19 (G III/75, 220, 237), is a literal borrowing from the Florentine. No doubt Spinoza in the *TTP* does not explicitly name Machiavelli; he cites only Tacitus and Quintus Curtius. But the precise confrontation of the two authors does not leave any doubt, to the point of suggesting that Spinoza has practically written by having in front of him the text of the *Discorsi* I/11 (*Della religione de' Romani*). One will conclude that, for Spinoza, Moses fulfilled in the Hebrew state exactly the same function as Numa Pompilius in the history of Rome: that of the true organizer of the state's continuity.

Yet it is no less important to see how Spinoza, who projects Machiavelli's historical schema onto the biblical text, at the same time leads to a profound transformation of the latter. Again, the very construction of chapter 17 is quite revealing here. Spinoza begins with numerous examples (Alexander, Augustus) that are all designed to show the utilization of religious representations and beliefs by a monarchical power seeking to protect itself against internal dissensions and rebellions, and to turn the power of its subjects against an external enemy. It is a question, he tells us, of a *"simulation," with the ambivalence that characterizes it: it deceives, but it is simultaneously unmasked as such. Can one be satisfied with these examples in order to understand the mechanism according to which today the absolute monarchies of "divine right" function? It indeed seems that the answer is "No": every politics (indeed every tactic) of recourse to religion refers to a more fundamental structure, to the fact that the mass is not only an object* but an *active* power, and consequently refers to a conception of the imagination that is not *instrumental* but *constitutive* (of a kind of life and knowledge). In other words, neither Machiavellian ruse—if it ever existed under this pure form—nor monarchical ideology (whose linkage with superstition the preface of the *TTP* described in such a vehement way) can be explained by themselves. In order to understand how the *place of God* (*vicem Dei*) can, in history and in political practice, be either occupied fictively or invoked as the location of an election or a guarantee of power, it must first be explained how this place is established.

This is what the constitution of Mosaic *theocracy* is going to show us in detail as a fundamental political regime. By giving to all the elements of the structure a simple and sensible configuration, this privileged example is going to illustrate gradually the simultaneity of two processes of constitution of the *imperium* (or of civil society) and of *religio* (or of the collective imaginary), whose conjunction alone forms a *populus* in its historical singularity. In addition, Spinoza insists on the fact that this entire constitution proceeds from *jus naturale*. And first of all in the sense that the Hebrews, because of exceptional (but neither unique nor supernatural) circumstances, no longer found themselves under the power of any other *natio*, of any "external" oppression. They were only with themselves; they could only rely on "their own forces." What, then, is the role of Moses here? It is the role of an initiator or, if one wishes, of a legislator, but, as the *TTP* has not ceased to explain, not the role of a superhuman situated outside of history. Moses' own ideology, at the cost of some conflicts and adjustments, winds up adapting itself precisely to the state of culture and ignorance, and to the *multitudo*'s demand for security. In this sense Moses, in the last analysis, *forms part* of the multitude. He is only the vector of an immanent causality: it is the "natural" power of the Hebrews themselves that, through its intermediary, is realized in the constitution of a given political regime.

To think about this constitution is definitively to arrive at think-ing about, on two levels or registers at once — that of utility and that of its imagi-nary representation — the "transfer of power" as a continuous process. It is thus to analyze the permanent *split* of a unity and also the *unity* of a double activity. There is in fact only *a single* civil society instituted by Moses. However, the fact that this civil society immediately assumes the form of a religious society also presupposes that the analysis can distinguish between two correlative causal chains; the remain-der of this analysis proceeds to show that they both produce *real* effects. In the ex-position that Spinoza proposes to us of the first fluctuations of the state form, dur-ing Moses' lifetime, it is a question of analyzing this double articulation, by giving it the form of a narrative of the moments of the foundation of the *imperium*. In fact, in this well-known succession (Theocracy I, Moses's quasi monarchy, Theocracy II), the first moments only have the value of a theoretical fiction: by themselves they are essentially unstable. They only represent the provisional components of Theocracy II, which alone constitutes a complete and relatively stable form, whose institutions no longer rest on the interventions of a single individual, but can endure by themselves. Therefore, if Spinoza, "rationalizing" the biblical narrative, spreads out the formation of the state over three successive "pacts," it is finally to put clearly into evidence the intrication of the levels, the double positioning of the material and imaginary functions of power (division of lands, regime of property, and mili-tary organization, on the one hand; interpretation of right or law in terms of divine will, on the other). In fact, the *first* pact only enables one to *name God* as holder and source of the common power. The *second* pact, by transferring all the powers to Moses, shows that the *place of God* (*vicem Dei*) must be metaphorically occupied by one or several men who exercise the functions of sovereignty. Finally, the *third* pact institutionally *divides* these powers in such a way that the *equilibrium* between the forces at the heart of the people permanently reproduces the conditions of obedi-ence to the divine law (hence the observance of the pact itself), and that, recipro-cally, the representation of the divine law permanently limits the tendency of leaders, of armed citizens, of confederated tribes and different powers established to en-croach on one other. To a certain extent one finds again the three moments of the definition of the pact in chapter 16, but in an inverted form.

I have spoken of a dialectic. From the moment that it is submit-ted to the efficacy of a structure, Spinoza can draw out some remarkable effects from it.

First, regarding the relations of the concepts of "democracy" and "theocracy." Let us cut to the chase: according to chapter 16, in its abstraction, every civil society, from the moment that it can be thought of as the realization of a pact, is *naturally* democratic. We now see *under what form* such a democratic power really—indeed even necessarily—exists in the conditions that are apparently the furthest removed from the civic ideal with which we associate this word: precisely under the form of a complete theocracy. Theocracy is the *imaginary* institution of society as democracy, that is, as the collective transfer of power of individuals to an *imperium* that is itself only their collective projection. Consequently, theocracy is its *real* historical establishment. But why *this* term, one will ask? On the one hand, it is a fact, to which the biblical text as much as Roman history, illuminated by one another and by a scientific method of interpretation, testifies. But, on the other hand, this fact is entirely *explicable*. No *populus* as such is original, that is, manifests a preestablished harmony or an originally *political* nature of man, but every *populus* is constituted from a *multitudo* and its characteristic powers (e.g., that of the imagination). Thus, every *populus* is the continuous regulation of the relation that the powers of the multitude maintain with nature of which they form a part, implying activity *and* passivity, agreement *and* disagreement, knowledge *and* imagination. Therefore— and this consequence is decisive for the *TTP*'s project—in history there is not a unique form of the *democratic imperium*, but there are necessarily *several*: as many as there are "regimes" corresponding to the imaginary representation of the common interest. On the other hand, every reflection on the forms that democratic institutions can assume in given historical conditions (for every multitude is not similar to that of the Hebrews) should pose for itself the question of the theological forms (or the forms of *theocracy*) that correspond to it, and of their control.

Second, Spinoza has now completely subverted the idealist representations of *reason* and *unreason* in history and politics. Better: if it had seemed to us that, under the "pragmatism" of the calculation of interests attributed first to individuals as the "motive" of their socialization (of their "escape" from the state of nature), something like a teleology or a ruse of reason was presupposed, we were still quite simply caught up in an idealist conception of this reason. Reason is not opposed as a contrary to the unreason (of passions, of the appetite). What is rational, that is, explicable, is the reality of the historical process by which individuals, who, for the most part (collectively and each for his own part), have by nature and by themselves only a representation woven with hopes and fears, constitute, however, in the very element of the imaginary a viable and productive combination of their forces. And what is rational in the second degree (as an idea of reflection) is the concept that the philosopher or historian can form from this combination, in other words, the definition of the *pact*.

But it is also the concept of *contradictions* of the pact. In fact, the third unavoidable lesson is that no pact is absolutely stable. As Heraclitus and Chairman Mao said, *one divides into two.* Being overdetermined, inscribed in a complex of theologico-political institutions, the pact contains the germ of a split. No doubt there is no "power of the negative" here: let us take care not to reintroduce another ideal teleology. The pact does not carry inscribed in its simple essence the promise of its own collapse. It remains that, without the internal contradiction of institutions, without *the form* that institutions give to the passional conflicts of the multitude, the external forces of production would be almost inoperative. Institutions by themselves have no other power than that of the masses, including when it is a matter of a power of decomposition. But, on the other hand, the power of the masses can destroy the *imperium* only if it finds in the institutions themselves the means of organizing itself into tendencies, into parties, in a word, to constitute itself into *imperia in imperio.*

Spinoza analyzes this dialectic, one knows, according to two great axes, whose correlation he shows: on the one hand the development of a struggle against civil, politico-military power and religious, ecclesiastical power; on the other hand, the development of a struggle between the established *summae potestates* and the *multitudo* itself as *plebs.* This is a struggle promoted by the *multitudo* and exacerbated by the tyrannical oppression of princes and by the privileges of ecclesiastical castes. Whence *seditiones,* whose importance is that they have the "war of religion" for a tyrannical form and that they take shape by following the appeal of a prophet who in his turn manages the *vicem Dei* and thus turns against the established power the very language of its legitimacy. On the one hand, the struggle of "those above" among themselves and, on the other hand, the struggle of "those below" against them necessarily assume the form of a mobilization of the religious imaginary implied in the pact itself. Spinoza concludes from this that, if every civil society has a democratic foundation, every civil society also includes the possibility of a monarchic evolution, whose counterpart is the autonomization of the religious apparatus and the development of tendencies to superstition.

III

However, by showing how Spinoza attaches to the overdetermined structure of the "pact" a causal dialectic that is capable of explaining the tendencies at work in the history of states, we have only drawn near the central difficulty, which, from one end of its enterprise to the other, the *TTP* does not cease to tackle: that of *obedience.*

This is a practical difficulty: from the moment that any *imperium* has no other "guarantee" than its own capacity to ensure that "men obey its commands" (*homines eius mandatis obsequantur*), what is the distinct mechanism of fear itself that can produce this effect? In religion itself—a fortiori in the extreme forms of superstition—there is an element of fear, which can turn against power. Consequently, there is a theoretical difficulty: how does one think about an internal obedience (of the soul), which refers, however, to the constitution of a power that is external to individuals taken one by one? Isn't it absurd to postulate either that the *obeying* individuals are only dealing with themselves (including and especially if for them the divine law is identified with practical love for one's neighbor), or that individuals obeying a third, externally constituted power, are, however, *free* by the very fact of this submission, and only act *ex proprio decreto*? In other words, is Spinoza a closet theorist of *voluntary servitude*? Or else, on the contrary, does he, through a sort of reductio ad absurdum of this concept, in fact tend to separate two "spheres" of individual existence, which authoritarian regimes (regimes of "censorship") misguidedly strive to confuse (and, in fact, in vain, for this confusion would be *against nature*): the regime of internal freedom and the regime of external obedience?

Everything depends, of course, on the articulation proposed between "right" (*jus*) and "law" (*lex*). Now in this regard the *TTP* sketches two inverse movements. The first—chapters 4 and 5—begin with a discussion of the usages of the word *lex*. There occurs, in these chapters, a drastic reduction. Once and for all, there would remain only a single adequate sense of the term *lex*: the one that designates a relation of forces between individuals, and in particular a political *imperium* (the fact of being *alterius juris*, of acting *ex alieno decreto*). Also, chapters 4 and 5 oppose, in a sharply contrasted presentation, the genesis of political authority, which in itself only implies the idea of command; the definition of genuine piety, which only concerns the internal inclination of the soul to the good and practical works of charity, for which each individual is his own judge; and finally, the knowledge of nature, which is also that of God, but has only to form the representation of a law (on the contrary, this representation can only make it delirious). And it is only next, in reference to the extreme barbarism of the Hebrews, that Spinoza shows how Moses had to amalgamate these distinct instances, by making moral precepts of the laws of the state itself (at the cost of their "externalization" in rites, ceremonies, therefore, the inversion of their meaning), and by founding the whole on a theology of creation and the election of the Hebrew people. Note that such a presentation does not refer to the idea of a pact. Also, this passage of the *TTP* is the one in which Spinoza seems closest to identifying the *imperium* as such with servitude, and democracy (or individual and collective liberation) with something hypothetically "beyond" the state, indeed, beyond politics ("if human beings were so constituted by nature as to desire nothing but what is prescribed by true reason, society would not need any laws" [*si homines a natura ita essent constituti, ut nihil, nisi id quod vera ratio indicat, cuperent, nullis sane legibus indigeret societas*] [GIII/73]).

However, the movement of chapters 16 and 17 is quite different. Here the context is no longer that of a critique of uses (almost all improper) of the word *lex* but that of a development of the power that the word *jus* expresses, passing from the *jus naturale* to the *jus civile*. Yet it is at the very heart of this development that the necessity of the law is reintroduced: at precisely the same time as the reference to the concept of *voluntas*. As opposed to Hobbes, for whom the contract (a metajuridical act sanctioned in the element of language, in imitation of an act of private right) presupposes the *Wille* of individuals as already constituted personalities (since only autonomous wills can reciprocally engage one another), we see Spinoza on the contrary pass from the desire and appetite that alone define the power of the individual *before* the pact to the *will* that expresses this power once the pact is in force. Better: what the pact institutes is a collective power that assumes *after the fact* the form of a relation between wills. Everything happens from now on in the element of the will: mutual recognition of citizens (the possibility for them mutually to engage one other), commandment, and obedience (hence also, at the limit, rebellion and transgression, in which is affirmed not a *conatus*, which is purely *physical*, but a *bad* will, a *pertinacia* or *contumacia*). Theoretically speaking, individual or collective *wills* do not exist before the pact but are constituted under its effect, this very effect that places the *summa potestas* in the place in which the law that must be observed is stated. *The very notion of will must therefore be understood as a retroactive effect of the pact*, an effect always already given and thereby irreversible, impassable, from the moment that in fact, historically, there is a "tacit or explicit" pact.

In other words, the existence of the pact is not only a *translatio* or a displacement of power (which a physics could account for); it is the transposition or metaphor (equally *translatio* in the sense of *translation*) from *jus* into *lex*. Yet if there is no *lex* except for the *wills* that recognize it as such (until its transgression), on the other hand, there are no *wills* except in reference to a *lex* (*humana* and/or *divina*) that institutes ends and values. The will is the consciousness (imaginary, as is every consciousness) of a desire accompanied by the representation of a law. This is why throughout the *TTP*, although Spinoza contests the doctrine of salvation by grace, he does not cease to base himself (as he will also do in part IV of the *Ethics*) on Paul's astonishing antinomian affirmation in the *Letter to the Romans*: before the law there is no sin, and, on the other hand, the constitution of the law poses at the same time the necessity of obedience and the necessity of transgression, that is, the constitution of the law establishes the two "relative" poles between which "acts" or "voluntary choices" (*decreta*) move in a permanent *fluctuatio*. He is not afraid to suppress everything that, in Paul's assertion, is in fact intended to justify an eschatological thesis (the idea of premeditated temptation by God), while entirely preserving the idea of a circular correlation between the representation of the law and the representation of decision, whether free or constrained, *ex proprio* or *ex alieno decreto*. In fact, it is the very structure of the imaginary that is here described as the world of *good* and *evil*, of *will* and *law*.

Thus, it is not important to Spinoza—and this is where he displaces every problematic of "voluntary servitude"—to oppose autonomy and heteronomy, spontaneity and obedience as two separate reigns. In fact, these are two inseparable modalities of the same consciousness of self and *alienus*, that is, of one's *neighbor*. Although perceived as original, the will is always *secondary*: it is the imaginary mode according to which individuals necessarily assume consciousness of their own power and the power of the others on which they depend. This is why the will is also always already *divided*: affirmation (hope) of sovereignty and recognition (fear) of subjection or submission. This form is just as much present when individuals are conscious of "obeying only themselves" (that is, they perceive other men as a freely chosen object of love, with which they identify) as when they perceive the rules of collective life as an external constraint accompanied by penalties. "Free" mutual recognition (from which can arise the representation of a "general will") and submission to a power that appears to be arbitrary are doubtless not practically equivalent (neither for the individual nor for society), for hope and fear do not exactly command the same works, but they presuppose *a common element*. What distinguishes the most oppressed *civis* from a *servus* is the fact that the power on which he depends still requires a "voluntary" recognition from him, and gives him the hope of not being *sibi inutilis*. But what distinguishes the citizen of a *libera respublica* from a pure "spiritual automaton" (or, if one likes, from a natural power immediately "agreeing" with others) is the fact that every pact of association establishes not only a *jus commune*, or a *certa ac determinata ratio ad existendeum et operandum*, but a *summa lex totius populi* to which he is submitted and that he "fears" to transgress.

Let us set aside here every equivocation: in the *translatio* from *jus* into *lex*, natural right, that is, the causality of the relations of power alone, is actually preserved. The causal connection goes from *jus* as *potentia* to *jus* represented as *lex*, from the power of individuals to the power of the sovereign, and from the latter to the representation of obligation (whether it be a question of the rights of the citizen or of private morality) without an effective exterior, the "miracle" of a supernatural intervention or a transcendental principle of morality, ever being introduced into this double chain. Spinoza repeats it as often as necessary: the *law* and the *will* are representations. The fact that individuals are constituted as historical actors only in the element of this representation does not imply that it is its own cause. Still less does it imply that it is the source or foundation of right (*jus*) and consequently of power (*imperium*). On the contrary, only an actual power can preserve it and put it into effect, that is, can represent itself as law. Consequently, not only does Spinoza take the exact opposite of a "theocentric" conception according to which sovereign power emanates from a divine transcendent authority, not only does he hold that the fact of power alone establishes a juridical order, but he deduces from it that, in order for a religious law to be in force in a given society, there must exist an established power that imposes it.

Why, in these conditions, is it necessary to define in general the fundamental law that is in force in a given state as a *divine* law? Why is it inevitable that obedience appear as a divine commandment, or as the consequence of a divine commandment, *even* when the political regime no longer has a theocratic form or no longer rests on the fiction of a "divine right" of the sovereign? Why not limit oneself to the idea of constitution of a legislative political authority, by giving to religious law the status of a particular form, which it could take *or not*, depending on the regimes? The response to this question (which is obviously politically crucial) is linked, it seems to me, to the reflection that runs through the entire *TTP* on *the very formalism* of the law. The entire law, in fact, and in particular the fundamental law that establishes all the others, that is, that stipulates obedience as such, necessarily has *the form of an enunciation*. This structure is obvious when one or several "real" individuals (Moses, Caesar, the pope, or the council of a republican state) issue a command and insist on its execution by virtue of the expression of their will. It is obvious again when, in a "metaphorical" way, the rules of individual existence are understood and taught as the decrees of a legislator or a divine judge. In the two cases, enunciation finally takes the form of a written *code*, which is inserted into a *narrative* of legitimation ("historical" narrative of the origins of the law).

But this structure (enunciation-prescription-narrative) is always present, under its most abstract and irreducible form, when the law is *inscribed in hearts* and has no other content that the moral precepts of universal reason. It is precisely a matter of *precepts*, and this normative *forma* constitutes an ineliminable residue. The "narrative" of the law is then simply the memory of each individual; it is the internal discourse in which he poses himself as the subject of an *obedientia* and, consequently, of a fear and a hope. It is the discourse by which he recounts to himself, in the sense of a personal *historia*, the necessity of obedience for salvation, and represents to himself the *attributes* that absolutely must be imitated and in this sense constitute the ideal *exemplar* of man. In other words, everyone fully obeys only *his* internal God. But such a narrative is none other than the singular mode according to which individuals can submit their will to a universal law *ex proprio decreto*. Whence the incredible formulation:

> I shall go further and maintain that every man is bound to adapt these dogmas to his own way of thinking, and to interpret them as seems easiest to him, without any hesitation, but with his fullest consent, so that he may the more easily obey God with his whole heart.... How salutary and necessary this doctrine is for a republic, so that men may live peacefully and harmoniously,... I leave everyone to judge for himself.
>
> [*quinimo unusquisque... haec fidei dogmata ad suum captum accomodare tenetur, eaque sibi eo modo interpretari, quo sibi videtur eadem facilius, sine ulla haesitatione, sed integro animi consensu amplecti posse, ut consequenter Deo pleno animi consensu obediat.... Quae doctrina, quam salutaris, quamque necessaria sit in republica, ut homines pacifice, et concorditer vivant,... omnibus judicandum relinquo.*] (G III/178f)

Constitute yourself in such a way that you cannot doubt the reasons of your action! This is why, even if, in a limit-situation, one can suppose that men would abandon every anthropological belief regarding the nature of God (or, what is not very different, would agree in order to postulate that their theological beliefs are indifferent to the very content of practical faith, and of value among themselves, from the moment they dispose of the same works), the common law should still be referred to the *name of God*. This name would designate quite simply the subject of enunciation, the place of the *He*—whoever he is—who stipulates love for the neighbor, the *ens supremum* that each individual loves and recognizes by observing a law as the condition of the common Good. Better: this name would designate quite simply the voices (*vox illa, quam Israelitae audiverent*) (ibid.) that establish a relation of direct interpellation between the I, subject of obedience (*subditus*), and the He, universal of the Law. This is why every political power (every sovereignty), at the same time that it establishes a relation of forces, from the fact alone that it absolutely states its right to be obeyed, must be presented as the interpreter of a superior commandment. Every legislator refers by its very form to an anonymous Legislator, whose only name is *God, Person,* the one who *is*.

One understands, then, why Spinoza confines himself neither to the motive of physical fear nor to the idea of a human, moral *natural law,* such as natural-right theorists (including Hobbes) postulate. For either the latter is only a surreptitious way of baptizing *human reason* what, for real men (in the imagination of real men), is called God, or else it is an attempt to deny the form of enunciation by reducing it to a given *general rule,* of which good actions would be the case-by-case application. But no demonstration, mathematical or experimental, can engender the form of the subject's interpellation, produce a certainty that would be a belief *(fides),* or subsume *my* actions under *the law: pious dogmas* are necessary. The result is that, if the power from which civil society (or the state) is constituted is only that of men themselves, if the causes of its stability and instability must not be sought elsewhere than in the variations of their natural power and powerlessness, the modality according to which this combination is brought about is always the representation of a law *at the same time internal* (inscribed *in the depths of hearts) and external* (revealed by an *ens supremum),* according to a double movement of introjection and projection. Which one could still express by saying that men make their own history—but to the extent that in the imagination they receive the law *(ratio sive causa)* under an inverted form *(lex sive finis),* as the *dictamen* of the Other. Only on this condition can they represent for themselves *order,* which they strive to realize in their institutions and in their works. By developing the concept of the *vera religio* (that is, the necessary kernel of every religion that actually tries to organize the relations of men among themselves and that stipulates nothing other than obedience), Spinoza had precisely drawn out from the totality of all narratives a *fundamental norm (fundamentum universale, lex divina naturalis, dictamen rationis)* capable *at the same time* of being completely interiorized by individuals (whether, rationally, they understand that *summum legis divinae praemium esse ipsam legem* [G III/62], or whether they find in diverse theological opinions the motive of love for the neighbor) and of being referred to a God (even if the latter's nature remains, for the imagination, indeterminate, that is, if its existence is posed absolutely).

An entire spectrum of experiences is thus circumscribed, whose possibility refers to the very structure of the politico-theological imaginary. It includes *two limits,* which Spinoza had characterized from the outset. On the one hand, the limit that *Moses* represents: maximal exteriorization of the law, almost total alienation of individual wills, interiority being concentrated in the faith of the prophet himself, subject and medium of a genuine collective hallucination. On the other hand, the limit that the figure of *Christ* represents, the "true model of life for all men," *os Dei*, that is, Voice of the voice that legislates in general, maximal internalization of the Law and of the enunciation by all and by each in particular, but always referred to the name of God. It is not improper to conclude that, if the allegorical and transhistorical figure of Christ has become historically the necessary referent of every *free* human obedience, it is because it represents this unavoidable condition of imaginary experience:

> The voice of Christ can thus be called the voice of God in the same way as that which Moses heard. In this sense it can also be said that the wisdom of God — that is, wisdom that is more than human — took on human nature in Christ, and that Christ was the way of salvation.
>
> [*Et ideo vox Christi, sicuti illa, quam Moses audiebat, vox Dei vocari potest. Et hoc sensu etiam dicere possumus, sapientam Dei, hoc est sapientam, quae supra humanam est, naturam humanam in Christo asumpsisse, et Christum viam salutis fuisse.*] (G III/21)

IV

In order to articulate in their unity and their irreducibility the two registers of the real and the imaginary, the two theses that we have attempted to reconstitute must be maintained simultaneously: *jus* is nothing but the expression, the consequence of the effects of natural human *potentia*; *jus* expresses itself as *lex*, that is, it represents itself in consciousness as the effect of a statement that is divine, "revealed," or stipulated to subjects endowed with "will." Abstractly speaking, the "pact" is nothing other than the formal concept of this double expression, which forbids as much the return to an imaginary (theological) conception of politics as the "physicalist" illusion of a politics without an imaginary component. The pact is neither a divine order in which the law or the legislator would create individuals and the social body itself, nor an artificialist mechanism in which the de facto power would arbitrarily use religion, and for that purpose in fact would *fabricate* it.

Let us note here that, in a theological representation of the state — such as medieval thought had elaborated it from the Pauline metaphor of the *corpus Christi* or the *corpus mysticum* — it is the members of the social whole themselves (ranks, corporations, at the limit individuals) who emanate from God across the action of his Word or his Law. From Spinoza's point of view, such a representation only expresses a superstitious variant of religious belief. Moreover, it eliminates the subjective moment of the will that must be explained, by making the *potestas* over the *subditi* who are not *cives* fall from the sky.

On the other hand, in an artificialist *contract* of the Hobbesian type, it is necessary to presuppose that the bilateral relations of individuals among themselves *suffice* to constitute a norm of right that would be *other* than their own chain to infinity, their own reciprocal exchanges. In order to escape a vicious circle, it is necessary to presuppose—as Hobbes precisely did—that the "transfer" of right occurs entirely for the benefit of a Third Party (an Arbiter) who is not actively involved in the contract. So that the very meaning of the word *right* is split: *on the one hand*, natural power, suppressed in the civil state; *on the other hand*, juridical rule, transcending nature. From Spinoza's point of view, this representation is idealist; for the historical sovereign, although different from "private" individuals, remains no less an individual—as Machiavelli has shown and as experience confirms—*in relation* with them, depending on the power they have "preserved" as men (in particular their power to think, hence, to imagine), and which cannot be reduced to zero.

Paradoxically, these two representations of the *political body* or of the *social bond*, the one mystical, the other secular and "disenchanted," have *something in common*: the idea of organic totality, of an integration of individuals as such into a finalized order. Against the theological representation, Spinoza holds that divine law *does not constitute individuals*, is not the real source of political power and the history of states, but only regulates voluntary *actions* (or works) as a normative representation. At the same time that he defines the law as an imaginary statement, he shows its ambivalence: generally it entails obedience, but on occasion also transgression, the other form of action in which the subject's freedom is affirmed. Against juridical artificialism, Spinoza poses the efficacy of the imagination for founding the rule of right, that is, he refers the constitution of the Third Party, of the arbiter of particular contracts, to the *effect of transcendence* that religious representations imply, or to the form of subjugation that they *introduce* into history, without history thereby becoming the *contrary* of nature, since religious imagination is an entirely natural power. In the two cases, his position takes on its meaning as an assertion that the constitution of societies is nothing other than the chain of actions and passions of the *multitude*: a multitude reducible to the totality of individual powers that compose it, but irreducible to a sum of bilateral relations (or of exchanges) among individuals. Which requires no less than a theoretically revolutionary concept of causality.

It then clearly appears that, if Spinoza's conception of the social relation cannot proceed from the concept of *pact*—in the *TTP* in any case—it differs *toto coelo* from all classical definitions of the *social contract*. This is what we had posed from the beginning. But if we recapitulate the elements that have just been set forth, it is easy to establish that in reality they constitute the development of a contradiction. The historical pact is a double pact, both civil and religious. Natural right, as a real power, is concentrated in a *summa potestas*, and as an imaginary power, is concentrated in a *summa lex*; the *potestas* is only effective to the extent that the individuals who have constituted it permanently recognize it as constituting a law for their will. This effect of aftershock structures civil society, but it also permanently introduces the possibility of a *de facto gap between right and fact*, between the universality and unconditionality of the law and the empirical behavior of those who embody its authority.

For any power (including ecclesiastical power), the introduction of religion into the state, the very fact of being posed as legitimate in reference to the order of unconditional values, is double-edged. On the one hand, it indeed permits obedience to be required and generally obtained and individuals' belief or *fides* to be mobilized — by the fact alone of the *place* occupied. But, on the other hand, it permanently opens up the possibility of a contestation: a questioning of the legitimacy of power, the particular form it assumes, or the dignity of those who exercise it. In a potentially infinite regress, the universality of the very enunciation of the commandment is always *beyond* the person who lends it its sensible body and its words. This is why Moses himself was challenged as interpreter of the God that the Hebrews would not even have known without him. For example, against the *imperium* to which God stipulates obedience, rises up the *pontifex* or the prophet, who shows that God has been betrayed by his elected, or that he has withdrawn his Grace on account of the elected's injustice. Against the *imperium* in general, the right to command in the name of the law or to interpret the law, rises up the rebellious *conscience* of individuals for whom no human power can *monopolize* divine speech or by itself embody justice. How does it happen that the very structure that ensures power also ensures its contestation?

In fact, this is not surprising, for this structure does not correspond to any natural finality or preestablished harmony. It is necessary instead to understand why *most of the time* it is the first aspect that carries it along. And therefore to turn again toward history. What historical *cement* can account for the relative stability of the pact, without having to invoke any other cause than the theologico-political complex itself? Spinoza tells us in an extraordinarily sharp way: it is *nationalism*.

The term "nationalism" is anachronistic, but it is the only one that seems to me to recover adequately the content of the *TTP*'s analysis, whereas the classical term "patriotism" would not suffice and could even lead to error. Again, we are going to see that here Spinoza occupies a singular—precisely *anachronistic*—position in relation to certain of his immediate predecessors and contemporaries, who have been included with him in the "natural right" tradition (but also, by a symptomatic vacillation, in the tradition of theorists of "reason of state"). Thus, it is remarkable that Grotius, who for the first time formalizes the *social pact* as the foundation of the juridical order, who prior to Spinoza (and, roughly speaking, in the service of the same political interests) defends the civil conception of the *jus circa sacra*, and who above all casts the bases of a modern "international" right in a mercantilist perspective, does not undertake the least analysis of what we would call the national phenomenon. De facto, the states among which for Grotius are established alternating relations of peace and war (which should be normalized) are indeed nations. But the concept that designates them is only that of a juridical *potestas*, which means that (as in Hobbes, if not in Machiavelli) the question of an identity other than formal is not posed: a "nation" is always only a sum of individuals and territories that *are found* (by means of conquest, choice, or heritage) and brought together under the authority of the same sovereign. In other words, it is always a dynastic concept of national unity that, paradoxically, is at work in this official theorist of the Dutch nation constituted at the end of a war of national liberation that had hardly ended. And despite his sociogeographical considerations on the *naturalness of peoples*—promises with a great future—he proceeds no differently than Jean Bodin. Spinoza's point of view is demonstrably different. This is not the place to go into the historical and psychological reasons that can explain it. It is a question instead of understanding well how fully the combination of the concepts of *imperium*, *religio*, and *natio* is brought about in his work.

    Natura nationes non creat: this means that Spinoza rejects in advance every historicism, every vitalism, every national animism. There is nothing in him of an *Urvolk*, an original people. Nor is there any spirit of a people *prior* to its political history, whose traces would be religion or mythology. But the whole context of this famous formula must be considered: if nature does not create nations, history produces nothing but nations, through the chain of natural causes itself:

> Why was this nation more stubborn than the others? Was it Nature? But surely it is not nations but individuals that Nature creates, and individuals are only divided into nations by the diversity of language, laws, and customs; and the last two, i.e., laws and customs, are the only factors which can give a nation a particular temperament, a particular nature, and finally particular beliefs.

> [*cur haec natio reliquis contumacior fuit? an natura? haec sane nationes non creat, sed individua, quae quidem in nationes non distinguuntur nisi ex diversitat linguae, legum et morum receptorum, et ex his duobus, legibus scilicet et moribus, tantum oriri potest, quod unaquaeque natio singulare habet ingenium, singularem conditionem, et denique singularia praejudicia.*] (G III/217)

Let us reread the *TTP* in light of these formulations without equivocation, starting with chapter 3 on the *vocatio Hebraeorum*. A complete theory of the national *ingenium* is progressively constructed in it. The components retained by Spinoza, in order to tie them together in a single ideo-passional "complex," are of four orders.

The first order is that of the *succession of generations*, hence, kinship, whose continuity and durability permit the *populus* to be represented as constituting a particular *natio*, separate and different from all others, having a common origin and perpetuating its identity by means of direct descent.

Second, there is the order of the *soil*, or the national territory, with which each people (obviously the Hebrews) identifies its communitarian existence (each nation has its *promised land*, its *natural borders*), and which it considers to be sacred.

The third order is that of the collective cult's *mores*, rituals, and "external signs."

Finally, what is probably the essential order — or rather the component that connects all the others — is the *native language*: not only insofar as it has its own grammar and its own words (the entire first part of the *TTP* studies the meaning of the Bible's words according to the properties of its original language and from this meaning deduces the Bible's function in the singular history of the Hebrew state), but insofar as the Bible is *preserved* by the vulgar, the mass of people whose cohesion it expresses and whose imaginary it translates into particular narratives of origin (such as the Exodus).

In chapter 8, bringing about a first stage of the constitution of the Hebrew state by Moses, Spinoza had insisted on the connection between the effectiveness of the "pact" and the fact that it concerned an engagement *for posterity*, that is, of the formation of a national ideology and its material instruments (texts). The pact, which has no other "guarantee" than its *present* force, is necessarily stated in terms of perpetuity:

> For by the first pact he had bound only those who were present, whereas by the second pact he also bound those who should come after them.... He therefore commanded that this book of the second pact be religiously preserved for future generations.

[*Nam, quia primo pacto non nisi praesentes, qui aderant, obligaverat, at secundo omnes etiam eorum posteros . . . ideo hujus secundi pacti librum futuris saeculis religiose servandum jussit.*] (G III/123)

The law is only effective if it is *written* in a determinate language, to which, in return, it confers a sacred nature, which means that the masses "live" or "inhabit" from inside, in an imaginary way, the very code of the enunciation. The *marks* of language, of territory, and also marks of the body (Jewish circumcision, the Chinese pigtail, and generally the identifying features concerning the body or clothing that fulfill for each people a symbolic function religiously preserved from father to son: *morum et rituum singulari* [G III/215]) become then the principle of a fixed distribution of love and hate between the *inside* (those who are submitted to the same law, and who by this fact bear its mark on their body, in their rituals, and especially in their language) and the *outside* (those who are excluded from the law, or recognize another law, and by this fact bear other marks). The same chain of causes and circumstances that is expressed in a determinate social pact in history leads to the constitution of this *ingenium nationis singulare*, just as other conditions wind up in its dissolution, as I recalled above.

Consequently, there is a new circle: no nation without *imperium*, without a state or the germ of a state; but no longer a state without nationalism. In each historical state, the cement of the relation of obedience between the *summa potestas* and the *multitudo* of individuals in the last analysis cannot be anything but the constitution of a national interest translated into a nationalist ideology. As long as this cement holds, the legitimacy of the sovereign is not genuinely contestable (prophets rebellious against the state pass for *false prophets*, whatever their virtue or miracles). On the other hand, when seditions or civil wars (social or religious) undermine the continuity of the state, this is expressed first by the disappearance of patriotism.

Under these circumstances, one understands better Spinoza's insistence on the history of the Hebrew people, the reason for which he insists on making this history begin with Moses (and not with Abraham), and the interplay of the correspondences with Machiavelli's discourse (itself haunted by the question of Italian unity, such as Rome had otherwise realized, and such as the church had destroyed by "electing" Italy as its apostolic headquarters). The history of the Hebrew people *non tantum, ut Jeremias . . . ait, ab urbe condita, set jam inde a legibus conditis* (G III/217) is the laboratory for the analysis of nationalism, of its contradictory causes and effects. And one finds, under a still more determinate form (closer to the apprehension of a *singular essence*) the circle of the real and the imaginary. Every nation's real singularity is necessarily lived as a unique privilege, a historical "election," or, better, a *calling* (*vocatio*), which implies a particular mission, to the exclusion of other peoples. The law is stated on and for a given land. The law's marks and the prophets' voices will henceforth form a circle of *certainty* (chapters 1 and 2) in which each individual inscribes the consciousness of his actions, between the promise of salvation and the fear of punishment. But, Spinoza adds, *non dubium est, quin omnes nationes prophetas habuerint, et quod donum propheticum Judaeis peculiare non fuerit* (G III/50): every nation has its mission and its prophets, that is, effects the same transposition for its own sake, by elaborating in its own way the signs of election. Whoever says *natio* says imaginary *electio* and *vocatio*; whoever says *vocatio* says signs or generic "features" of identification. From the fact that the individuals who in the state of "nature" (insofar as *natura* is opposed to *natio*) are not at all distinct from one another (*nisi somniare velimus, naturam olim diversa hominum genera procreavisse* [G III/47]) become collectively different, they can also do the same thing quite differently: to imagine God in a singular way, and consequently to believe *ex pleno animi consensu* that his commandments are indeed addressed to them:

> (Moses) did indeed concede that there were beings who... acted in God's place; that is, beings to whom God gave the authority, right, and power to guide nations, to look after them and care for them. But he taught that this being whom it was their duty to worship was the highest and supreme God, or (to use the Hebrew phrase) the God of Gods.... in virtue of this supreme right and power he had chosen the Hebrew nation for himself alone, together with a certain territory... leaving other nations and lands to the care of other gods standing in his place. For this reason he was called the God of Israel and the God of Jersusalem... while other gods were called the gods of other nations. For this same reason the Jews believed that the land which God had chosen for himself demanded a special form of worship, quite different from other lands; indeed it could not suffer the worship of other Gods.

> [(Moses) concessit quidem, dari entia, quae... vicem Dei gerebant, hoc est entia, quibus Deus authoritatem, jus et potentiam dedit ad dirigendas nationes et iis providendum et curandum; at hoc ens, quod colere tenebantur, summum et supremum Deum, sive (ut Hebraeorum phrasi utar) Deum Deorum esse docuit... et pro hoc summo suo jure et potentia sibi soli Hebraeam nationem elegisse, certamque mundi plagam... reliquas autem nationes et regiones curis reliquorum Deorum a se substitutorum reliquisse; et ideo Deus Israelis, et Deus.... Hierosolymae, reliqui autem Dii reliquarum nationum Dii vocabantur. Et hac etiam de causa credebant

Judaei, regionem illam, quam Deus sibi elegerat, cultum Dei singularem et ab aliarum regionem cultu prorsus diversum requirere, imo nec posse pati cultum aliorum Deorum.] (G III/38–39)

A supplementary, essential, link is thus added to the circle of the constitution of the *imperium* that assumes the figure of the pact: from the power of individuals to collective right, from collective right to the imaginary of the law, from the latter to the imaginary of a singular law, that is, of a national election. And vice versa. Only then are we in a position to understand what is the mechanism, or rather what is the passional dynamic, at work in history. In fact, if *potentia* apparently summoned only the concepts of interest and reason, if the *lex divina naturalis* referred only to a passional spector still unilateral, proceeding from *fides* to love and from hope to fear, then a *lex divina* we shall risk calling *nationalis* (that is, imagined as a historical *vocatio*) requires at the same time the deployment of the passions of love and hate, which are in reality inseparable. Men as such are neither "good" nor "wicked"; they are good *and* wicked, that is, they cannot love without hating: to love all the more intensely as they hate more intensely, as if the "quantity" of positive and negative affect had to present a kind of constant equilibrium.

The key question becomes, then, that of the distribution of this affect. What is it to construct (or to preserve) a state? It is to form a real/imaginary pact in terms of which the affects of love and hate cease to be distributed accidentally by encounters, fluctuating at every moment, but, channeled by institutions (by means of an apparatus of power that is at the same time a *psychic apparatus*), fixed by sacred ideals and cultural conformisms (hence communitarian rituals), incorporated into the proper "style" of a language (this very style that the prophets attribute to God), are distributed on *objects* situated on both sides of a border that is itself imaginary/real between "friends" and "enemies," fellow citizens and strangers (*cives/hostes*). Such a division is possible only in a multitude, for positive identification and its correlate, generic hatred, are mass phenomena (similarly, rituals, mores, and the linguistic circulation that preserves and transforms the meaning of words are also mass phenomena). The analysis of this process is at the center of chapter 17:

> It was God alone, then, who held sovereignty over the Hebrews, and so this state alone, by virtue of the pact, was rightly called the kingdom of God, and God was also called the king of the Hebrews. Consequently, the enemies of this state were the enemies of God. . . . He who forsook his religion ceased to be a citizen and by that became an enemy, and he who died for his religion was regarded as having died for his country.

[*Imperium ergo Hebraeorum Deus solus tenuit, quodque adeo solum ex vi pacti regnum Dei jure vocabatur, et Deus jure vocabatur, et Deus jure etiam rex Hebraeorum; et consequenter huius imperii hostes, hostes Dei. . . . Qui a religione deficiebat, civis esse desinebat, et eo solo hostis habebatur; et qui pro religione moriebatur, pro patria mori reputabatur.*] (G III/200)

And further on:

> And that the armed forces should be formed from the people alone. These armies did not swear allegiance to their commander or the high priest, but to their religion, that is, to their God; and so they were called the armies or hosts of God, and God in turn was called by the Hebrew people the Lord of Hosts. This was why in great battles, where the fortunes of the entire people depended on the issue, the ark of the covenant was borne in the midst of the army, so that the people, seeing their king almost as if present, might fight to the utmost of their strength.

> [*. . . et ex solo populo exercitus formare, qui non in fidem imperatoris, nec summi pontificis, sed religionis sive Dei jurabant; qui adeo exercitus, sive ordines Dei vocabuntur, et Deus contra apud Hebraeos Deus exercituum; et hac de causa arca foederis in magnis proeliis, a quorum discrimine totius populi vel victoria vel clades pendebat, in medio exercitu ibat, ut populus, regem suum quasi praesentem videns, extremis viribus pugnaret.*] (G III/209)

A people, an army, a God. Every people has its Joan of Arc. Every people loves itself ("my country, right or wrong"), because, in the collective imagination, it is exclusively loved by God (*Gott mit uns*). But, through an ambivalence characteristic of all passional life, the principle of external exclusion also becomes the principle of the exclusion of the *internal enemy*. One understands why in chapter 16 Spinoza had postulated *in general*, as a rule constitutive of every state, that

> if anyone has attempted to perform any public function without the knowledge and authority of the supreme council, he has infringed the sovereign's right and committed treason, even though his action . . . was certain to lead to the commonwealth's improvement; and he is rightly condemned.

> [*si quis ergo solo suo arbitrio, et inscio supremoconsilio, negotium aliquod publicum aggressus est exequi, quamvis inde incrementum civitatis . . . certo sequeretur, jus tamen summae potestatis violavit, et majestatem laesit, atque jure merito damnatur.*] (G III/197–98)

Just as the state of war and the state of peace are not separated in time by an impassable divide, neither are "internal security" and "external security" practically separable. From which it follows that respect for laws can be not only sanctioned by a prince but approved and wanted by the multitude itself, for failures are, in the final analysis, likened to the rupture of national unity and to a threat against its mystical *body*. Spinoza then develops his analysis of the fusion of theological and patriotic passions:

> So much for the reasons which kept the captains within due bounds. We must now see how the people was restrained; although the basic principles of the state indicate this most clearly. For even a cursory examination will immediately show that they must have inspired such extraordinary devotion in the minds of the citizens that it would have been almost impossible for any of the latter to think of betraying or deserting his country, and they must all have been ready to suffer death rather than an alien rule. For once they transferred their right to God, and believed that their kingdom was God's kingdom, and that they alone were God's children, the other nations being his enemies, and therefore the object of their implacable hatred . . . nothing could be more abhorrent to them than to swear allegiance and promise obedience to some foreigner. . . . Hence the love of the Hebrew people toward their country was not simply love but piety, and it was so fostered by their daily ritual that it must have become second nature. . . . It therefore amounted to a daily reprobation of them [the Gentiles]; and this must have inspired in the Hebrew people continual and ineradicable hatred, for a hatred which springs from great devotion or piety, and is itself believed to be pious, is undoubtedly greater and more persistent than any other. And the common reason for the continual growth of hatred, that is, the fact that it is returned, was also present; for the Gentiles must have regarded the Hebrew people with the most bitter hatred. How greatly all this — their freedom from human government, their devotion to country, their absolute right against, and hatred for, the Gentiles (a hatred not only permitted but even regarded as pious), the hatred of the Gentiles for them, the uniqueness of their customs and rites — how greatly, I say, all this must have strengthened the minds of the Hebrew people to endure every hardship for their country with remarkable constancy and courage, reason teaches as clearly as possible, and experience itself has testified.
>
> [*Haec de rationibus, quae principes intra suos limites continebant. Videndum iam, qua ratione ratione populus retinebatur; sed hanc etiam imperii fundamenta clarissime indicant: si quis enim ad ea vel leviter attendere velit, videbit statim, haec amorem adeo singularem in civium animis parere debuisse, ut nihil difficilius aliquis in mentem inducere potuerit, quam patriam prodere, vel ab ea prodere; sed contra*

*omnes ita affecti esse debuerint, ut extrema potius quam alienum imperium pater-
entur. Nam, postquam suum ius in Deum transtulerunt, suumque regnum Dei
regnum esse, seque solos filios Dei, reliquas autem nationes Dei hostes esse crediderunt,
in quas propterea odio infensissimo affecti erant . . . nihil magis abhorrere potuerunt,
quam in fidem alicuius extranei jurare, eique obedientiam promittere. . . . Amor
ergo Hebraeorum erga patriam non simplex amor, sed pietas erat, quae simul et
odium in reliquas nationes ita quotidiano cultu fovebantur et alebantur, ut in naturam verti debuerint. . . . Quare ex quotidiana quadam exprobratione continuum
odium oriri debuit, quo nullum firmius animis haerere potuit: utpote odium ex
magna devotione seu pietate ortum, quodque pium credebatur; quo sane nullum
maius nec pertinacius dari potest: nec causa communis deerat, qua odium semper
magis ac magis incenditur, nempe eius reciprocatio; nam nationes eos contra odio
infensissimo haber debuerunt. Quantum autem haec omnia, videlicet humani imperii libertas, erga patriam devotio, in omnes reliquos ius absolutum, et odium non
tantum licitum, sed eitiam pium, omnes infensos habere, morum et rituum singu-
laritas, quantum, inquam, haec Hebraeorum animos firmare valuerint ad omnia
singulari constantia et virtute pro Patria tolerandum, Ratio quam clarissime docet,
et ipsa experientia testata est.]* (G III/214–15)

It is under this theologico-patriotic imaginary of the predestination of a people and
its land that the right of property and the equality of political rights contribute to
the reinforcement of respect for the law, in other words, to the institution of obedience to the state in a lasting way. From the moment that love for one's neighbor is
simultaneously hatred for the stranger (indeed hatred for that which in everyone
could be or could become "foreign"), obedience to the law actually becomes *voluntary*: internalization and externalization, in practice, form only one thing. This is
why I have spoken of *nationalism* and not only of *patriotism*. The idea of patriotism,
in fact (through an obviously self-serving fiction), includes only love for country,
indeed even love for a country thought of as the embodiment of universally human
values and not its necessary correlate: hatred for the foreigner. What constitutes the
characteristic force of Spinoza's explanation (but the discussion also obviously calls
for it!) is the identification *in general* of nationalist passion with a development of
the theological imaginary, and turning it into the internal, necessary impetus of the
duration of states. This is what distinguishes Spinoza from Machiavelli, at the very
moment he is inspired by him or borrows sources from him (Tacitus, Titus Livy) in
order to combine them with his own sources (*Exodus, Deuteronomy*, Paul, Flavius
Josephus). For Machiavelli (at least in the *Discorsi*) finally wants to see in religion
only a particularly effective means in the service of a patriotic *virtù* that is to a certain extent above the passions of love and hate.

It is also what, by the very fact of the radicality of the analysis, was to pose for Spinoza a difficult problem when he was drawing contemporary political conclusions. By discovering in the Hebrew *theocracy*—whose concept he completely refounds—both the primitive force of democracy and the explanation of its contradictions, Spinoza has gone over "to the country of the enemy." That is, he has set about to oppose to his Calvinist adversaries (or rather to the Calvinist adversaries of the political "party" whose friend he is, the party of the liberal regents) not a *counterideology* of the foundations of the state's legitimacy (as Hobbes did, *mutatis mutandis*), but *another analysis* of the very notions on which their ideology rested. In which he illustrates assuredly what is in his foundation a philosophical approach: not the refusal of a partisan position but an investigation of the very conditions of possibility of the partisan position. But this project is not the only one. It is doubled by another, directly strategic, project that the internal analysis of the text also obliges us to consider, although it appears extremely risky (and hardly corresponds to the image of a philosopher whose rule of life had been "prudence"). This second project is one of *detaching*, in its critical circumstances (in which precisely the rulers' national capability was questioned), the Calvinist mass (imbued with "theocratic" conceptions) from its collusion with the monarchist party, in order to rally it in the name of patriotism to the republican camp, on the condition of finding a terrain common to the republic and the mass's religion, which would imply *also* that the republic be reformed in a "democratic" sense.

However, in doing so he could not fail to create a series of frightening theoretical difficulties for himself: How, in fact, to tie together, in a transformed "pact," a civil law that is still *national* and a religious law that is irreversibly *universal*, which is not adapted to the imaginary of any people in particular, which does not state the common law in any national language, and which consequently detaches the narrative of its origins from the election of a people and its land, in order to transfer them onto a universally "human," that is, metaphorical level? The *jus circa sacra* conferred on the state—an institutional solution again taken up from the republican tradition, which Spinoza enriches with an explicit definition of the "dogmas" necessary for the unanimity of the diverse Christian sects or churches— only displaces the difficulty. No doubt this purification eliminates as many foci of internal conflict and regroupment for forces transversal to states, competing for their power. No doubt, by completely internalizing the *voice* that stipulates obedience, it wards off the risk of the *imperium in imperio* or of contestatory prophetism. But, whereas, on the one hand, the state can thus present *itself* as the institutor and interpreter of a civil, that is, national religion; on the other hand, the univeralism of faith is accentuated, that is, a rift is opened between the subject of morality and the subject of patriotic *pietas*. The distinction established between *external cult* (organized by the state) and *internal cult* (attached to every individual's effort to attain knowledge) risks inscribing the latter within a cosmopolitan perspective.

More profoundly, the difficulty is that of the *passional motive* of obedience. For each individual, only a theoretical reasoning demonstrates the necessity of reconciling *fides* toward the state and *charitas* toward all men. Won't the *neighbor* according to Christ and the *citizen* according to the state remain irremediably distinct? What will be for the multitude the *object of hate* without which there is no passionate love (any more than there is hope without fear), if the foreigner must always be considered as a brother in obedience to the divine law and in hope of salvation, that is, if the ritual marks only have a relative meaning?

This difficulty can be connected with those raised by the theoretical role conferred by Spinoza on the schema of three typical forms of the state (hence of the "pact") — *theocracy, monarchy, democracy* — that underlie the whole *TTP*. Theocracy, we have seen, is *already* a form of democracy: this characteristic corresponds to the sacralization of the soil and the election of the *entire* people, who maintain in it the "theological hatred" of foreigners. It is understandable why, by comparison, monarchy represents an alienation and a weakening. With the sacralization of the monarch, one individual's interest is substituted for the interest of all (Spinoza also tells us that defensive wars attempt to transform themselves into wars of conquest), and patriotism is perverted into the desire of sacrifice for the sovereign, which means that the reciprocal love of *cives* and their common hatred of the *hostis* are mediated by love for the sovereign and hatred for *his* enemies. At the limit (the one described in the Preface to the *TTP*), love for country sees its significance inverted: from the imaginary form of self-preservation, it becomes a form of self-hatred. And the monarch who embodies the common passion of individuals can assume the form of their enemy.

What could be, in this regard, the passional regime of an *evolved* democracy? How should one understand the *TTP*'s repeated suggestion that the forms of "theological hatred" observable in the history of the Hebrew state (with its incredible ability to resist external threats) are linked simultaneously to a certain cultural *infantilism* and to a primitive, autarkic economy? There is, it seems, a certain "archaism" in the pure theocratic form. But isn't this archaism always still necessary to the modern state? Astonishingly silent on certain aspects of Dutch national politics (like colonialism), which, however, play a decisive role in it, Spinoza indicates to us that, in a state like the United Provinces, the collective *conatus* does not tend so much to the defense of borders as to universal commerce. The fact is, though, that internal and external circumstances have not made the necessity of national unity disappear. Spinoza nowhere suggests that the nation-form is itself an archaism.

A civil religion coupled with the universal love for one's neighbor does not allow one, in fact, to *name* God as the "king" or protector of a race and a land. It empties the cry of *Gott mit uns* of all affective force. If it is true that a theocracy is *already* in some way a democracy, no doubt such a democracy must always *still* include a "monarchical" element (when circumstances require the unconditional unity of the commandment). Or in other, intentionally provocative, terms: no doubt a *true religion* — in the double sense of the term — must be not only a civil religion but a *civil superstition*. But then the cycle of the historical formations of the imaginary would have to be traversed again, *in the opposite direction.*

These seem to be the difficulties that have definitively determined the *TTP*'s aporia and thus contributed to impelling Spinoza to other paths.

Translated by Ted Stolze

T   E   N

The Theoretical Function of Democracy in Spinoza and Hobbes

Alexandre Matheron

I HAVE no intention of treating the question of democracy in Spinoza and Hobbes in its entirety, for this question is far too vast. Everyone knows, for example, that Hobbes prefers monarchy to democracy, whereas Spinoza prefers democracy to monarchy. It would be easy to show in detail how Spinoza, on this point, takes pains to refute one by one all the arguments advanced by Hobbes. Moreover, Hobbes was inspired to a great extent by Pieter de la Court's refutation in *Political Balance* of Hobbes's arguments. But it is not this aspect of the problem that I will examine. I will be content to presuppose it. The problem I would like to raise concerns, not the judgment made by Hobbes and Spinoza on democracy with respect to its practical advantages or disadvantages, but the theoretical role they eventually make it play in their respective doctrines of the foundations of political legitimacy in general. In other words, to what extent in each of them is the recourse to democracy indispensable in order theoretically to found the other forms of sovereignty? We shall see that, on this subject, Hobbes and Spinoza followed an evolution simultaneously parallel and inverse: parallel regarding the premises and inverse regarding the conclusions.

But in order really to understand the significance of this problematic, a few words about its origin are in order. This origin, in one sense, is prior to the very appearance of the notions of sovereignty and social contract. It is to be sought in a very old principle traditionally admitted as a commonplace: the principle according to which the political community *as such*, as a *collective person*, has the highest conceivable human authority over its own members. Thomas Aquinas, for example, tells us that the consent of the entire multitude has more power, in legislative matters, than the authority of the prince himself, for the prince is authorized to legislate only insofar as he represents the multitude, insofar as he assumes its juridical personality (*in quantum gerit personam multitudinis: Summa theologica*, Ia IIae, Q 97, A3). Of course in Saint Thomas there is neither sovereignty nor a social contract. But when these two notions do appear together, they will be combined with this traditional principle so as to make possible the establishment of the common problematic that Hobbes and Spinoza had to confront.

The one who brought this about most systematically was Grotius. In effect, contrary to what Rousseau will say in book I, chapter 5, of the *Social Contract*, Grotius knows very well that for a people to give itself a king, it must first itself be constituted as a people. What fooled Rousseau is that Grotius treated the question in two different places, and by beginning at the end. But in book II, chapter 5, of *De Jure Belli ac Pacis* Grotius *explains* precisely how a people is constituted. A people is constituted by a contract of association: all the heads of family convene among themselves to form a political society with a view to ensuring civil peace and common defense, and each of them transfers to *the community as such*, for everything concerning this end, the natural right that he had to direct his own actions — it being understood that every decision taken with a majority of voices will be presumed to express the will of the community itself; so that we are, ipso facto, in a democracy. And under these conditions, in accordance with the traditional principle, the people, expressing itself through the voice of its assembly, necessarily has the highest conceivable human authority over its own members, which now means an absolute sovereignty. The people is sovereign, as is every individual in the state of nature. The people's sovereignty is necessarily absolute in its content, since by definition it covers the totality of public affairs, and it is necessarily absolute in its duration, since nothing can put an end to it other than a voluntary decision by the people itself. But the people can decide to transfer to someone else the absolute sovereignty it has over its own members in any way it likes. What one possesses in absolute property one can give to whomever one wants, in whole or part, with or without conditions — and that goes for power as much as for property. Whence the possibility of a contract of submission, all of whose aspects Grotius had already explored in book I, chapter 3. The sovereign people, if it so desires, can unconditionally transfer all of its sovereignty to a king or an aristocratic council, which will then become absolute sovereign without restriction. But the people can also, if it so desires, transfer all of its sovereignty under certain conditions that the king or council will be obligated to respect; in this case the sovereignty of the king or council will be absolute in its content but no longer in its duration, at least if it has been stated that the king or council will lose absolute sovereignty in the event the agreement should be violated. Finally, the people can decide to transfer only a part of the attributes of its sovereignty and retain for itself the remaining part (by reserving for itself, for example, the right to establish taxes), in which case there will no longer be absolute sovereignty in any sense. Therefore, every possibility is open. From the very fact that democratic sovereignty is necessarily absolute, the other forms of sovereignty can be anything at all: everything depends on the clauses of the contract.

We find Hobbes and Spinoza confronted with this problematic. They both admit with Grotius, and for analogous reasons, the necessarily absolute character of democratic sovereignty: Spinoza made no innovation on this point. But the conclusions they draw from it are very different from those drawn by Grotius. Concerning the other forms of sovereignty, they both attempt to reduce all solutions to a single one, either absolutist or antiabsolutist. This reduction can be obtained in two ways: either by denying Grotius's thesis that monarchy and aristocracy derive from democracy or, on the contrary, by maintaining and reinterpreting the same thesis. From which, in principle, three possible positions may be derived, which could be summarized in the following way: (1) Other forms of sovereignty derive from democracy, which consequently necessarily transmits to them its absolute character. (2) Other forms of sovereignty do not derive from democracy but are constituted in precisely the same way, and, consequently, for the same reasons, they are necessarily absolute. (3) Other forms of sovereignty derive from democracy, and, consequently, since they are *only* derivations, they can never be absolute. Logically, there is a fourth conceivable position, but it has not been used. In fact, Hobbes moved from the first position to the second; and Spinoza, by means of a conceptual transposition that constitutes all his originality, moved from the second position to the third.

II

The first position is the one Hobbes takes in *De Cive*. I do not believe that he had adopted it gladly. But he had been *obliged* to adopt it in order to eliminate a difficulty that his theory of the social contract, as it was expounded in this work, did not allow to be resolved rigorously. A difficulty, I should say, which concerns only republics of *institution*. I will leave completely to the side republics of acquisition, which pose no problem.

Concerning republics of institution, then, the mechanism of the social contract argued in chapter 5, sections 6 and 7, is apparently very simple: it is defined solely in terms of a *transfer of right*. Individuals, by an agreement they make with one another, hand over to a single man or a single assembly the right they naturally had to use their own forces as they wished, in order to allow it to ensure civil peace and the common defense. Whence it happens that every sovereignty is necessarily absolute in its content. The end with a view to which we have contracted would be unrealizable if the totality of public affairs did not depend on a single will, and whoever desires the end implicitly desires the means. Thus, every division of sovereignty is excluded. But this implies nothing, and Hobbes will specify in chapter 6, section 13, that we are obligated to obey the sovereign *in all matters*; no theorist of absolutism has ever claimed anything else. On the one hand, then, we have the right to resist the sovereign if he wants to kill us or if he orders us to commit suicide. We have agreed to give him the means to *kill others* but not to kill ourselves or to let us kill, for every agreement of this kind is automatically void and cannot be included within the social contract. And, on the other hand, in a much more general way, we can conceive of an infinity of cases in which our disobedience would not take away from the sovereign any powers with which the social contract obligates us to furnish him. For example, Hobbes says, if the sovereign has condemned my father to death, and if he orders me to execute him; I have the right to refuse, for he will find specialized professionals to do this work anyway. I have agreed to give the sovereign the means to execute all those condemned to death, eventually including my father, but I have acquitted myself of all my obligations on this point by paying my taxes — thanks to which the sovereign can recruit his executioners.

Now here it is that the difficulty really appears. For in Hobbes's view — and this is a crucial point — the sovereign *has all the rights*, even if we are not obligated to respect all his rights. For example, he has the absolute right to have me put to death if I have refused to execute my father, and in doing so he will commit no injustice against me. But, if this is the case, at least in *De Cive*, it is for a *purely negative* reason: it is because the sovereign *is not* a party to the social contract, which has been concluded only among subjects, and consequently has agreed to nothing. Whoever has abandoned no right has all the rights, just as in the state of nature. But why, precisely, is it *logically impossible* for the sovereign to be a party to the social contract? For, finally, when one has rights, one always has the right to abandon them. It is true, of course, that the sovereign cannot make any agreement incompatible with the exercise of sovereignty. For example, if he promised not to raise taxes without the consent of his subjects, his promise would be void, for it would mean that he simultaneously accepted and did not accept sovereignty, and one cannot *want* what is logically contradictory. But would that happen if he made any agreement that would prevent him from exercising his sovereignty *at all*? For example, why couldn't he agree never to have those condemned to death executed by their own sons? Or, in a more general way, why couldn't he agree never to punish those who disobey an order that they are not obligated to obey? This time, it would no longer be contradictory, and, according to the strict logic of chapters 5 and 6 of *De Cive*, the agreement would be valid. Yet the result would be catastrophic. For, if it were so, the authority of the sovereign would indeed remain absolute in its content, but it would cease to be absolute in its duration. If one day he happened to violate his agreement, there would be a rupture of the contract, the subjects could consider themselves free from all their obligations, and we would return to the state of nature, which is what precisely should be avoided. Therefore, it must be admitted that the social contract of *De Cive*, considered by itself, could not constitute a juridical instrument perfectly adequate to the end it was intended to realize, and, consequently, that it was important to complete it by means of something else.

Hobbes provides us with this complement in chapter 7. And he provides us with it precisely by resorting to the hypothesis of an *original democracy*. Every political society of institution, he tells us, is *necessarily* democratic at the beginning. It is not always a matter, of course, of a historical priority, but it is indeed a matter of a logical priority. From the fact alone that individuals are assembled in order to designate together a sovereign, even if this sovereign is finally a king, they have implicitly agreed to submit to the decision of the majority; and consequently, by this fact alone, they have established a democracy, even if it must last only an infinitesimal moment. Yet in the particular case of democracy it is *obvious* that the sovereign cannot be a party to the social contract; for the sovereign is the assembly of the people insofar as it is a *collective person*, which did not exist in the state of nature, and with which, consequently, individuals have not been able to contract. Therefore, the democratic sovereign really *cannot agree to anything*. It is true that, if the assembly of the people next transfers sovereignty to a king or an aristocratic council, this king or council can now declare to make an agreement toward it: toward this assembly alone and not toward each subject taken individually, since it is with the assembly that it contracts. But, as soon as sovereignty has been transferred, the assembly of the people ceases to exist as a collective person. No one can be obligated for anything toward a person who no longer exists. At any rate, the king or council is thus freed from every agreement as soon as it becomes sovereign. But the subjects are obligated to obey it, for they have agreed *with one another* to obey the assembly of the people, which has precisely ordered them to obey the king or the council as itself. And this is how the necessarily original democracy necessarily transmits to other forms of sovereignty its necessarily absolute nature.

But it is true that, from Hobbes's own viewpoint, this solution was hardly satisfactory. One could show (but I am not going to do it!) that it conceals at least ten logical fallacies, almost all of which arise from the fact that the doctrine of the juridical personality is not yet elaborated in *De Cive*. But, at any rate, it is obvious that the *theoretical* privilege accorded to democracy contained something extremely troubling for Hobbes: it was paradoxical to derive the legitimacy of the best form of sovereignty from that of the worst form. And here is, I think, one of the reasons, at least, for the revision Hobbes brought to bear on his theory of the social contract in *Leviathan*.

In chapter 17 of *Leviathan*, in fact, the social contract is no longer defined solely in terms of the transfer of right. It consists first of all and essentially in an *authorization*, which only *implies* a transfer of right. To authorize someone to carry out an action in my name, Hobbes explains in chapter 16, is to recognize this action as my own. It is to assume its full juridical responsibility for the case in which the one I have chosen to represent me would carry it out. This absolutely does not mean that I abandon the right to perform or not to perform this action; quite the contrary, I retain it, and it is *by virtue of my own right* that my representative will act, not by virtue of his own right. To him I *grant the use of my own right*, which for this reason remains mine. The only right I have abandoned is that of refusing to be the author of this action if it is performed. And the social contract is the generalization of this mechanism: subjects gather together (which, as in every convention, has *irreversible* juridical effects) to *authorize all the actions of the sovereign without exception*, provided that he declare or allow it to be understood that they are related to civil peace and common defense (which obviously he will always do). From which Hobbes deduces in chapter 18 that the sovereign, as required, can agree to nothing, but it is no longer at all for the same reason as in *De Cive*, and original democracy no longer has anything to do with it. It is because, if the sovereign has declared to agree not to perform a certain action, and he performs it anyway, this will not be *his own action* but that of each of his subjects. Consequently, he will not himself have violated any convention. He has the right to do everything materially without committing any injustice, because *juridically he does nothing*.

Regarding the transfer of right implied in authorization, the former comes quite simply from the fact that certain (but not all) of our actions bind us. In fact, every time that the sovereign gives me an order, it means that he declares that he is going to take a right away from me in order to have the means to ensure civil peace and the common defense. Therefore, everything happens juridically as if I myself had agreed to abandon this right with a view to this end. Which will have, as chapter 16 had stated, exactly the same effects as a declaration of abandonment of ordinary right, neither more nor less. From which Hobbes can conclude in chapter 21 that authorization binds us neither more nor less than the social contract of *De Cive*. Since one cannot be bound to commit suicide, I retain the right to resist the sovereign if he wants to kill me, although I had authorized him to kill me. Also, since every agreement is void if it has no relationship with the end with a view to which one has agreed to contract, I retain the right to disobey the sovereign if my disobedience does not take away the means of ensuring civil peace and the common defense, although I had authorized him eventually to punish me for it.

In *Leviathan*, then, Hobbes was able to resolve the problem of *De Cive* by eliminating every reference to the hypothesis of an original democracy. From the standpoint of the theory of legitimacy, all forms of sovereignty have exactly the same status: they are all equally absolute, not because they would derive from democracy, but because they are all instituted by the same act of unlimited authorization, which this time is juridically impeccable and thus no longer needs a complement. Simply put, it is *preferable* to institute a monarchy when one can.

III

Starting from here, what is Spinoza's position going to be? Everyone knows, of course, what an immense conceptual transposition he undertook regarding the notion of right. For Spinoza right is quite precisely power, and this should be taken literally. To say that I have the right to perform an action is strictly equivalent to saying that I desire to perform it, that I have the physical and intellectual capacities to perform it, that no external obstacle prevents me from performing it, and that consequently I actually perform it. I will not develop this point, but I will consider it as established. Spinoza uses this new concept of right to reinterpret Hobbes's theory of the social contract and demolish it from within. And I believe that he did so twice. In the *Theologico-Political Treatise*, he translated the social contract of *De Cive* in terms of power, but with results partly analogous to those of *Leviathan*, at least theoretically; and in the *Political Treatise*, he translated the social contract of *Leviathan* in terms of power, but with results partly analogous to those of *De Cive*—analogous, of course, having taken account of this transposition that, in another sense, inverts everything.

In chapter 16 of the *TTP*, then, the social contract is defined exclusively in terms of the transfer of right, as in *De Cive*. This is why Spinoza can also still speak of contract. But *transfer of right* here means *transfer of power*—by means of which there is no longer anything to apply: a group of individuals living in the state of nature decide with a common agreement to transfer to a sovereign all the power that everyone had at his disposal before so as to defend himself individually. In other words, they decide to create once for all, and irreversibly if possible, a new relation of forces that will give to this sovereign an irresistible power. Spinoza, here, considers the example of democracy, but he will state a little later that this is only an example. All the consequences I have deduced from my hypothesis, he will tell us, apply word for word to all other forms of sovereignty without exception.

And these consequences actually allow Spinoza to resolve the problem of *De Cive* quite simply, without any recourse to an original democracy. From the hypothesis stated by Spinoza, in fact, one immediately deduces that any sovereign has agreed to nothing, and that the subjects are obligated to obey him in all things. For if they had wished to make an agreement with him that had obligated him juridically, they would have had to retain for themselves enough force to constrain him to respect it, which they precisely have not wanted to do, since, by hypothesis, they have transferred all their power to him. But, despite the expression *to obey in all things*, the subjects in reality will not have more obligations than in *De Cive* and *Leviathan*. They are not obligated to obey, here and now, what is commanded to them *in fact* here and now; and it is not very likely that any sovereigns give orders that are *too absurd* (that they order, for example, that those condemned to death be executed by their own sons). They are generally not so stupid as to ignore the fact that, if they did so, the country would indeed quickly become ungovernable and that they would thus lose the irresistible power by means of which their sovereignty is defined—which again would make us fall outside of the hypothesis from the start. Spinoza states simply, against Hobbes, that there is *even less* danger to fear in democracy than everywhere else, for it is almost impossible that a great number of men would agree on something absurd. Therefore, in appearance, everything is resolved. From *De Cive*'s theoretical hypothesis of the social contract reinterpreted in terms of power, Spinoza was able to conclude, just as in *Leviathan*, that all the forms of sovereignty are exactly on the same plane regarding their foundation. Democracy is *preferable* because the subjects are freer in it, but it enjoys no theoretical privilege regarding the question of the foundations of legitimacy.

Yet the question is going to come to life again. For the previous conclusions are valuable only *to the extent* that the hypothesis of chapter 16 conforms to reality. Spinoza tells us at the beginning of chapter 17 that this theoretical hypothesis is never *completely* confirmed in practice, although it is always more or less approximately confirmed. It was an *abstract* hypothesis, which neglected the resistances of human nature, just as the theory of falling bodies neglects the resistance of the wind. In reality, no one could ever transfer all his power to someone; in all existing societies, the subjects, in fact, always retain enough force to make their sovereign afraid. Yet we must indeed take into account, in a second moment, what we had first neglected in the first approximation. And under these conditions, the first problem is posed, which Spinoza will treat partially after the *TTP*: what exactly is transferable? And how can that which is transferable be, in practice, irreversibly transferred? But this problem poses another, much more fundamental, problem, about which Spinoza does not say a word in the *TTP*: when all is said and done, *what exactly is a transfer of power?*

Spinoza analyzes this problem in the *Tractatus Politicus*. But the result of this analysis is at first glance rather surprising. In fact, if I transfer my power to another, I obviously fall *under the power* of another. Now, Spinoza tells us in chapter 2, section 10, we fall under another's power in only two kinds of cases: either when he has chained, disarmed, or enclosed us, or else when we *desire* to act according to his desires because he has succeeded in inspiring fear or hope in us. But the first case has no relationship with a transfer, since our will doesn't intervene. In the second case, by contrast, our will does intervene: we voluntarily put our own power at the disposal of another. But, in reality, is it truly here a *transfer*? No, certainly not. For physically our power remains our own. We do not abandon it but retain it, and it is precisely because we retain it that another needs us in order to realize his own ends. By contrast, here we do indeed have something rather analogous to the *authorization* of Leviathan. In *Leviathan*, we have seen, I authorized another to act in my own name by granting him the use of a right that remained mine. He used this right by doing something, and whatever he did, it was I, juridically, who did it. Also, I did not have the right to contest having done it. Now, if we replace *right* with *power*, and *juridically* with *physically*, the following is precisely what happens here: I grant to another the use of a power that remains mine, and he uses it to accomplish something. Whatever he accomplishes, it is I, physically, who do it, and obviously I cannot deny having done it. The only difference with *Leviathan* is that this equivalent of authorization is *never* irrevocable. As soon as I cease to hope or to fear, I cease to put my power at another's disposal, and he can no longer do anything.

But when this equivalent of authorization is given at the same moment by a large number of individuals to the same person, it actually has as a *consequence* a *transfer of power*, just as the authorization of *Leviathan* implied a transfer of right. For it modifies the relations of force. The one who benefits from it, as long as he benefits from it (but no longer), has at his disposal a great enough power to inspire fear and hope in each of the members of the group considered individually, and consequently to decide to grant it again the use of his individual power. Authorization entails a transfer, which itself reproduces authorization, and so on. And this is what the *genetic definition of sovereignty* given to us in chapter 2, section 17, expresses: the right of sovereignty is the right defined not by the power of the sovereign but by the power *of the multitude*. The possessor of sovereignty, if one can say it, is not the sovereign but the multitude itself. The sovereign is only the holder of sovereignty, and he holds it precisely to the extent that the multitude agrees to put it at his disposal. Without it, he could do nothing and would therefore no longer have any right. Everything he does as sovereign is in reality done by the multitude, just as all the actions of the sovereign of *Leviathan* were by right those of his subjects. But, of course, contrary to what happened in Hobbes, this equivalent of authorization is not given *once for all to all* of the sovereign's actions: it is given, at every moment, to each of his particular actions, by the fact alone that most of his subjects agree to cooperate actively or passively with him. And it is precisely for this reason that the *TP* no longer speaks of the social contract. Political society is not created by a contract; it is engendered and reengendered at each moment by a consensus that must be permanently renewed.

Now this interpretation of the social contract of *Leviathan* in terms of power is going to lead Spinoza, without any paradox, to rediscover the thesis of the priority of democracy that was the thesis of *De Cive*. It is even a question, most of the time, of a historical priority: Spinoza says so in chapter 8, section 12. But this very frequent historical priority can itself be explained, much more profoundly, by not only a logical but an *ontological* priority: a little like substance is by nature prior to its affections. Spinoza points this out to us in chapter 7, section 5. No one, he tells us, yields authority to another, whether one wants to or not: the ambition of domination and envy are universally widespread passions. As a result, he adds, the multitude would never transfer sovereignty to a single man or to some number of men if it could itself realize the agreement in its own midst. From which it happens that the existence of every nondemocratic regime is explained by the conjunction of two factors: on the one hand, the power of the multitude, which *desires* to live with a common agreement, which consequently *attempts* to find a terrain of understanding among all its members, which thus *attempts* to organize itself into a democracy; and, on the other hand, external causes that prevent it from directly realizing this tendency and obligate it to satisfy it by diverted paths and by resorting to a mediator. Every political society, then, has two causes: a democratic *conatus* that, all things being equal, would flow onto an institutionalized democracy, and external causes that modify this *conatus* by sometimes giving it nondemocratic affections. Now, since right is identical to fact, every causal explanation is at the same time a *juridical legitimation*. Therefore, as in *De Cive*, the legitimacy of all other forms of sovereignty really derives from the legitimacy of democracy.

But the difference with *De Cive* is that these other forms of sovereignty can *never* be absolute. In *De Cive*, in fact, the original democracy was a *transitive* cause of other regimes. It disappeared right after having produced its effect, by transmitting to it the totality of its characteristics. Whereas, on the contrary, in the *TP*, it is a question of an *immanent* cause. The origin is always there, for the democratic *conatus* always functions; if it didn't, there would no longer be a state. Whence it happens that in every nondemocratic regime sovereignty is necessarily divided (in fact, and therefore by right) between its possessor and its holder. It is not a question, of course, of a vertical division. Implementing every attribute of sovereignty depends simultaneously, in each particular case, on the sovereign's decision and on the multitude's active or passive acceptance. This is obvious in a monarchy: kings are always naked, as chapter 6, section 5, forcefully explains. But aristocracy, too, as chapter 8, section 4, explains, must take account of popular pressure, even if the latter is expressed informally. Aristocracy is *nearest* the absolute, but it does not reach it, for in aristocracy possessor and holder coincide. Every particular form of sovereignty can be defined as being the power of the multitude *insofar* as it is held by someone: "insofar as it is the power of the multitude" (*potentia multitudinis quatenus*). But the only absolute sovereignty is the "power of the multitude insofar as it is held by the multitude itself" (*potentia multitudinis quatenus a multitudine ipsa tenetur*).

Translated by Ted Stolze

E L E V E N

Reliqua Desiderantur:
A Conjecture for a Definition of
the Concept of Democracy
in the Final Spinoza

Antonio Negri

AS IS well known, Spinoza's death abruptly interrupts the *Tractatus Politicus* at paragraph 4 of chapter 11, at the very moment he begins to reflect on democracy. In paragraph 1 Spinoza considers the concept of democracy and how it differs from the concept of aristocratic government; in paragraphs 2 and 3 he defines the conditions of participation in democratic government by rigorously emphasizing the characteristics of its legality; in paragraph 4 he finally begins to deepen the rules of exclusion. That is all. The incompleteness of the development is such that one can hardly speak of a sketch or a vigorous introductory outline. At the same time, it remains the case that in these few pages we witness the emergence of at least two strong concepts: the definition of democracy as *omnino absolutum imperium* at the beginning of paragraph 1 and, in paragraphs 2 and 3, the rigorous legalism of a positivist construction of the conditions of democratic participation. Thus, between the incompleteness of the text and the force of the concepts that nonetheless emerge, a great tension is objectively expressed, and from now on a certain disquiet of the reader seems inevitable. Sharing this disquiet, I would therefore like to deepen the research in order to try to understand how the concept of democracy could have been expressed in the *TP*.

Toward this end we can travel two paths. The first consists of seeking in Spinoza's other works, in particular in the *Tractatus Theologico-Politicus*, the definition of the concept of democracy. On the other hand, concerning the definition of the concept of democracy, one could regard any reference to the *TTP* as irrelevent, especially if one thinks—as I believe I have shown in my *Savage Anomaly*—that in the development of Spinoza's thought, the *TP* represents a philosophical project that is more mature or has a completely different nature.[1] The second path consists, then, in freely thinking about the concept of democracy in light of the dynamic of Spinoza's metaphysics.

Could the metaphysical hypothesis be proven more correct than philological repetition? Perhaps. In any case, and not only relative to this passage (but almost always when one travels the paths of the metaphysical tradition), it is legitimate to suppose that historicity is given here only as the always different emergence and diffusion of moments of conceptual innovation, of rupture with dominant ideologies, of transformative differences, inside the constructive project, and of the power of the rational structure. The work's vitality perhaps allows for this constitutive hermeneutic.

Most interpreters have followed what I would call the first path. This reading considers the last four paragraphs of the *TP* as a simple reference to what the *TTP* says about democracy. It matters little that the *TTP* speaks about the democracy of the Jews rather than about democracy *tout court*. Better: in this way certain difficulties of Spinoza's reading can be resolved, in particular those posed in the first four paragraphs of chapter 11 through the interconnection between the affirmation of the absoluteness of the concept of democracy and the positivist demonstration that immediately follows. On the horizon of the demystification of sacred history that the *TTP* represents, democracy can in fact be read as a progressive ethico-political concept, all the denser in morality as, by suppressing the transcendence of the foundation, the critique highlights such a reversed trace, the presence of a very ancient vocation and an always renewed human project. The absoluteness of the concept of democratic government is thus gradually deployed and finds its ethical justification. Moreover, on this dense horizon, the legalism can in turn be regarded as a legitimate consequence, a progressive and positive accumulation of rules of consent, participation, and exclusion. It is in this direction that a second generation of Spinoza's interpreters seems to me to proceed,[2] just as attentive to the sacred dimension of the secular concept of democracy and to its humanist secularization as the first generation of political interpreters in the nineteenth century was sensitive to the liberal and positive dimension of this concept.[3] The Straussian interpretation mediates between the first and the second generation of interpreters.[4]

Yet there exists a series of general reasons that prevent one from following the first path. The *TTP* and the *TP*, in fact, take part in two different phases of Spinoza's thought. Whereas the *TP* is a kind of constitutive project of the real, the *TTP* represents an intermediary and critical stage in the development of Spinoza's metaphysics. Be that as it may, I do not want to insist too strongly on this difference, so that I can also avoid once again being criticized for building a kind of Chinese wall between them. However, not to regard the solution of continuity as radical does not mean to forget that it exists.[5] We will therefore privilege another series of considerations. From this point of view, the impossibility of giving to the concept of democracy in the *TP* a definition drawn from the *TTP* results from a series of data like, for example, the different description in the two treatises of the forms of state, figures of government, their different evaluation — but above all from the disappearance in the *TP* of any reference to the contractarian horizon. If one wants to formulate some hypotheses regarding the concept of democracy in the *TP*, and the way in which it could have been developed, it seems to me that one would have to consider not the similarities but the differences between the two treatises. But since some other authors have largely and definitively addressed these questions,[6] I would especially like to insist at the beginning on the difference in conceptual and semantic horizon that the disappearance of the contractarian theme determines in the *TP* in order to understand the significance of this absence. It is clear that by proceeding in this way it is a matter of accumulating elements that enable one to verify if, at the level of the *TP*'s problematic, it would be possible to give an original definition of the concept of democracy that would be simultaneously historically determined, conceptually complete, and metaphysically structured.

The fact that the contractarian theme is present in the *TTP* does not constitute a problem. On the other hand, the fact that the contractarian theme is not present in the *TP* does pose a problem. I mean that in the seventeenth century social contract theory was so widespread that its affirmation imposes itself as an evidence, its rejection, on the contrary, less so.[7] Thus, we can pose two questions at the outset. First, what does the contractarian theme mean in the seventeenth century; better, what are the general meanings, the fundamental variations, the ideological tensions it offers? Second, within the framework of natural rights theory and classical political theory, who rejects the contractarian problematic and why, or who assumes it under a weakened form or who exhausts it in utilizing it? In short, what classes of meaning does the acceptance or rejection of the contractarian problematic imply?

The response to these questions is not simple. In fact, an ideological problematic of the complexity and extent of the contractarian problematic was lived according to different modalities, and only a profoundly reductive vision could envisage a unilateral development. Yet it is possible to point out certain major functions assumed by this theory in the seventeenth century. In this regard it is fundamental to recognize that contractarian theory is not sociological in nature, unless in a way that is marginal and open to innovations or to the subversion of the paradigm. But contractarian theory is instead immediately juridical: this means that its function is not to explain human association and the constitution of political society but to legitimize the constitution of political society and the transfer of power from civil society to the state. Social contract theory is an explicit sociological fiction that legitimizes the actual nature of power and thus provides the basis for the juridical concept of the state.[8]

Two remarks are in order. First, social contract theory has a character that is certainly transcendental (in other words, it is applicable to every state), but it is formally limited. This means, second, that among the meanings attributable in this age to the notion of the state, the monarchical concept, that is, the concept of the unity, absoluteness, and transcendence of the title of power (and often equally of the exercise of power, but without a univocal relation) is fundamental (hegemonic and exclusive of others). I say the monarchical concept in opposition to the republican concept in order to emphasize the transcendence of power against every constitutive, dynamic, participatory conception. Variants are formed on this basis. The monarchical concept is, in fact, the concept of the state's substance. Therefore, it cannot be a concept of the form of government. From then on the theory of contractarian transfer and that of the formation of sovereignty by means of a transfer contain the possibility of developing different figures of the form of government. Then there can exist, so to speak, a monarchical monarchy, an aristocratic monarchy, and even a democratic monarchy: it is in this sense that a century later Rousseau can lead social contract theory to its fulfillment.[9] In addition to having a function of juridical legitimation that I would call foundational and formal, social contract theory has, then, a historically and conceptually specific determination; it is substantially predisposed to the legitimation of the different forms of government in which the absolutist state of modernity is represented.[10]

What we have just said is confirmed negatively by the response to the second question we posed: what are the political currents and currents of ideas that ignore or are opposed or that in any event do not accept these specific functions of social contract theory? It seems to us that we can pinpoint essentially two of these currents in Spinoza's universe: those tied to the tradition of republican radicalism of the culture of humanism and the Renaissance, and the one originating from the democratic radicalism of Protestantism, mainly Calvinist Protestantism. On the one hand, Machiavelli; on the other hand, Althusius. But if Machiavelli's position is no doubt more radical, the Althusian acceptance of the contract is explicitly dedicated to the denunciation of every idea of alienation of power, and the contract cannot be dissolved by the association of subjects: the subject of the sovereignty is "the total people associated in one symbiotic body from many smaller associations" (*populus universus in corpus unum symbioticum ex pluribus minoribus consociationibus consociatus*).[11] In these two cases, in short, we witness the triumph of an idea of politics that, without formally excluding the idea of a transfer of power, subordinates it to the material determinations of the social, of practices, of the multiplicity and specificity of powers.[12] Note that the political realism present in these traditions has nothing to do with those theories of the relativism of values that in this same period constitute and dominate political science. In Machiavelli and Althusius, beyond the considerable diversity of the cultural universes in which they participate (and in Spinoza himself, when in the first pages of the *TP* he banters with the political philosophy of his time), political realism is not at all a relativism of values but a resolute adherence to the truth of the concrete: it is not the definition of a social negative that only an absolute power can discern by giving it a meaning, but a theory of the truth of action, of the absoluteness of its horizon. Machiavelli and Althusius have little in common with the juridical subtleties of contractarianism, or with the cynicism of the "politicians" that is the latter's condition and complementary theoretical figure.[13] When Althusius and Machiavelli finally meet in the Levellers or in Harrington's thought, they express, on the other hand, the luminous power of a positive conception of being, the strong republican conviction of the originally human character of institutions and the perfectability of society—in short, they express a frank republican materialism.[14] This is also the case with Spinoza.

In conclusion, we can say, then, that social contract theory is in general a theory of the absolutist state, whereas the rejection of the theory, or its usage in terms excluding the idea of a transfer of power, represents republican traditions that are polemical vis-à-vis every representative ideology and every statist practice of alienation. To the statist absolutism affirmed by social contract theories, as a consequence of the relativity of social values that preexist their normative self-determination by the state, is opposed, in the realist positions that reject the theory of normative transfer, a conception that proposes the social as absoluteness. The same metaphysical absoluteness that is characteristic of the horizon of truth. At the horizon of this truth, the truth of fact, the truth of action.

Yet the social contract is present in the *TTP*. However, this does not mean that its presence is important to the point of determining specific developments of Spinoza's political theory, or that it forces the latter into the generic framework of the political philosophy of the period. The presence of social contract theory in the *TTP* (in certain respects it is almost not noticed, not conscious of possible effects, dependent on the hegemonic currents of the century) limits, though, the possibilities of a radically innovative orientation.[15] In the *TP*, on the other hand, to the absence of a contract theory corresponds a complete freedom of theoretico-political development. By this we mean that the affirmation according to which right and politics immediately participate in the power of the absolute is essential in the *TP*. Right and politics have nothing to do with the negative and dialectical essence of contractarianism; their absoluteness testifies to and participates in the truth of action:

> Now from the fact that the power of things in Nature to exist and operate is really the power of God, we can easily see what the right of nature is. For since God has the right to do everything, and God's right is simply God's power conceived as completely free, it follows that each thing in Nature has as much right from Nature as it has power to exist and operate; since the power by which it exists and operates is nothing but the completely free power of God. (*TP* II/3)

To ask ourselves what can be the *democraticum imperium* in the *TP*, beyond the limits of the contractarian horizon, will mean, then, not to substitute the lack of indication by the materials treated in the *TTP* but, on the contrary, to proceed by conjectures by deepening the study of the extent to which Spinoza belongs to the republican tradition.

It is thus in the absence of every version of contract theory that Spinoza in the *TP* speaks of democracy as the absolute form of state and government. Yet outside of contractarian theory, how can a philosophy of freedom be embodied in an absolute form of government; or, on the contrary, how can an absolute form of power be compatible with a philosophy of freedom—better, with the very concept of republican democracy? From this standpoint it seems that by rejecting the contractarian problematic Spinoza must confront a certain number of difficulties.

We have seen how the contractarian theme is tied to a certain conception of the state that Spinoza rejects. However, it is not in the expression of the rejection and the protestation that Spinoza's difficulties arise — rejection and protestation are the echo of the imaginative force and the republican ethical flavor as well as an implicit threat: "without freedom there is no peace." The difficulties appear instead at the propositional stage, when one rejects, as Spinoza does, this specific passage of the alienation of freedom generally required by the contractarian conception: an alienation that, although it constitutes sovereignty by means of a transfer, restores to subjects a freedom or a series of rights that have been transformed from natural rights into juridical rights (in the transfer and by sovereignty). But without this movement, how can absoluteness and freedom be made compatible? Better: how can freedom be elevated (from below, without transfer) to absoluteness? The maintenance of natural freedom, contractarians explain, is only possible whenever it is relativized and redefined juridically. The absoluteness of freedom, of freedoms, is otherwise chaos and a state of war. If democracy, according to Spinoza, is an organization constitutive of absoluteness, how can it simultaneously be a regime of freedom? How can freedom become a political regime without renouncing its own naturalness?

In order to respond to these questions and know if it is possible to escape these difficulties, first we have to clarify the concept of absoluteness, as an attribute of democracy. What does the determination *omnino absolutum* mean insofar as it is an attribute of the *democraticum imperium*? The responses concern at least two levels: the first is directly metaphysical; the second is the one on which the concept of absoluteness is confronted with the usage that Spinoza makes of the term in political theory, thereby distinguishing it from other usages, and in particular from those that refer to contractarian theory.

From the perspective of general metaphysics, Spinoza's concept of the absolute can be conceived only as a general horizon of power, as the latter's development and actuality. The absolute is constitution, a reality formed by a constitutive tension, a reality all the more complex and open as the power that constitutes it increases:

> If two men unite and join forces, then together they have more power, and consequently more right against other things in nature, than either alone; and the more there be that unite in this way, the more right will they collectively possess. (*TP* II/13)

We are thus at the heart of Spinoza's metaphysical conception — the logically open determination of the fundamental ontology constitutes its essential determination. "Absolute" and "power" are tautological terms. Power, as an open determination, in movement toward this absolute that, on the other hand, it actually constitutes, is already presented in the *TTP* beyond the biblical legend as a history of the Jewish people. In the recognition of the development of this human power, one notes the fundamental passage of Spinoza's thought, from the first to the second foundation of the system.[16] This human power next appears in the first chapters of the *TP* as the basis of collective existence, of its movements — in other words, of society and culture. The absolute, then, has power as its very essence and becomes existence by virtue of the realization of power. This is the definition of the absolute from the metaphysical point of view. But in the framework of this problematic it seems superfluous to insist on the implications of the definition: it is enough to recall, always in very general terms, that if the concept of absoluteness is reduced to that of power, it is obviously reduced to that of freedom. The terms "power" and "freedom" are superimposed onto one another, but the extension of the first is equivalent to the intensity of the other. Always in very general terms.

These considerations become extremely useful from the moment that we consider the term "absoluteness" according to the specificity of Spinoza's political thought. From this perspective the *absolutum imperium*, in fact, will become a term that, by signifying the unity of power, will come to assume it as the projection of the *potentiae* of subjects and to define its totality as life, always open, internal, as the dynamic articulation of an organic totality. Let us consider, then, this *absolutum imperium* that Spinozan democracy constitutes, from the perspective of a series of political problems as much traditional as characteristic of the science of his time. We shall see with what originality this definition is inscribed in the problematic context cited and how much it manages, within its own movement, to redefine adequately the problem of freedom.

The first point of view is that of the *absolutum imperium* from the perspective of the legitimacy of power: the themes *titulum* and *exercitum*. It is under these two categories that the legitimacy of power is traditionally defined, and it is in relationship to these two categories that legitimacy can be evaluated, in its extension, in its articulations, in its forms of existence — legitimacy and legality, but also their contrary, namely, illegitimacy and tyranny. Yet the absoluteness of democratic government in Spinoza is so strong and so real that it does not permit this distinction. On the other hand, it is extremely equivocal, for it is based not only on the determinations of freedom but on the form of its state organization. Generally, the exercise of power in Spinoza is closely associated with its tenure. Therefore, it is not possible to offer distinctions or articulations of this relationship. Democracy is in particular the absolute form of government because tenure and exercise are

originally associated with it. The power of being thus manifests itself in all its uni-
fying force. In a modern language, we would say that such an absolute conception
of democratic power realizes the unity of the formal legality and material efficacy of
juridical organization and demonstrates its autonomous productive force.[17]

The second point of view is that of the *absolutum imperium* in
the causuistic tradition of the forms of power. A certain ancient and classical tradition, as we know, presents each form of government under two figures, one positive, the other negative. The absoluteness of Spinoza's definition of democracy denies this possibility. Not that Spinoza does not envisage the possibility of a corruption
of each form of government, and in particular of democracy: but the process of corruption is not separable from the unity of the life of a form of government; it is not
the product of an alterity. It is, on the contrary, the life or rather the death of the
same organism. For example, in *TP* II/1 Spinoza considers the Roman institution of
dictatorship, which, arising as a function of the stabilization of the republic, has a
tendency to develop into an independent figure. The development of dictatorship is
an abstract and dangerous tendency. To the extent that dictatorship tends toward
absoluteness, it not only manages to restore the republic but also fixes conditions
that are antagonistic to the absolute power of the democratic demand and thus establishes a state of war. On the contrary, the administration of a state of emergency
and the need of renewal must be conceived within the framework of the conditions
of normal life of the republican absolute. The power of the absolute form of government in this case can transform the possible state of war into a movement of organic refoundation and then restore vigor to the state. Just as by reconsidering the
problematic of *titulum/exercitium*, the figure of the absoluteness of the state is given
to us simultaneously, here before this dynamic of development, of corruption and
refoundation, so too the power of the absolute form of government is given to us in
a diachronic schema that is dynamic and temporally constitutive: "It is clear then
that the condition of this kind of state [the aristocratic] will be best if it is organized
so as to approach most closely to the absolute" (*TP* VIII/5).

The third point of view is that of the *absolutum imperium* from
the internal perspective of the administration of the state, or again the concept of
magistracy and the magistrate. Here absoluteness also derives directly from the definition of the state. This means that Spinozan democracy, whatever the forms of organization of responsibilities and controls and the functions in which it is represented, can in no way be defined as a constitutional democracy, that is, as a form of
government founded on the division and equilibrium of powers and on their reciprocal dialectic. In Spinoza the conception of the magistrate and the magistracy, on

the contrary, is absolutely unitary. Certain functions of control and equilibrium are not excluded, but they do not derive from a constitutional situation of fragmented or dialectical power. These functions, on the other hand, can be figures of expression of constitutive power, fragments or versions of the unitary tension of the system. Inside the latter, just as each subject is a citizen, so too is each citizen a magistrate — but the magistracy is the moment of revelation of the highest potential of unity and freedom.[18]

We could continue by showing many other points of view from which the Spinozan absoluteness conceptually and actually includes the concept of power and its functions. But we would not add much to what we have already said. Whatever the point of view, the same experience is repeated. Absoluteness is the power that develops and maintains itself, unitarily, productively. Democracy is the highest form of expression of society. For it is the most expansive form in which natural society is expressed as political society: "For absolute sovereignty, if any such thing exists, is really the sovereignty held by the entire multitude" (*TP* VIII/3). Yet in such a full dimension, by traversing the *multitudo* of subjects, democracy becomes absoluteness, for it puts all social powers into motion from below, and from the equality of a natural condition. Democracy as an *omnino absoluta* form of government means, then, that there is no alienation of power — neither in relation to its exercise, nor in relation to its formation or the specificity of executive action, that is, the specificity of the figure of magistracy. The absolute is nonalienation, better, it is, positively, the liberation of all social energies in a general *conatus* of the organization of the freedom of all. Continual, permanent. Every political formation knows such mechanisms as organizational phases, functions of control, and representative mediations. But from the perspective of absoluteness these mechanisms do not form dialectical interruptions; they no longer organize passages of alienation. Power, however, develops on an open horizon, and these mechanisms participate in articulations of this horizon. This is a collective action that reveals the nature of power and defines the relationship between natural society and political society.

However, we have not yet responded to the question about the compatibility between absoluteness and freedom. Aren't we in the presence of a totalitarian utopia? Doesn't the refusal of the contract wind up producing purely and simply an absolutist projection of freedom in completely developed power in such a way that every distinction and determination vanishes? I do not think that this objection can be formulated yet. It remains true that until now the response has only been sketched and that it necessitates a supplementary path. In other words, after having shown the characteristics of absoluteness and how the only possible foundation of value is consolidated in it, without being able to escape it, after having shown the impossibility of every alienation and how servitude arises from alienation, Spinoza's discourse traverses a second foundational passage. This discourse poses, in other words, the problem of the subject of this collective action that constitutes democratic absoluteness. Now this subject is the *multitudo*. It is therefore around the theme of the *multitudo* that the problem of the relationship between freedom and absoluteness should be reconsidered.

In 1802, during the same period in which he was preoccupied with Spinoza, and more particularly with his political thought, Hegel wrote a *System der Sittlichkeit*.[19] In this system the idea of "absolute government" is developed as an exaltation of the internal unity of power. This movement provokes certain effects contrary to those we have observed in Spinoza: the refusal of alienation in Spinoza is absolute. In Hegel, though, every recognition of the singularity of needs and of subjects is absorbed into the metaphysics of the absolute across an exemplary development of dialectical movement. The absolute is given, as a result, as *jouissance*. Consequently, Hegel ceaselessly repeats, absolute government is beyond singularities; it must reject their negative determinations. Otherwise, the *absolutum imperium* would dissolve into the vulgarity and ignorance of the mass, and to the transcendental unity of subjects would be opposed a mere "heap" of individuals. Absolute government is thus the idea of an absolute movement that becomes absolute tranquility, absolute identity of the living, absolute power that surpasses every singular power. Absolute government is infinite and indivisible totality. The transfer to the alienated generic that in contractarianism was the result of the transcendence of the negativity of the social process is here the presupposition of social movement. It is not by chance that monarchy is the form of absolute government.

This course does not concern Spinoza. The relationship between power and the absolute in the *TP* is expressed according to two movements. Certainly, as we have seen, one movement pushes with great force toward absoluteness in the strict sense, toward the unity and indivisibility of government, toward its representation as one soul and one mind:

> The first point to be considered is this. Just as in the state of nature the man who is guided by reason is most powerful and most fully possessed of his own right...so also the commonwealth which is based on and directed by reason will be most powerful and most fully possessed of its own right. For the right of a commonwealth is determined by the power of the multitude guided as if by one mind. (*TP* III/7)

But the other movement of power is plural; it is the reflection on the powers of the *multitudo*. The life of absolute government is endowed in Spinoza with a systole and diastole, with a movement toward unity and a movement of expansion.

Spinoza specifies, after having followed the path of unity, that if absoluteness is not confronted with the singularity of real powers, it closes back onto itself. It is only from this closure, by traversing and being marked by its substance, it is only by seeking in this interrupted flow a normative source, that it will be possible to rediscover social subjects. Its effects will be disastrous: the latter will no longer be citizens but subjects. Thus it is for Hegel and all authors who accept, whatever the philosophical figure proposed, the idea of transfer and alienation as the foundation of sovereignty. From this point of view the refinement of the dialectical passage, in relation to substance, is not something very different from the vulgar fiction of the theory of contractarian transfer. In these two cases we find ourselves before the mystery of the transfer — mysterious because one does not communicate across it but ideally transforms the fact of association, which is presented as a normative source and as the basis of a hierarchical organization — as the surreptitious foundation of science. The union of the one and the multiple, of totality and the infinite, of the absolute and the multitude is given as a synthesis, as presupposed. (No, the Hegelian course does not concern Spinoza, and paradoxically, at the very moment that he recuperates Spinoza's terminology, Hegel is more "Spinozist" than Spinozan — and why not? He is also a little "acosmic.")[20] In fact, here the very idea (and practice) of the market emerges as a hegemonic idea. By traversing contract theory or dialectical theory, during different phases, the idea of the market is close to the idea of the state. In these two cases the productive cooperation of subjects and their reciprocal vital association are mystified into an organization of value, of the norm, of command; and human association is thus subordinated to the capitalist function of exploitation.[21]

In Spinoza all this is denied in principle. Just as the metaphysical relationship between totality and infinity is submitted to analyses and is ceaselessly reformulated as a problem, just as the relationship between unity and multiplicity in physics is conceived and developed on an open horizon, a horizon of confrontation, of wars, of violent associations — so too, in politics, the relationship between absoluteness and *multitudo* is posed in extreme terms, which are paradoxical but no less decisive for that: it is an open relationship. We shall see that it is a relationship of hope and love: "The good which everyone who seeks virtue wants for himself, he also desires for other men; and this desire is greater as his knowledge of God is greater" (*E* IVP37). In the *TTP* the term *multitudo* appears only six times and has not yet acquired a political dimension: it is a sociological, nonpolitical concept.[22] At any rate, it does not constitute a political subject. Here, in fact, its problematic is less important, for the concept of democracy, the *praestantia* (*TTP* XVII/Title) of which enthralls, lives on a displaced, perhaps even degraded, terrain in relation to the political clarity of the *TP* and the theme of absoluteness. In the first treatise the democracy of the *multitudo* is a kind of original essence. It declines, develops, disappears, is degraded in the history of the Jews, and it is articulated with theocracy, but in substance it remains as a model, as a political prototype, as a fundamental regime. The contractarian definition accentuates the static dimension of the model. Moreover, in the *TTP* Spinoza does not speak about forms of government other than democracy (*TTP* XVI), except incidentally; and so he does not need to distinguish the figure of political subjects. In the *TP*, on the other hand, the point of view is completely different: it is a constitutive, dynamic, democratic point of view. Here the *multitudo* constitutes above all the limit toward which political reason tends — from the solitude of the monarch to aristocratic selection to democratic absoluteness — a limit that is given precisely insofar as power is adapted to the power of the *multitudo*. *Omnino absolutum* is the power that is adapted to the *multitudo* — At the risk of employing a pleonastic turn of phrase, we could say to "all" of the *multitudo*, which thus becomes subject, an elusive subject, as can be every indefinite but ontologically necessary concept.

The critics who have attacked the concept of the *multitudo* as subject and as the central metaphysical attribution of Spinoza's doctrine of the state have correctly insisted on the concept's elusive nature. On the other hand, no doubt apologists for the *multitudo* have sometimes exaggerated by considering it almost as an essence or as a schema of reason.[23] But the material elusiveness of the subject-*multitudo* does not prevent effects of subjectivity from being expressed in Spinoza. Thus, the *multitudinis potentia* founds the *imperium* or preserves it through the direct creation of right (*TP* II/27). And the totality of civil right, in the expression of which arises the state's constitution, is produced and legitimized by the *multitudo* (*TP* II/23) — and so forth (*TP* III/9, 18, etc.).

Even if it is elusive, the *multitudo* is thus a juridical subject, a necessary attribution of the social, a hypothesis of unity and political construction (*TP* III/7). But at the same time the *multitudo* remains an elusive totality of singularities. Such is the crucial paradox — the one formed between the physical, multiple, elusive nature of the *multitudo* and its subjective, juridical nature that creates civil right and constitution. This relationship is unsolvable. One observes here the radical impossibility of taking this image of the *multitudo*, and the juridical effects it implies, in the direction of Rousseau's general will (Spinoza carries out this demonstration in *TP* IV and V.)[24] No, the relationship between the absolute and the *multitudo*, between the two versions of power is not concluded: the one concentrates the unity of politics, the other spreads out toward the multiplicity of subjects.

The concept of the *multitudo* logically concludes Spinoza's politics to the extent that it brings to an end neither its dynamic nor its idea. In other words, it shows in conclusion the absolute of Spinoza's politics as opening, as the incapacity of slowing down or mystifying the process of the real. Spinoza's politics participates in a genuine Copernican revolution: the infinite is the *multitudo*, a continuous movement is its power—an infinite movement that constitutes a totality but is identified in it only as the actuality of a passage; it is not closed but opened; it produces and reproduces. The opposite of a Ptolemaic and theological conception, according to which a principle (necessarily an alienation) is supposedly in a position to unify the world. It is thus the opposite of the Hegelian conception of the relationship conceived as a resolved relationship between totality and infinity. It is precisely on the noncompletion of this relationship, such as it is posed by Spinoza, against every theology and against every idealism, that the politics of the *TP* is a genuine disutopia, a Machiavellian hypothesis of freedom, a radically democratic proposition of the subversion of the social. Every value, every choice, every political act must be deployed on the basis of the incomplete relationship between the absoluteness of power and the multiplicity of propositions, needs, and experiences. The rational tendency lives between the folds and in the complexity of this necessary incompleteness, but it lives in it fully. An extraordinary optimism of reason dominates the scene. This philosophy of Spinoza in the *TP* is already the philosophy of the Enlightenment; it is the philosophy of Voltaire and Diderot in a highly metaphysical form.

But alongside this extreme tension of the rational tendency and its optimistic orientation, there is the pessimism of the consideration of the concrete—not a preconceived pessimism but a realist conception of the always different and always variable effects of the will and its relationship to the real. The circle does not close again: such is politics—continuous confrontation of an absoluteness that reason requires and of an irresolute multiplicity that experience obliges us to consider. Optimism of reason and pessimism of the will.

In the *Ethics* the term *multitudo* appears only once, in VP20S: "*in multitudine causarum*" The term is therefore detached from any direct reference to political thought, and yet it arises within the framework of a demonstration that can be linked to political thought: the demonstration of the power of the mind over the affects in the construction of the intellectual love of God, a demonstration that this power is all the stronger as the number of individuals that we imagine engaged in this process is increased. Beyond the pure semantic reference — "the multitude of causes" — the appearance of the term *multitudo* is thus not insignificant. Rather, it indicates a typical movement of Spinoza's thought: in this infinite context of fluctuations and affections, what arises for the mind is the necessity of governing them, of organizing them from the perspectives of power; and finally, wherever we think we have identified the development of an ascetic tension, there is on the contrary the construction of a collective horizon. This theoretical movement, which ensures that the spiritual tension extends to the collective, is essential and produces effects of displacement that are extremely characteristic (and seldom emphasized) in Spinoza's philosophy.[25] Anyway, what is important to emphasize here is how this oscillation, this contradictory dimension, this paradox are typical of the concept of the *multitudo*. Let us try to develop more on this question.

The concept of the *multitudo* is first of all a physical power. Considering its very definition, it is situated in the physical context of the *Ethics*, and especially on that knot between parts II and III, at which we have tried (elsewhere) to identify the central moment of the "second foundation" of Spinoza's metaphysics.[26] In this context, the horizon on which the concept of the *multitudo* is formed and presented is therefore very specific. A horizon of bare corporeality and savage multiplicity. A world of physical interconnections and combinations, of associations and dissociations, fluctuations and concretizations, according to a completely horizontal logic, constituting the paradoxical intersection of causal and fortuitous dimensions, between tendency and possibility: here is the original dimension of the *multitudo*. It is clear that this physical horizon cannot support any mediation whatsoever. To its force alone is entrusted the possibility/capacity of refining the level of associations, of developing the multiplier of intersections of the composition, of attaining always higher degrees of complexity. Social consistency (and therefore the consistency of political combinations) is entirely internal to this continuity; better, it is the result of the physical dynamic of the world.[27] The sociopolitical concept of the *multitudo* therefore contains in filigree the entire series of these movements, of these previous progressive constructions. It suffices to recall that, in order to understand how the artificial dimension of the contractarian proposition is disjointed in the face of the inexhaustible material dimension of the social flow — in Spinoza's social physics the contractarian thematic can only result as completely incidental.[28]

A simple deduction can now lead us to other considerations. If what we have said is true, the tendency of Spinoza's political philosophy — which consists in running throughout the flow of the multitude and establishing in this flow a series of increasingly complex distinctions, up to those that concern the forms of government—becomes a very violent confrontation. We mean that each rupture of the flow and every establishment of a rigid form is an act of violence in relation to the tendencies of Spinoza's physics. However, this horizon of contradiction and these theoretical movements of displacement are productive. Here, in fact, we can summarize another series of the elements that are typical of Spinoza's conception of the *multitudo*; after having considered it as a physical power, we can consider it henceforth as a natural, better, an animal power. What it represents is the reign of fear, of violence, of war—but these are, in fact, only passions, these acts and these situations that can permit us to follow the entire progression of the movement of the *multitudo*. A movement never pacified, always open:

> For the human body is composed of a great many parts of different natures, which constantly require new and varied nourishment, so that the whole body may be equally capable of all the things which can follow from its nature, and hence, so that the mind may also be equally capable of understanding many things at once. (*E* IVP45Sch)

And even if we admit that by passing from the simple *conatus* to the *cupiditas*, from the physical realm to the animal realm, to the border of dislocation, a certain corrective to dispersion is introduced,[29] nonetheless it seems to us to be extremely difficult to grasp the possibility of leading these mechanisms and processes, which are simultaneously contradictory and complex, to an internal unity. The result again, in particular, is the difficulty of defining the concept of the *multitudo* as a political subject. So that it seems that the *multitudo* can be a political subject only as an idea of reason or as a product of the imagination.[30] By contrast, concretely, the *multitudo* is a continuous and contradictory mixture of passions and situations—and then, across a new dislocation, an accumulation of will and reason, which, as such, constitute institutions (*E* IVP37S1 and 2). But this process only imperfectly allows for the power of subjects to be deployed from the perspective of concrete constitutional situations and constitutes here a definitive element of juridical and political affirmation. All in all, the formation of the political subject is postulated as a tendency in an indefinite interweaving of subjective intersections. From this point of view, plurality has an advantage over unity. Reason, thought, would like the *multitudo* to be presented as a single soul: this demand of reason traverses the natural field on which social life unfolds but does not manage to overcome its violence and dispersion once and for all:

"From this it is clear that just and unjust, sin and merit, are extrinsic notions, not attributes which explain the nature of mind" (*E* IVP37S2).

After having considered the *multitudo* from the physical and animal point of view, there is a third level of possible considerations, which allows the final consequences of the previous developments to be measured: it is a question of the *multitudo* from the point of view of reason. We have just seen how the demand of reason—which we can here define from now on as a proposition of the absoluteness of the moment of democracy—cannot manage to become real because of certain physical and animal limits. In Spinoza the "will of all," even if it were given, could never become a "general will"—and this anti-Rousseauian conclusion is a premise of his thought. This does not mean, however, that the concept of the *multitudo* does not itself contain a certain rationality, and therefore a certain power. *Multitudo* is neither *vulgus* nor *plebs*.[31] On the other hand, the becoming-real, in Spinoza's politics, has the power and limit of fact. Neither more nor less. If the absoluteness of the democratic claim does not manage to embrace the development of freedoms, it must nonetheless permit the life in common of singularities, reciprocal tolerance, the power of solidarity. This passage is fundamental. It poses the actual nonsolution of the relationship between absoluteness and freedom as the foundation of one of the highest values of the republican tradition: tolerance. The nonsolution of the problem of the political subject becomes the foundation of tolerance, of respect for consciences, of freedom to philosophize. The *multitudo*, in its paradoxical nature, is the foundation of democracy insofar as it allows each individual to introduce into society his own values of freedom. Each singularity is a foundation. Tolerance for Spinoza does not here represent a negative virtue, as a residual morality.[32] If in the *TTP* tolerance concerned intellectual freedom especially, here it becomes universal right.

This aristocratism, which, in the motto *libertas philosophandi*, stands out in the very title of the *TTP*, seems dissolved into the concept of the *multitudo*. What is claimed here is a republican right and what is proposed is the very condition of democratic politics. An equal right for all. Once again, each singularity stands out as a foundation. It is possible, says Spinoza (*TP* XI/2), in a city in the aristocratic regime for the number of members chosen for government to be greater than that of a city in a democratic regime. But even if all the inhabitants of the city participated in the aristocratic form of administration, the city would remain aristocratic, and this total participation would not be an absolute government. Absolute government is founded not on a "choice" (even if the choice of everyone) but on the *multitudo*, on the foundation of the freedom of the individuals who compose this *multitudo*, hence on the mutual respect of the freedom of every individual. The *multitudo*, considered from the point of view of reason, is thus the foundation of tolerance and universal freedom.

These conclusions, relative to the concept of the *multitudo*, thus do not suppress its aporetic nature; on the contrary, they accentuate it. The *multitudo*, placed between absoluteness and freedom, between civil right and natural right, between reason and the contradictory materiality of the constitutive movement of being, has an ambiguous definition; its concept cannot be concluded. Each of the elements of its definition lives — if it is considered through the prism of the *multitudo* — at the same time as all the other elements. The democratic regime, whose absoluteness consists above all in the fact of being founded in an entire and exclusive form on the *multitudo*, is thus absorbed into this aporia. But this aporetic form is extremely productive — and it is precisely this disequilibrium between absoluteness and freedom that allows the democratic regime to be the best. Yet it also returns to Spinoza's political theory to move with equilibrium in the oscillation between the *multitudo* and the idea of the absolute:

> Those who confine to the common people the vices that exist in all human beings will perhaps greet my contentions with ridicule, on the ground that "there is no moderation in the vulgar, they terrorize if they are not afraid," that "the common people is either a domineering servant or a domineering master," that "it has no truth and judgment in it," and so on. But nature is one and common to all: we are deceived by power and education. Hence, "when two men do the same thing we often say that the one may do it with impunity but not the other; not because the person who does it is different." Pride is characteristic of rulers. If men are made arrogant by appointment for a year, what can we expect of nobles who hold office without end? (*TP* VII/27)

For once Spinoza here allows himself a sarcastic remark.

The political universe is a universe of action. The fact that democracy appears as the objective aporia of the absolute and freedom, and that this aporia is posed as the dynamic condition of the political process, far from resolving the problem and the difficulties of the definition of democracy, aggravates it. When the absoluteness of this form of government is reflected onto the necessity of action, hence onto subjects, it seems to become its limit. For if it is necessary to act, it is by knowing that the aporia is always inherent in the action: the aporia is then transferred from objectivity to subjectivity. The subject must act while recognizing the incompleteness of the universe in which it acts. At any rate, it must act. But how? According to what lines of orientation and following what perspectives and what projects? To conjecture about democracy so as to cover the space henceforth only indicated in the *TP*, from the *reliqua desiderantur* on, means to give a response to these questions. My hypothesis is that Spinozan democracy, the *omnino absolutum democraticum imperium*, must be conceived as a social practice of singularities that intersect in a mass process—better, as a *pietas* that forms and constitutes the reciprocal individual relations that are established among the multiplicity of subjects that constitute the *multitudo*.

I arrive at this hypothesis by considering, as we have seen until now, that Spinozan democracy has no contractarian structure, that it therefore constitutes a process that remains as open as the nature of the subject (*multitudo*) that governs it is incomplete. But the absoluteness of government is a concept that is equivalent to an indivisible figure of power. According to this logical presupposition, absoluteness is the indivisibility of the process, an indivisibility that is applied to the complexity of the power of subjects, since the process of power is founded, articulated, and develops on the powers of the *multitudo*. If the concept of the *multitudo* is therefore presented to us objectively as an ambiguous concept, perhaps even as a schema of the imagination (certainly in an inadequate way from the point of view of the definition of a solid political subject), the latter is on the other hand articulated subjectively and is a project and a convergence of *cupiditates*, to the extent that under the aegis of reason, the latter are materially displaced from the individual good to the collective good. In short, the republican reinvention of Spinozan democracy is not given only because the definition in the abstract is open to the ontological power of the *multitudo*. Concretely, the dramatization of the concept of the *multitudo* is completely assumed and dissolves into its components. Consequently, the definition of democracy is reduced to the constitutive power of subjects. Yet this constitutive power of subjects is ethical.

In *E* IVP37S1 the subject, by pursuing its own virtue and by understanding that it will enjoy this virtue all the more by desiring it equally for others, lives—reversed from the point of view of singularity—the objective and constitutive tendency of politics. Of politics, of the absolute, of democratic politics. Yet the subject explicitly assumes here *pietas* as an instrument of ethical reason from this perspective. What is *pietas*? It is the "desire to do good generated in us by our living according to the guidance of reason" (*E* IVP37S1). To act morally according to reason, which *pietas* represents here, is deployed, then, in honesty, that is, in action benevolently and humanely conducted in harmony with itself and others. One acts in this way by loving the universal, but this universality is the common name of numerous subjects. *Pietas* is thus the desire that no subject be excluded from universality, as would be the case if one loved the particular. Moreover, by loving universality and by constituting it as a project of reason across subjects, one becomes powerful. If, by contrast, one loves the particular and acts only out of interest, one is not powerful but rather completely powerless, insofar as one is acted on by external things. The tendency toward the universal is a passage across the universal: a passage so human that it includes all human beings, a development of the *cupiditas* that articulates subjects and objects into a dynamic and tendential form:

> To man, then, there is nothing more useful than man. Man, I say, can wish for nothing more helpful to the preservation of his being than that all should so agree in all things that the minds and bodies of all would compose, as it were, one mind and one body; that all should strive together, as far as they can, to preserve their being; and that all, together, should seek for themselves the common advantage of all. (*E* IVP18S)

In part IV of the *Ethics* this conviction of the usefulness of man for man and of the ontological multiplication of virtue in the human community is ceaselessly repeated (see especially *E* IVP35, C). It doubtless represents one of the essential points of Spinoza's thought. Anyway, if it were not so (as certain interpreters claim), it is certain that this conviction constitutes the framework of Spinoza's political thought. The *multitudo* is thus nothing but the interconnection of subjects having become an ontological project of collective power. But at the same time, the concept of the *multitudo* is linked to the ambiguity of the imagination and translated into the theory of political action. This is then the theoretical genesis of Spinozan democracy.[33]

This indication is no longer generic. The same passages of the *Ethics* (especially IVP37) that introduce the ontologically multiplicative function of *pietas* and honesty into the tendency toward the collective in fact simultaneously and directly lead to the definition of the state. In addition, it is no longer necessary to insist on the insufficiency of formalist definitions of the state, nor to emphasize the still unfinished character of the political approach of the *Ethics* (see especially *E* IVP36S2; P40; P45C2; P54S; P58S; P63S; P70; P72S; P73S). What is especially important to emphasize in these two points of view is that the insufficiency of solutions corresponds to the emergence of an extreme tension on the metaphysical ground. The relation *pietas/respublica/democraticum imperium* is here obviously unresolved, whatever the efforts supplied so as to resolve the problem. Thus, in the final propositions (71, 72, 73) of part IV of the *Ethics* we find ourselves before a series of incessant, pointless reformulations of proposition 37: the repetition does not resolve its incompleteness. The continual referral of political virtue to generosity, to the rejection of hate, anger, and contempt, in short, to love for the universal does not come any closer to resolving the problem (*E* IVP45, 46); in other words, the reference to a series of passions that, if they are valuable as indications of a direction, nonetheless do not correspond to the necessity of its completion. The former appear, on the other hand, as particular, unilateral, and abstract functions. Finally, at this level of complexity, one can no longer pretend to confront the problem from the standpoint of individuality and consequently resolve it ascetically. In this respect, part V of the *Ethics* has nothing to teach us. On the contrary, it seems, however, that one finds oneself before an operation that suppresses the collective framework of the development toward society—a kind of lapse in argumentation. Yet the problem was posed. Of course, one could object that it had already been posed in the *TTP*, in which in the very wording of the *Treatise* (if wanting to indicate the spirit of the work we are content to emphasize one of the most extrinsic elements), *pietas* with the *libertas philosophandi* and *pax* are mentioned among the fundamental values that are concentrated in the preservation and in the reproduction of the republican enterprise. But *pietas* is still a form of devotion rather than a foundation of political action. By contrast, at the end of the *Ethics* and thus at the beginning of the project of the *TP* the problem appears in all its *import*.[34]

But in the part available to us, even the *TP* does not succeed in resolving the problem of the relationship between the ontological power of the collective and the freedom of individuals. The concept of the *multitudo*, as we have seen, poses the problem by leaving it open. But all the conditions for a solution are given. In fact, there is missing only a final passage that consists in a specific description of the function that *pietas* assumes in this context. Let us imagine that description. First, in order to be in conformity with the premises and the density of the problem, it is clear that the description of *pietas* will not, so to speak, have the actual aporetic consistency of the problem itself. On the other hand, it should displace it, take hold of it again so as to situate it within the perspective of construction. Thus, it will finally offer us the problem of democracy as an operational horizon, an operational horizon that shows the possibility that *pietas* may become a social practice, a constitutive determination. Yet it is enough for us to add a few words concerning *pietas*, for most of these characteristics are henceforth given, and the fundamental problematization is the one that brings them together from the constitutive point of view, in the dynamic displacement. One could say that the initial exclusion of the social contract is recuperated and that an original, dynamic, and open situation is now presented, a situation inside of which is the active construction, the building of a kind of social contract. Not the social contract as myth, but the social constitution, the association, and collective becoming of the ethical moment. We shall make only a few remarks concerning *pietas*. As a passion and an extremely strong ontologically constructive moral behavior, *pietas* is the precise opposite of *superstitio* and *metus*: *pietas* suppresses them. *Pietas* forms part of the positive series that *potentia* expresses across reasonable *cupiditas*, in order to transform *cupiditas* itself into *virtus*; and *pietas* carries this multiplier of friendship and love into *virtus*, the way to realize this ontological surplus that the collective determines. From this point of view, *pietas* is the soul of the *multitudo* and expresses an inverted but complementary ambiguity in it. If the *multitudo* is a collective term that, in order to become absolute, needs to reconstruct itself across the singularities that constitute it, *pietas* is a singular concept, open in an ontologically constitutive way to the *multitudo*. The framework is repeated: "the more we comprehend singular things, the more we comprehend God"; "nevertheless, in God there is necessarily an idea that expresses the essence of this or that human body, under a species of eternity" (*E* V P24, 22). Is it possible to think that democracy can be represented *in reliquis* as the limit toward which tend the absoluteness of the mass and the constitutive singularity of *potentiae*, in other words, the *multitudo* and *pietas*?

Whether this limit can be determined, whether the natural process of the *cupiditates* can have a termination, fixed in a positivist manner, and whether — in the absoluteness of the democratic process — the activity of the *jure contendo* can have a status of *jure conditio* — this is what Spinoza seems incidentally to deny in *TP* XI/3, in which he affirms: "We can conceive different kinds of democracy. My purpose, however, is not to discuss them all, but to confine myself to only one. . . ." It seems to me that the negation of an exclusive figure of democracy as absolute regime is in conformity with the ontological underpinning of Spinoza's thought, and that consequently the metaphysical bases of that powerful legalism that we have emphasized from time to time in the second and third paragraphs of this chapter are missing here — a legalism that serves here to fix the conditions of participations and/or of exclusion from the democratic administration of government and from the active and passive exercise of the electorate. A legalism that constitutes the framework of this unique and particular form of democracy that Spinoza would consider analyzable: a legalism, hence, extremely effective, for it constitutes precisely (in the strict sense) the very object of scientific consideration, but not, for all that, exclusive, definitive, sufficient, founded. It is interesting to observe the successive development of Spinoza's argumentation, in other words, paragraph 4 of chapter 11, and to understand how the argumentation that has appeared until now to be legalist contradicts itself:

> But perhaps someone will ask whether it is by nature or by convention that women are subject to men. For if this is due solely to convention, I have excluded women from the government without any reasonable cause. However, if we consult actual experience, we shall see that it is due to their weakness.

In other words, Spinoza will explain what follows in terms of the nature of woman. The institution is thus factually the extrinsic figure of an irrepressible natural process, foundational and not founded. Therefore, it is not interesting here to follow the argumentation further.[35] It is much more important to signal that the legalism, the purely institutional reasoning, does not constitute an argument.

This appears all the more clearly when we pass from the uncertainty and incompleteness of these final paragraphs to the consideration of the metaphysical framework of the concept of democracy. We have seen how the absoluteness of the political process is incapable of coming to an end. But it is clear that the unstable equilibrium of a concept of democracy filtered across the *multitudo* and *pietas* does not constitute a strange emergence in the life of Spinoza's thought. On the other hand, in Spinoza's philosophy we always find ourselves before moments of great disequilibrium: the guiding thread that ties together *conatus* and *potentia*, *cupiditas* and *virtus* does not manage to conceal the veritable catastrophes that are determined on these knots. The relationship between the objective disposition of the *multitudo* and the subjective determinations of *pietas* can appear now just as disproportionate. Yet the space deployed between the two of them can seem too great. The completion of the relationship can then be represented as simply antinomic. But why oppose the tendency of the freedoms, powers, and absoluteness of the form of government? Why not consider the incompleteness of the relationship between social practice and the juridical subject of power as a metaphysical condition of absoluteness? Why can't the *absolutum* be the presence of the political process in its complexity? I do not believe that it is necessary to be stopped short by these difficulties. Instead, I believe that the repetition of this situation of theoretical contradiction and this succession of moments of logical struggle in Spinoza's system constitute the driving force of its thought and a fundamental theme of its propositional power. For, in fact, the disproportion and the extreme tension of concepts are torn from the heavens and forced to live in the world. The operation of the secularization of power—which is deployed with so much effectiveness from the *TTP* (as Strauss and now Tosel have shown)—accomplishes here a qualitative leap; better, to use a terminology that seems more appropriate to me, it is displaced. In the *TP*, in fact, the absolute does not repeat the theological fullness of the traditional concept of power, not even in the form of the highest secularization.[36] Here there exists, on the other hand, the substantial difference that in subjective terms we postulate between the concepts of emancipation and liberation—here, objectively, power is not only emancipated from its image and its theological form but is freed from them. This is why, when it is presence and deed, the absolute can present itself as a limit, as the very powerful margin of a contradiction in action, a free constitution. Spinoza's political discourse does not thereby become at all banal, as if it consisted of the pure recording and the missing solution of real difficulties. Better: faced with the hysteria of the contractarianism that it thinks it can escape, across a fiction, the dystony of the real constitutive experience of politics, Spinoza pushes as far as possible the description of disequilibrium and the definition of the resulting tension. On the one hand, then, the form of a maximal objectivity, of a metaphysical framework that reconstitutes across an enormous movement, and its disequilibria, its disproportions, the quite violent relationships that move between physics and ethics, between individuality and sociality, and the syntheses that constitute it, in short, the absolute. On the other hand, a subjectivity that does not stop at the desire of preservation and perfection of its own being, which is not reduced to, nor ends up in, individualist figures, but poses the problem of the good and salvation within composition and recomposition, by deploying itself among all the world's powers—in short, freedom. We know that the perfection of this relationship is unrealizable. The concept of the *multitudo* is an example of imperfection. But we shall always have attempted to try again. The possible democracy is the most complete image of the disutopia of the absolute relationship. Democracy is a "prolix method."

To conclude: Spinoza's religiosity is often mentioned with respect to the *TTP* and *TP*. In fact, a genuine atheist religiosity runs throughout Spinoza's hypothesis of democracy: *Nemo potest Deum odio habere* (*E* VP18). This hypothesis has been felt to live in the relationship between absoluteness and freedom, in the contradiction that constitutes it, in the constructive struggle that democracy requires. One senses that it is endured, as the disproportion, the metaphysical abyss, the theology without theology are endured—but above all it is felt as the tension of a genuine hope. If there exists here a biblical spirit, it is not at all that of the secularized version of the *TTP* but instead that of the extremely profound materialist *pietas* of the Book of Job:

But human power is very limited and infinitely surpassed by the power of external causes. So we do not have an absolute power to adapt things outside of us to our use. Nevertheless, we shall bear calmly those things which happen to us contrary to what the principle of our advantage demands, if we are conscious that we have done our duty, that the power we have could not have extended itself to the point where we could have avoided those things, and that we are a part of the whole of Nature, whose order we follow. If we understand this clearly and distinctly, that part of us which is defined by understanding, that is, the better part of us, will be entirely satisfied with this, and will strive to persevere in that satisfaction. For insofar as we understand, we can want nothing except what is necessary, nor absolutely be satisfied with anything except what is true. Hence, insofar as we understand these things rightly, the striving of the better part of us agrees with the order of the whole of Nature. (E IVApp32)

Translated by Ted Stolze

Notes

1. Negri (1991, 183–89).
2. Balibar (1994); Tosel (1984).
3. Solari (1949); Ravà (1958); Eckstein (1933).
4. Strauss (1952; 1965). If the first generation of interpreters in the twentieth century essentially considered Spinoza to be the father of liberalism, the second generation mainly retains the analysis of the process of engendering freedom. The attention of the second generation of interpreters bears more particularly on the passage from the *TTP* to the *TP*. Midway, during the 1930s, is the critical work of Leo Strauss, who shows how Spinozan democracy is at the same time the product and the image of the development of a specific form of religious alliance and social association, between theocracy and Jewish militancy. It is pointless to recall here the importance of Leo Strauss's interpretative contribution—this interpreter as brilliant as he was reactionary, who brought about a continual reversal of all the materialist developments in the history of political thought. It is more worthwhile to dwell on the analyses of the second generation, for whom between the *TTP* and the *TP* a genuine process of secularization was accomplished. Marramao (1983) has recently shown that the process of secularization must be understood as the processes by which a preexisting theological kernel becomes worldly. Marramao sees in the political philosophy of the seventeenth and eighteenth centuries the fundamental moment of such a process. This seems particularly obvious when one finds oneself before the political theories of Protestant origin in which the secularization of the religious theme often constitutes an

explicit program. But can one transform this historical recognition into a hermeneutical function? I do not think so, and I regard Marramao's approach as profoundly ambiguous — since there exists no continuity of ideological problematics, especially if they are religious, which must not be subordinated to innovative events, as well as to the complexity of the real, to the totality of the political relation and in general of the relations of force that are determined in historical time, and since nothing guarantees us, in the process of secularization, the semantic continuity of the concepts considered. The insistence that, in contemporary philosophical literature, can be observed regarding this continuity seems to have instead an ideological content: secularization is less considered as a "laicization" of the religious theme than as a natural-rights permanence of the religious problematic. This remark seems more particularly to be applicable to the entirety of Leo Strauss's thought. But it is then still more obvious that Spinoza's thought cannot be grasped under Strauss's interpretative categories. André Tosel's recent work, despite the strong influence of Strauss, seems to me to be free from this ideology and to accomplish, in the radical dimension of Spinoza's approach, not a confirmation of the continuity of religious thought, from the perspective of secularization, but an atheist and materialist rupture against every laicization and theological permanence.

5. In my *Savage Anomaly* (Negri 1991) I have vigorously insisted on this double "foundation" of Spinoza's system, and thus on the solution of continuity existing between a first and second phase of his thought. I have the impression that beyond the inadequate and sometimes risky philosophical demonstration, beyond certain difficulties that arise from the confrontation with an interpretative tradition that is strictly continualist and systematic, my intervention has had a certain impact, and has perhaps even generated some support. I deeply want to thank those who have emphasized in a critical way the crudeness of my approach, while considering it relevant and having a certain heuristic value. I think that it would be necessary to deepen the research on this terrain, and this essay is also meant to contribute to such a deepening. As much as I thank those who have reserved a critical reception for the thesis of the internal discontinuity of Spinoza's metaphysics, so too do I reject the accusations, often acerbic, that have been formulated against my reading of the "second foundation" of Spinoza's thought and against the formation, between the *Ethics* and the *TP*, of a constitutive perspective of being, founded on collective subjectivity. See recently in this regard Saccaro Battisti (1984). I would like to return to this theme at a later point.

6. Droetto (1958), Matheron (1988).

7. On the diffusion of social contract theory, see Gierke (1958), Gough (1957), and Strauss (1953). On this argument I refer to these now classic texts in order to emphasize essentially the unilateral character of the interpretation of the contractarian problematic of the seventeenth and eighteenth centuries, which we also find in almost every author — from Georg Jellinek to Léon Duguit, from Paul Janet to Giorgio Del Vecchio, from Carl Friedrich to Robert Derathé, from Norbert Bobbio to Hans Welzel. By the unilateralness of interpretation I mean not only the fact that during these centuries the contract is regarded as a hegemonic figure of political theory but also that its content is reduced to a substantial unity, in juridical terms.

8. The entire tradition and finally (but with their own authority) Hans Kelsen and Bobbio, Niklas Luhmann and John Rawls have insisted and continue to insist with great effectiveness on the immediately juridical character of the contractarian hypothesis. This insistence is generally motivated by reference to the highest justification of the contractarian thematic in the history of thought, namely, the Kantian definition. Here the hypothetical character and the juridical function of original agreement are immediately apparent. See Vlachos (1962, 236ff). The transcendental character of the contractarian hypothesis is thus fundamental, and the transcendental dimension is immediately juridical. One could add that in this case philosophical thought has made of Kantianism simultaneously an exclusive method and a kind of idea of reason, which separates historical concepts (Negri 1962). So that the position of anyone who has explicitly grasped the sociological function of contractarianism and has turned it into a representation of the class struggle — as have Harrington or the Levelers — is truly marginal. See in this regard also Macpherson (1962), Zagorin (1954), and Blitzer (1960). The development of political thought as well as the contractarian function in the seventeenth century can be considered differently, if instead of the contractarian thematic one considers the diffusion and fortune of Machiavellism. One knows how much Machiavelli's thought was badly understood in a programmatic way by the interpretation of "politicians" (on this point see especially Procacci [1965]). Machiavelli's thought, however, was read and applied by political science in another perspective, that is, from the republican standpoint; see especially in this regard the unfinished but very rich interpretation of Raab (1964).

9. Derathé (1950).

10. In Negri (1970) the research aims to establish certain historiographical criteria that might allow the variants of the absolutist model of the modern state to be considered. It is pointless to refer here to the vast bibliography that it is useful to consult in this regard. It suffices to recall that a correct methodology must continually compare the ideological alternatives — often numerous — with the urgencies and determinations that emerge from concrete praxis. The thesis defended in the essay cited is that the history of modernity and the ideological variants of the absolutist state must be read as so many expressions of the profound crisis that characterizes the century. The humanist Renaissance had expressed a radical revolution of values, but this "rise" of modern man, this emergence of his productive singularity and the first image of his collective essence, were rather quickly put back into question by the development of the class struggle and the impossibility of the nascent bourgeoisie's fighting on two fronts. A series of alternatives was therefore determined in relation to this problem. What must essentially be recalled is that the first organization of capitalism and of the modern state constitutes less the capacity of structuring this new productive energy than its crisis, a purely negative dialectic (in every alternative that is not a rupture and an anomaly, as is the case, on the contrary, in Spinoza) of this original *Aufklärung*.

11. Althusius (1964, *Preface*).

12. Gierke (1939); Friedrich's "Introduction" to Althusius (1932).

13. Popkin (1979); Spink (1964).

14. Macpherson (1962).

15. Matheron (1984) considers the affirmation of the contractarian problematic in Spinoza in the *TTP* as an adherence to the juridical terminology of the age and as an instrument adapted to the position of the conditions of validity of right. According to Tosel (1984), on the other hand, the contract and its affirmation in Spinoza are a means to subordinate the religious alliance to the properly political pact—by revealing in this way the practico-political nature of the religious. It is clear, in any case, that the affirmation of the contract blocks the metaphysical process: in Matheron by suggesting that the analysis of conditions of validity can be different from the analysis of the determinations of the effectiveness of right; in Tosel by preventing religion from being set aside once and for all and religion from being grasped only in the deed, in the ethical unfolding of the divine, and not in the emergence of ancient truths.

16. It is not impossible for me here to push the demonstration of the political plane to a properly metaphysical plane, as I have already done (Negri 1991). From a general point of view it is at any rate important to refer to what Deleuze affirms (1990)—that is, that Spinoza's way moves toward an absolute presence of being—in order to understand how this process of redefinition of being necessarily contains a mechanism of transformation of political categories. If I may be permitted an image, it seems to me that one can say that Spinoza's path moves toward a greater and greater nakedness of being. I am not alluding only to the fall of the functions of the attribute in the second phase of Spinoza's thought, and I no longer insist only on the pragmatic definition, which is more and more

determinate and constitutive of being; I speak above all of the conception of substance and of a depth that is emptied more and more to the extent that the surface is enriched. Traditional metaphysical thought, by which we have been formed, only perceives with great difficulty the considerable effects of the simple presence of the divine substance.

17. It is strange that Hans Kelsen, the most important and most coherent theorist of the problems of validity and efficacy in the unity of juridical organization, did not (to my knowledge) see a precursor in Spinoza. This is probably due to the weight exerted by neo-Kantian reductionism (of phenomenalism and formalism) in the evaluation of Spinoza's thought. Kelsen's philosophico-juridical thought is, however, much richer than his neo-Kantian matrix. In the final phase of his thought, Kelsen adheres in particular to a juridical realism that is extremely fascinating in its absolute "superficiality." Here the unity of the validity and of the juridical efficacy, the formative force of executive acts, refers back to a metaphysics of constitution, possible Spinozan references it would be interesting to study. See in this regard Negri (1977).

18. The concept of "magistrate," as an immediate formulator of right, as *defensor pacis*, instead of a simple executor of right and simple operator of legality, is typical of every conception of nonmonarchical right and state (in the sense mentioned above, i.e., nonabsolutist) in the seventeenth century. This very concept of magistrate, which we would consider internal to Spinoza's political thought, hardly appears at all during these same years as a difficult and essential problem in the liberal Locke; we see it, on the contrary, develop in the republican Harrington. Concerning Locke, see Viano (1960); for Harrington, see John Toland, "Introduction" to Harrington (1770). It remains to be seen up to what point in these latter positions the problematic of the magistrate represents the continuity of the premodern figure or else represents a new foundation of its function as an expression of the will of the people—as is certainly the case in Spinozan democracy.

19. Hegel (1923, 415–99). See Spinoza (1802–3, xxxvi): *eadem de causa, ne in nostra hac editione jure aliquid desideretur, sequitur, quam Vir Cl. mihique amiccimus Hegel mecum communicare voluit, Notarum Spinozae marginalium ad tractatum theologpolit. gallica versio* (I, 429) *collata cum iisdem latine ex originali a Cel. de Murr pubblicatis.* But also see Hegel (1969, I, 65, 74ff) and *passim* Hegel (1928, 371).

20. Macherey (1979); Negri (1991).

21. "For what is most useful to man is what most agrees with his nature . . . i.e., . . . man" (*Nam, id homini utilissimum est, quod cum sua natura maxime convenit . . . , hoc est . . . , homo*) (*E* IVP35C1). There is no doubt that this Spinozan proposition in its very literalness could be attributed to Marx. But the problem here is not philological, and we would not know how to add much to the philology of the Spinoza/Marx relation already fully developed by Rubel (1977). The problem is entirely philosophical. The question could be posed in the following terms. By considering as totally unacceptable the reference of Marx's thought to natural rights theory, the question that presents itself is that of the quality and of the figure of radically constitutive natural rights theory, a natural rights theory of power, of the productive force, and of political realism. From now on a quite vast literature, whose highest expression is represented by the writings of Deleuze and Matheron — and recently by Tosel — leads us to these conclusions. In the study of the Spinoza-Marx relation a supplementary step could be taken if one grasped the materialist reversal of Spinozist natural rights theory in relation to our current political problematic. But if the forms of research trying to retrace in Spinozan materialism a germ of the critique of political economy are revealed to be apologetic and pointless, the Spinozan reading of the eminently sociopolitical organization of exploitation is, by contrast, undoubtedly relevant. In other words, in the postindustrial age the Spinozan critique of the representation of capitalist power corresponds more to the truth than does the analysis of the critique of political economy. Without forgetting, in fact, the importance of Marxian economic analysis, today the tension toward liberation represented by Spinoza's philosophy has a capacity of demystification and extraordinary demonstration. At the apogee of capitalist development, in fact, it seems to me important to rediscover the critical force of its origins.

22. Balibar (1994); Saccaro Battisti (1984); Tosel (1984).

23. I do not hesitate to situate myself (Negri [1991]) among the apologists for the *multitudo* — and to make at this point a necessary self-criticism, but, as one will be able to observe in the rest of my argument, in a sense contrary to the one asked of me. This means that it does not seem to me that I have insisted too much on the foundational power of the *multitudo*. On the contrary, and I accept on this point Balibar's critique (1984), I have too little brought to light the dynamic of this ontologically constitutive subjectivity. I do not believe that I have insisted too much on the mechanisms that lead the *multitudo* to subjectivity; I have only emphasized too little the processes that are opened from this subjectivity. It is now a matter of proceeding in this sense. A first line, as we shall see further on, is the one that, in the pluralist dynamic of the *multitudo*, leads toward the concept of tolerance, as the condition of existence of this same political subjectivity of the *multitudo*. The second line of research is the one that, from a still more elementary and ontologically important formative layer, leads to the ethical dialectic of singularities in the form of the collective and to the

expression of *pietas*. On these themes, and more generally on the way in which the ethics and politics are interconnected with the problem of salvation, see Matheron's (1971) fundamental research.

24. I refer here especially to the French interpretative current directed by Madeleine Francès, an interpretative current that, despite certain remarkable contributions, has in my opinion reduced the Spinoza-Rousseau relation to utterly unacceptable terms. As a caricatural expression of this interpretative current, see the translation of the Spinozan *civitas* by "nation" (Spinoza 1954).

25. Negri (1991, 175–76). This proposition (VP20), which appears at the center of the ascetic construction of the cognitive process, inverts the sense of it: Knowledge rises to the dignity, to the higher level of being only to the extent that it traverses the level of imagination, the social level, and lets itself be constructed by them. Love toward God, at the moment when it is reproposed as a vertical tension above worldiness, is held back and flattened in the horizontal dimension of imagination and sociability, and it is nourished only by them (173). Such is the mechanism of displacement of meaning that dominates Spinoza's metaphysics: one can never insist enough on this point.

26. Negri (1991, 86ff, 144ff).

27. The construction of the concept of the *multitudo* in Spinoza must be situated inside his physics. See *E* IIP13. See in particular the corollary to Lemma 3 and the definition and scholium to Lemma 7. This means that at the basis of the concept of the *multitudo* is the entire dialectic of the multiple and dynamic construction of the individual. The constructive way naturally does not stop at the physics: the same method is applied next through successive displacements, on the terrain of the construction of the passions, and is then deployed across the entire *Ethics*. In part IV, finally, from proposition 19 until proposition 73, the social passage from *cupiditas* is determined. Here at last the conditions of the concept of the *multitudo* are given together.

28. In short, Spinoza's political conception is consistent with associationist and mechanistic physics; the moments of displacement enrich it without weakening the method. This method and development exclude, consequently, every possibility of insertion of the social contract, or at least of that specific form of contract that concludes in normative transcendence. On this point one measures the difference between Spinoza's thought and Hobbes's. In Hobbes, a contractarian and absolutist politics (Strauss [1936]; Warrender [1957]) is superimposed in a forced and insidious way on a rigorously mechanistic physics (Brandt [1928]). It is obvious that the problem of consistency, or, at least, of a political philosophy and a natural philosophy, cannot be in any case posed abstractly, especially if one considers the philosophy of mechanism in the seventeenth century (on this see Negri

[1970], 149ff). Concretely, however, the options are varied, and Spinoza's desire for consistency leads to freedom, whereas Hobbes's rupture leads to the theory of necessary servitude.

29. See in this regard the interesting hypotheses and remarks recently proposed by G. Bocco (1984, 173ff).

30. On the theory of the imagination in Spinoza we now have the contributions of Mignini (1981) and Bertrand (1983), contributions whose tenor and orientations are uneven but nonetheless very interesting. On the basis of this research and the very important role they accord in the theory of the imagination, I believe I can fend off the accusations directed at me (Negri [1991]) on the exaggerated role attributed to the imagination in my analyses of Spinoza's political thought.

31. Saccaro Battisti (1984).

32. I have dealt at length with the variants of the conception of tolerance in the seventeenth century (Negri [1970]). I refer to this volume equally for the bibliography. A single remark, which is perhaps not as misplaced as it might seem: In 1970 the literature on tolerance was quite rich and always current. In 1985, despite the important quantity of writings on and against totalitarianism, there existed practically no important writing on tolerance. Being here on the point of showing that tolerance represents one of the contents of the absolute Spinozan government and that this attribution is perfectly correct, it remains for me to specify in conclusion that the recent bibliography on totalitarianism, by avoiding the theme of tolerance, risks belonging to totalitarianism itself.

33. Matheron (1984, 249ff) and Balibar (1984, 5–7, 46–47), with great clarity, become conscious of this genealogy. The intimate relationship between Spinoza's metaphysics and politics allows the ethical relationship of the *multitudo* to be developed in these very modern forms of the genealogy. On the other hand, Saccaro Battisti (1984), by isolating Spinoza's politics, repeats the ambiguity of objective definitions. The incredible aspect of Spinoza's theory of politics is his insistence on the subjectivity of actors. It is for this reason that, strictly speaking, in Spinoza there can only exist a democratic politics.

34. By developing these theses I only complete what I had shown in my *Savage Anomaly*. These pages should be placed most particularly at the beginning of chapter 8 of my work, in order to make more precise certain arguments. In this context of discussion I had tried to define how a series of contradictory pairs of political realism (*prudentia/multitudo, libertas/securitas, conditio/constitutio*) could be dissolved on the basis of the concept of "free necessity" attributed to the subject, during this phase of Spinoza's thought. This argument, absolutely correct, is, however, rather abstract: it must be completed on the moral side, on the side of ethical analysis. But here it is the *pietas* that shows the richness and completeness of the concept of "free necessity."

35. Matheron (1977) has fully analyzed Spinoza's passages relating to the question of women.

36. This is the moment of extreme opposition between Spinoza's thought and Hobbes's: more than anything, it is before the problem of divinity that they express the radical opposition that, beginning with them, characterizes the two fundamental currents of European political thought. But in the face of this problem, Hobbes affirms and Spinoza erases even the memory of the existence of God. The two tendencies are radically opposed. In Spinoza the secularization of the idea of power effaces the most distant theological reminiscence. In Hobbes, to the lack of physical and metaphysical reasons there corresponds the necessity of divinity, and in him, the reactionary, a certain order of reasons of the heart is opposed to the arguments of reason when it cries: long live God!

Works Cited and Select Bibliography

Albiac, Gabriel. 1979. *De la añoranza del poder o consolación de la filosofia*. Madrid, n.p.

———. 1987. *La sinagoga vacía: Un estudo de las fuentes marranas del espinosismo*. Madrid: Libros Hiperion.

———. 1993. *La synagogue vide: Les sources marranes du spinozisme*. Paris: Presses Universitaires de France.

Alquié, Ferdinand. 1981. *Le rationalisme de Spinoza*. Paris: Presses Universitaires de France.

Althusius, Johannes. 1932. *Politica Methodice Digesta of Johannes Althusius (Althaus)*. Cambridge, Mass.: Harvard University Press.

———. 1964. *Politica*. Edited and translated by Frederick S. Carney. Indianapolis, Ind.: Liberty Fund.

Althusser, Louis. 1970. *Reading Capital*. London: New Left Books.

———. 1976. *Essays in Self-Criticism*. London: New Left Books.

———. 1992. *Journal de captivité*. Paris: STOCK/IMEC.

Alwicher, Norbert. 1971. *Texte zur Geschichte des Spinozismus*. Darmstadt: Wissenschaftliche Buchgesellschaft.

Auvray, P. 1968. "Richard Simon et Spinoza." In *Religion, érudition, critique à la fin du XVIIe siècle*. Paris: Presses Universitaires de France.

Baader, Franz von. 1963. *Sämtliche Werke*. 16 vols. Aalen: Scientia.

Balibar, Etienne. 1985a. "Jus, Pactum, Lex: Sur la constitution du sujet dans le 'Traite Theologico-Politique.'" *Studia Spinozana* 1:105–42.

———. 1985b. *Spinoza et la politique*. Paris: Presses Universitaires de France.

———. 1989. "Spinoza, politique et communication." *Cahiers philosophique* 39:17–42.

———. 1990. "Individualité, causalité, substance: Réflexions sur l'ontologie de Spinoza." In Curley and Moreau 1990, 58–76.

———. 1992a. "Heidegger et Spinoza." In *Spinoza au XXe siècle*, 327–43. Paris: Presses Universitaires de France.

———. 1992b. "A Note on 'Consciousness/Conscience' in the *Ethics*." *Studia Spinozana* 8:37–53.

———. 1994. "Spinoza, the Anti-Orwell: The Fear of the Masses." Translated by Ted Stolze, revised by James Swenson and Etienne Balibar. In *Masses, Classes, Ideas: Studies on Politics and Philosophy before and after Marx*, translated by James Swenson, New York: Routledge.

Bennett, Jonathan. 1984. *A Study of Spinoza's* Ethics. Indianapolis, Ind.: Hackett.

Bertrand, Michèle. 1983. *Spinoza et l'imaginaire*. Paris: Presses Universitaires de France.

Blitzer, Charles. 1960. *An Immortal Commonwealth: The Political Thought of James Harrington*. New Haven, Conn.: Yale University Press.

Bocco, G. 1984. "L'enigma della sfera in Baruch Spinoza: Saggio sulla genealogia dell'adeguazione." *Aut Aut* 202–3.

Brandt, Fritjof. 1928. *Thomas Hobbes's Mechanical Conception of Nature*. London and Copenhagen: Hachette.

Brann, Henry Walter. 1977. "Spinoza and the Kabbalah." In *Speculum Spinozanum, 1677–1977*, edited by Siegfried Hessing, 108–18. Boston: Routledge and Kegan Paul.

Breton, Stanislaus. 1977. *Spinoza: Théologie et politique*. Paris: Desclée.

Brunschvicg, Léon. 1951. *Spinoza et ses contemporains*. 4th ed. Paris: Presses Universitaires de France.

———. 1953. *Le progrès de la conscience dans la philosophie occidentale*. Vol. 1. Paris: Presses Universitaires de France.

Bultmann, Rudolf. 1969–70. *Foi et compréhension*. 2 vols. Paris: Seuil.

Cajetan, Tommaso de Vio. 1964. *Commentary on Being and Essence*. Translated by Lottie Kendzierski and Francis C. Wade. Milwaukee, Wis.: Marquette University Press.

Curley, Edwin. 1988. *Behind the Geometrical Method: A Reading of Spinoza's* Ethics. Princeton, N.J.: Princeton University Press.

Curley, Edwin, and Pierre-François Moreau, eds. 1990. *Spinoza: Issues and Directions. The Proceedings of the Chicago Spinoza Conference*. New York: Brill.

Curtius, Quintus. [1946] 1962. *History of Alexander*. 2 vols. Translated by John C. Rolfe. Cambridge, Mass.: Harvard University Press.

De Barrios, Miguel [Daniel Levi]. 1680. *Libre alvedrío, / y harmonia del cuerpo / por disposicion de Alma. / Dirigida / Al Infinito Criador. / En el Ara de su Divina Carroça*. Brussels: Baltasar Vivien.

Deleuze, Gilles. 1969. "Spinoza et la méthode générale de M. Gueroult." *Revue de Métaphysique et de Morale* 4:426–37.

———. 1988. *Spinoza: Practical Philosophy*. Translated by Robert Hurley. San Francisco: City Lights Books.

———. 1990. *Expressionism in Philosophy: Spinoza*. Translated by Martin Joughin. New York: Zone Books.

———. 1993. "Spinoza et les trois 'Ethiques.'" In *Critique et clinique*, 172–87. Paris: Minuit.

Den Uyl, Douglas J. 1983. *Power, State, and Freedom: An Interpretation of Spinoza's Political Philosophy*. Assen, The Netherlands: Van Gorcum.

Derathé, Robert. 1950. *Rousseau et la science politique de son temps*. Paris: Presses Universitaires de France.

Derrida, Jacques. 1974. *Of Grammatology*. Translated by Gayatri Chakravorti Spivak. Baltimore, Md.: Johns Hopkins University Press.

———. 1976. *Of Grammatology*. Baltimore, Md.: Johns Hopkins University Press.

Doz, A. 1976. "Remarques sur les onze premières propositions de l'*Ethique* de Spinoza: A propos du Spinoza de Martial Gueroult." *Revue de Métaphysique et de Morale* 81:221–61.

Droetto, Antonio. 1958. "La formazione del pensiero politico di Spinoza e il suo contributo allo sviluppo della dottrina moderna dello Stato." In Benedetto Spinoza, *Trattato politico*, edited by Antonio Droetto, 7–129. Turin: Giappichelli.

Dunin-Borkowski, Stanislaus, Graf von. 1910. *Der junge de Spinoza: Leben und werdegang im lichte der weltphilosophie*. Münster: Aschendorff.

Eckstein, Walther. 1933. "Zur Lehre vom Staatsvertrag bei Spinoza." *Zeitschrift für öffentliches Recht* 13:356–68.

Foucault, Michel. 1972. *The Archaeology of Knowledge*. New York: Pantheon.

Gardet, L. 1969. *La cité musulmane*. Paris: Vrin.

Gardet, L., and M. M. Anawati. 1948. *Introduction à la théologie musulmane*. Paris: Vrin.

Giancotti, Emilia. 1985. *Baruch Spinoza: 1632–1677*. Roma: Riuniti.

———., ed. 1985. *Proceedings of the First Italian International Conference on Spinoza*. Naples: Bibliopolis.

Gierke, Otto von. 1939. *The Development of Political Theory*. Translated by Bernard Freyd. New York: Fertig.

Gimferrer, Pedro. 1968. *La muerte en Beverly Hills*. Madrid: Editorial Ciencia Nueva.

Gough, J. W. 1957. *The Social Contract*. 2nd ed. London: Oxford University Press.

Granada, Fray Luis de. 1922. *Obras*. 3 vols. Madrid.

Grelot, Pierre. 1965. *Bible et théologie*. Paris: Desclée.

Gueroult, Martial. 1968. *Spinoza, I: Dieu*. Paris: Aubier Montaigne.

———. 1974. *Spinoza, II: L'Ame*. Paris: Aubier Montaigne.

———. 1977. "Spinoza, tome 3 (Introduction generale et première moitié du premier chapitre)." *Revue philosophique de la France et de l'étranger* 102:285–302.

Harrington, James. 1770. *The Oceana of James Harrington, and Other Works*. London: Booksellers of London and Westminster.

———. 1992. *The Commonwealth of Oceana and a System of Politics*. Edited by J. G. A. Pocock. New York: Cambridge University Press.

Hegel, G. W. F. 1923. *Schriften zur Politik und Rechtsphilosophie*. Hamburg: Meiner.

———. 1928. *Vorlesungen über die Geschichte der Philosophie*. Stoccarde: Fromann.

———. [1952] 1969. *Briefe von und an Georg Wilhelm Friedrich Hegel*. Vol. 1, *1785–1812*. Hamburg: Meiner.

———. [1969] 1976. *Science of Logic*. Translated by A. V. Miller. New York: Humanities Press.

———. [1892] 1983. *Lectures on the History of Philosophy*. Translated by E. S. Haldane and Frances H. Simson. 3 vols. Atlantic Highlands, N.J.: Humanities Press.

———. 1991. *The Encyclopaedia Logic: Part I of the Encyclopaedia of the Philosophical Sciences with the Zusätze*. Translated by T. F. Geraets et al. Indianapolis, Ind.: Hackett.

Heidegger, Martin. 1958. *What Is Philosophy?* Translated by William Kluback and Jean T. Wilde. New York: Twayne.

———. 1985. *Schelling's Treatise on the Essence of Human Freedom*. Translated by Joan Stambaugh. Athens: Ohio University Press.

Herrera, Alonso [Abraham Cohen]. 1650. *Sepher Sha'ar Ha-Shamayim*. Translated by Isaac Aboab. Amsterdam.

———. 1655. *Sepher Beth 'Elohim*. Translated by Isaac Aboab. Amsterdam.

———. 1678. *Sha'm Ashomayim seu Porta Caelorum. In qua dogmata cabbalistica Philosophorum proponentur et cum philosophiae Platonis conferentur*. Sulzbach, Germany: Typis Abrahami Lichcenthaleri.

Hobbes, Thomas. [1905] 1989. *Metaphysical Writings*. Edited by Mary Whiton Calkins. La Salle, Ill.: Open Court.

———. 1991. *Man and Citizen* (De Homine *and* De Cive). Edited by Bernard Gert. Indianapolis, Ind.: Hackett.

———. 1994. *Leviathan, with Selected Variants from the Latin Edition of 1668*. Edited by Edwin Curley. Indianapolis, Ind.: Hackett.

Karppe, S. 1901. *Etude sur les origines et la nature du Zohar*. Paris: Alcan.

Kolakowski, Leszek. 1969. *Chrétiens sans église: La conscience religieuse et le lien confessionnel au XVIIe siècle*. Paris: NRF.

Lefort, Claude. 1972. *Le travail de l'oeuvre, Machiavel*. Paris: Gallimard.

Lloyd, Genevieve. 1994. *Part of Nature: Self-Knowledge in Spinoza's Ethics*. Ithaca, N.Y.: Cornell University Press.

Macherey, Pierre. 1979. *Hegel ou Spinoza*. Paris: François Maspero.

———. 1992. *Avec Spinoza*. Paris: Presses Universitaires de France.

———. 1994a. *Introduction à l'Ethique de Spinoza: La cinquième partie, les voies de la libération*. Paris: Presses Universitaires de France.

———. 1994b. "Spinoza est-il moniste?" In Revault d'Allonnes and Rizk 1994, 39–53.

Macpherson, C. B. 1962. *The Political Theory of Possessive Individualism: Hobbes to Locke*. New York: Oxford University Press.

Malet, André. 1966. *Le Traité Théologico-Politique de Spinoza et la pensée biblique*. Paris: Les Belles Lettres.

Marramao, Giacomo. 1983. *Potere e secolarizzazione*. Rome: Riuniti.

Matheron, Alexandre. 1971. *Le Christ et le salut des ignorants chez Spinoza*. Paris: Aubier Montaigne.

———. 1977. "Femmes et serviteurs dans le démocratie spinoziste." In *Speculum Spinozanum*, edited by Siegfried Hessing, 368–86. Boston: Routledge and Kegan Paul.

———. 1978. "L'anthropologie spinoziste." *Revue de Synthèse* 99:175–88. Reprinted in Matheron 1986, 17–27.

———. 1983. "L'*Anomalie sauvage* d'Antonio Negri." *Cahiers Spinoza* 4:39–60.

———. 1984. "Spinoza et la problematique juridique de Grotius." *Philosophie* 4:69–89.

———. 1985a. "Le 'Droit du Plus Fort': Hobbes contre Spinoza." *Revue philosophique* 2:149–76.

———. 1985b. "La fonction théoretique de democratie chez Spinoza et Hobbes." *Studia Spinozana* 1:259–273.

———. 1986. *Anthropologie et politique au XVIIe siècle (études sur Spinoza)*. Paris: Vrin.

———. 1988. *Individu et communauté chez Spinoza*. 2nd ed. Paris: Minuit.

———. 1990. "Le probleme de l'evolution de Spinoza du *Traité Theologico-Politique* au *Traité Politique*." In Curley and Moreau 1990, 258–70.

———. 1991a. "Essence, Existence and Power in *Ethics* I: The Foundations of Proposition 16." In Yovel 1991, 23–34.

———. 1991b. "Physique et ontologie chez Spinoza: L'énigmatique réponse à Tschirnhaus." *Studia Spinozana* 6:83–109.

———. 1992. "Philosophie et religion chez Spinoza." *Revue des Sciences Philosophiques et Théologiques* 76, no. 1:56–72.

———. 1994. "L'indignation et le conatus de l'état spinoziste." In Revault d'Allonnes and Rizk 1994, 153–65.

Méchoulan, Henri. 1970. "Spinoza à la charnière de deux mondes: Orthodoxie et héterodoxie." *Revue de Synthèse* 99:129–40.

———. 1976. "Morteira et Spinoza au carrefour du socinianisme." *Revue des Etudes Juives* 135:54–65.

Meinsma, K. O. 1983. *Spinoza et son cercle.* Translated by S. Roosenburg and J.-P. Osier. Paris: Vrin.

Mignini, Filippo. 1981. *Ars imaginandi: Apparenza e rappresentazione in Spinoza.* Naples: Edizioni Scientifiche Italiane.

———. 1984. "Theology as the Work and Instrument of Fortune." In *Spinoza's Political and Theological Thought,* edited by C. de Deugd, 127–36. Amsterdam: North-Holland.

Moreau, Pierre-François. 1977. "Jus et Lex: Spinoza devant la tradition juridique d'après le dépouillement informatique du *Traité politique.*" *Raison présente* 43:53–61.

———. 1985a. "La notion d'*imperium* dans le *Traité politique.*" In Giancotti 1985, 355–66.

———. 1985b. "Spinoza et le *jus circa sacra.*" *Studia Spinozana* 1:335–344.

———. 1990a. "Concorde et sociabilité dans la *Korte Verhandeling.*" In *Dio, l'uomo, la libera: Studi sul "Breve trattato" di Spinoza,* edited by Filippo Mignini, 375–79. L'Aquila: Japadre Editore.

———. 1990b. "Fortune et théorie de l'histoire." In Curley and Moreau 1990, 298–305.

———. 1994a. *Spinoza: L'experience et l'éternité.* Paris: Presses Universitaires de France.

———. 1994b. "Métaphysique de la gloire: Le scholie de la proposition 36 et le 'tournant' du livre V." *Revue philosophique* 1:55–64.

———. 1994c. "The Metaphysics of Substance and the Metaphysics of Forms." In Yovel 1994, 27–35.

Negri, Antonio. 1962. *Alle origini del formalismo giuridico.* Padua: Cedam.

———. 1970. *Descartes politico o della ragionevole ideologia.* Milan: Feltrinelli.

———. 1977. *La forma-stato.* Milan: Feltrinelli.

———. 1991. *The Savage Anomaly: The Power of Spinoza's Metaphysics and Politics.* Translated by Michael Hardt. Minneapolis: University of Minnesota Press.

———. 1994a. *Spinoza subversif.* Paris: Kimé.

———. 1994b. "Démocratie et éternité." In Revault D'Allonnes and Rizk 1994, 139–51.

Norris, Christopher. 1991. *Spinoza and the Origins of Modern Critical Theory.* Cambridge, Mass.: Blackwell.

Orobio de Castro, Isaac. MS. *Epistola invectiva contra Prado.* Paris: Bibliothèque Nationale.

Osier, Jean Pierre. 1987. "L'hermeneutique de Spinoza et de Hobbes." *Studia Spinozana* 3:319–47.

Pacchi, Arrigo. 1965. *Convenzione e ipotesi nella formazione dellafilosofia naturale di Thomas Hobbes.* Firenze: La Nuova Italia.

Popkin, Richard H. 1979. *The History of Skepticism from Erasmus to Spinoza.* Berkeley: University of California Press.

Procacci, Giuliano. 1965. *Studi sulla fortuna di Machiavelli.* Rome: Inst. storico per l'età moderna e contemporanea.

Raab, Felix. 1964. *The English Face of Machiavelli: A Changing Interpretation, 1500–1700.* London: Routledge and Kegan Paul.

Ravà, Adolfo. 1958. *Studi su Spinoza e Fichte.* Milan: Giuffré.

Ravaisson, Félix. 1953. *Essai sur la métaphysique d'Aristote.* Edited by Charles Devivaire. Paris: Vrin.

———. 1959. *Spinoza et Juan de Prado.* Paris: Mouton.

Revah, I. S. 1958. "Spinoza et les héretiques de la communauté judéo-portugaise d'Amsterdam." *Revue d'Histoire des Religions* 154:173–218.

———. 1959–60. "Les Marranes." *Revue d'Etudes Juives* 118:29–70.

Revault d'Allonnes, Myriam, and Hadi Rizk, eds. 1994. *Spinoza: Puissance et ontologie.* Paris: Kimé.

Rubel, Maximilien. 1977. "Marx à la rencontre de Spinoza." *Cahiers Spinoza* 1:7–28.

Saccaro Battisti, Giuseppe. 1984. "Spinoza, l'utopia e le masse: Un'analisi di 'plebs,' 'multitudo,' 'populus,' e 'vulgus.'" *Rivista di Storia della Filosofia* 1.

Schelling, F. W. J. 1936. *Philosophical Inquiries into the Nature of Human Freedom.* Translated by James Gutmann. La Salle, Ill.: Open Court.

———. 1950. *Lettres sur le dogmatisme et le criticism.* Translated by S. Jankelevitch. Paris: Aubier.

Scholem, Gershom. 1973. *Sabbatai Sevi: The Mystical Messiah.* Translated by R. J. Zwi Werblowsky. Princeton, N.J.: Princeton University Press.

Solari, Giorgio. 1949. *Studi storici di filosofia de dritto.* Turin: Giapichelli.

Spink, J. Stephanson. 1960. *French Free-Thought from Gassendi to Voltaire.* London: Athlone Press.

Spinoza, Baruch. 1802–3. *Opera quae supersunt omnia.* 2 vols. Edited by H. E. G. Paulus. Jena: Academische Buchhandlung.

———. 1925. *Spinoza Opera.* 4 vols. Edited by Carl Gebhardt. Heidelberg: Winter.

———. 1954. *Oeuvres complètes.* Edited by Roland Callois, Madeleine Francès, and Robert Misrahi. Paris: Gallimard.

———. 1958. *The Political Works.* Edited and translated by A. G. Wernham. New York: Oxford University Press.

———. 1966. *The Correspondence of Spinoza.* Edited and translated by Abraham Wolf. London: Frank Cass.

———. 1985. *The Collected Works of Spinoza.* Vol. 1. Edited and translated by Edwin Curley. Princeton, N.J.: Princeton University Press.

———. 1989. *Tractatus Theologico-Politicus.* Translated by Samuel Shirley. New York: Brill.

———. 1994. *A Spinoza Reader: The Ethics and Other Works.* Edited and translated by Edwin Curley. Princeton, N.J.: Princeton University Press.

Strauss, Leo. 1936. *The Political Philosophy of Hobbes: Its Basis and Its Genesis.* Oxford: Oxford University Press.

———. 1952. "How to Study Spinoza's *Theologico-Political Treatise.*" In *Persecution and the Art of Writing,* 142–201. Glencoe, Ill.: Free Press.

———. 1965. *Spinoza's Critique of Religion.* New York: Schocken.

Tosel, André. 1984. *Spinoza ou le crépuscule de la servitude.* Paris: Aubier Montaigne.

———. 1985a. "Quelques rémarques pour une interprétation de l'*Ethique.*" In Giancotti 1985, 143–71.

———. 1985b. "La théorie de la pratique et la fonction de l'opinion publique dans la philosophie politique de Spinoza." *Studia Spinozana* 1:183–208.

———. 1990. "Y-a-t-il une philosophie du progrès historique chez Spinoza?" In Curley and Moreau 1990, 306–23.

———. 1994. *Du materialisme de Spinoza.* Paris: Kimé, 1994.

Vallée, Gérard, ed. 1988. *The Spinoza Conversations between Lessing and Jacobi: Texts with Excerpts from the Ensuing Controversy.* Translated by Gérard Vallée et al. New York: University Press of America.

Vaughn, C. E. [1925] 1960. *Studies in the History of Political Philosophy before and after Rousseau.* Vol. 1, *From Hobbes to Hume.* New York: Russell and Russell.

Viano, C. A. 1960. *John Locke: Dal razionalismo all' illuminismo.* Turin: Einaudi.

Vlachos, George. 1962. *La pensée politique de Kant: Métaphysique de l'ordre et dialectique du progrès.* Paris: Presses Universitaires de France.

Warrender, Howard. 1957. *The Political Philosophy of Hobbes: His Theory of Obligation.* New York: Oxford University Press.

Yovel, Yirmiyahu. 1992. *Spinoza and Other Heretics.* 2nd ed. 2 vols. Princeton, N.J.: Princeton University Press.

———. 1994. *Spinoza on Knowledge and the Human Mind.* New York: Brill.

———, ed. 1991. *God and Nature: Spinoza's Metaphysics.* New York: Brill.

Zac, Sylvain. 1965. *Spinoza et l'interprétation de l'écriture.* Paris: Presses Universitaires de France.

Zagorin, Perez. 1954. *A History of Political Thought in the English Revolution.* London: Routledge and Kegan Paul.

Contributors

Gabriel Albiac

is professor of philosophy at the Université Compultense de Madrid.

Louis Althusser

was for many years the director of the philosophy program at the École normale supérieure.

Etienne Balibar

is professor of philosophy at the Université de Paris-X.

Gilles Deleuze

was professor of philosophy at the Université de Paris-VIII. Among his many books are *Difference and Repetition*, *The Logic of Sense*, and, with Félix Guattari, *Anti-Oedipus*, *A Thousand Plateaus*, and *What Is Philosophy?*

Emilia Giancotti

was professor of the history of modern and contemporary philosophy at the University of Urbino and president of the Italian Association of the Friends of Spinoza.

Luce Irigaray

is a psychoanalyst and feminist who is the author of *Speculum of the Other Woman* and *This Sex Which is Not One*.

Pierre Macherey

is professor of philosophy at the Université de Lille-III.

Alexandre Matheron

is professor at the École normale supérior de Fontenay-Saint-Cloud.

Warren Montag

is associate professor of English and Comparative Literature at Occidental College, California. He is the author of numerous translations and essays on such topics as Spinoza, Hobbes, Althusser, Foucault, Lacan, Derrida, and postmodernism.

Pierre-François Moreau

is professor of philosophy at the École normale supérieure de Fontenay-St. Cloud.

Antonio Negri

is professor of political science at the Université de Paris-VIII (St. Denis).

Ted Stolze

teaches in the Philosophy Department at California State University, Haywood. He has translated essays by Pierre Macherey and Etienne Balibar and is currently working on a manuscript about Spinoza's politics.

André Tosel

is professor of the history of philosophy and director of the Centre for Research on the History of Systems of Modern Thought at the Université de Paris-I (Panthéon-Sorbonne).

Index

Aboab, Isaac, 130, 141
Aeschylus, 26
Affect, xix, 13, 14, 21, 22, 23, 24, 26 27, 28, 30, 32, 126, 127, 199, 233
Affection, 22, 23, 24, 30, 31, 38, 56, 67, 80, 90, 136, 233
Alain (Émile Chartier), xiii
Albiac, Gabriel, xvi
Alexander, 99, 100, 182
Alphakar, 154
Alquié, Ferdinand, xiii, xiv
Althusius, 223
Althusser, Louis, ix, x, xii, xv, xvi, xvii, xviii, xix, 175
Aristocracy, 209, 217, 219, 231
Aristotle, 42
Attribute, xvii, 11, 12, 18, 29, 38, 49, 54, 55, 56, 57, 58, 65, 66, 67, 68 ,69, 70, 71, 72, 73, 74, 75, 76, 77, 78, 79,80, 81, 82, 83, 84, 85, 86 , 87, 88, 89, 90, 91, 92, 93, 101, 124, 130, 135, 138, 161, 190, 199, 217, 235

Bacon, Francis, 74
Balibar, Ètienne, x, xvi, xix
Bennett, Jonathan, x
Bible, the, 156, 157, 159, 160, 163, 165, 167, 196
Blanchot, Maurice, 31
Bodin, Jean, 191
Body, 12, 13, 14, 18, 22, 23, 24, 25, 26, 27, 29, 30, 39, 40, 41, 42, 50 51, 53, 54, 56, 57, 58, 59, 60, 103, 110, 117, 124, 125, 127, 139, 155, 156, 157, 163, 166, 172, 187, 193, 194, 204, 215, 217 223, 234, 238, 240, 241

Boehme, Jacob, 120
Borgia, Cesar, 14, 15
Boxel, Hugo, 88
Breton, Stanislaus, 11
Bruno, Giordano, 132
Burgensdijk, 154
Burke, Carolyn, 45

Caesar Augustus, 182, 189
Calvin, John, 154
Cassirer, Natorp, l52
Chekhov, Anton, 21
Common Notion, 28, 30, 31, 32, 158
Conatus, 112, 113, 134, 135, 137,
Contract, xix, 180, 193, 194, 209, 211, 213, 214, 216, 223, 224
Crescas, 154
Curley, Edwin, x
Curtius, Quintus (Tacitus), 99, 101, 181, 202

da Costa, Uriel, 10, 134, 154
Darius, 99, 100
De Barrios, Miguel (David) Levi, 115
de Blyenberg, William, 116, 117, 118, 119, 120, 125
de Gaza, Nathan, 121
de Granada, Fray Luis, 131, 133
de la Court, Pieter, 207
de Luria, Isaac, 120, 121
de Prado, Juan, xi, 133, 134, 141
de Vries, Simon, 78, 82

Death, xviii, 17, 19, 27, 38, 40, 138, 140, 141, 155, 201,
210, 211, 227
Deleuze, Gilles, ix, x, xii, xiv, xv, xvi, 75, 88, 123, 136, 139
Democracy, xvii, xix, 183, 204, 205, 207, 211, 212, 213,
214, 215, 217, 219, 220, 221, 222, 225, 227, 228, 231,
235, 237, 239, 240, 241, 242
Den Uyl, Douglas J., x
Derrida, Jacques, ix, xvi, 10
Desargues, Gerard, 30, 31
Descartes, Rene, xi, xiii, 5, 18, 30, 31, 57, 59, 66, 69, 70,
71, 72, 78, 86, 87, 89, 129, 137
Desire, xvii, xviii, 6, 7, 16, 51, 125, 126, 135, 136, 140,
148, 149, 150, 153, 154, 159, 161, 179, 187, 215, 217,
230, 242
Dilthey, 158
Dionysius, 133
don Alonso (Abraham Cohen of Herrera), 130
Dunin-Borkowski, 130

Eckhart, Meister, 38
Engels, Friedrich, 6, 62
Essence, xvii, 3, 6, 11, 21, 30, 31, 33, 37, 38, 39, 40, 41,
42, 44, 52, 54, 55, 56, 57, 58, 59, 61, 66, 67, 68, 70, 71,
73, 74, 75, 76, 7, 78, 79, 80, 81, 87, 98, 112, 117, 120,
122, 123, 124, 125, 130, 133, 134, 135, 136, 137, 138,
147, 148, 173, 177, 185, 198, 224, 226, 231, 240
Eternity, 30, 60, 165
Ethics, xi, xii, xiii, xv, xvii, 21, 24, 26, 27, 28, 29, 30, 31,
61, 73, 75, 76, 78, 80, 82, 86, 101, 103, 110, 120, 123,
125, 128, 129, 132, 133, 134, 135, 138, 150, 163, 164
165, 171, 187, 238, 239
Euclid, 12, 163, 164, 165
Experience, xiii, xiv, 5, 13, 97, 98, 99, 111, 125, 141, 148,
150, 154, 171, 175, 192, 201, 232, 241
Expression, xiii, xiv, xvi, xvii, 21, 26, 27, 29, 52, 53 61, 86,
89, 101, 102, 110, 114, 117, 149, 228
Extension, 7, 11, 41, 44, 49, 55, 56, 57, 58, 59, 69, 70,
71, 72, 79, 82, 84, 85, 89, 91, 92, 93, 110, 131, 138,
226

Fear, 17, 38, 102, 103, 104, 148, 174, 177, 178,184, 186,
188, 190, 191, 198, 199, 204, 215
Fichte, Johann Gottlieb, 111
Fischer, Kuno, 56
Flavius, Josephus, 202
Ford, John, 139
Foucault, Michel, ix, xiii, xvi, xvii, xviii, 3
Freedom, xviii, 4, 5, 13 14, 18, 44, 45, 55, 60, 104, 109,
110, 111, 112, 113, 114, 115, 132, 133, 138, 139, 140,
141, 155, 173, 186, 193, 201, 224, 225, 228, 229, 232,
235, 236, 239, 241, 242
Freud, Sigmund, 14, 18, 19

Galileo, 56
Galois, Evariste, 31
Geometrical Method, 24, 30, 31, 65, 76, 83, 84, 86, 102
Gill, Gillian, 45

God, xii, xiii, xvii, xviii, 7, 9, 10, 11, 12, 18, 23, 29, 30, 31,
37, 38, 39, 40, 41, 42, 43, 44, 45, 54, 55, 56, 58, 60, 69,
75, 76, 78, 79, 81, 86, 87, 88, 92, 113, 114, 115, 116,
118, 119, 120, 129, 130, 131, 132, 133, 135, 137, 138,
141, 148, 149, 156, 157, 160, 162, 163, 176, 180, 181,
182, 183, 188, 190, 191, 192, 198, 200, 201, 205, 224,
230, 233, 240
Goethe, Johann Wolfgang von, 25
Don Gonzalo de Córdoba, 130
Good and Evil, 100, 109, 111, 114, 115, 117, 118, 121,
122, 123, 124, 126, 147, 188
Gramsci, Antonio, 14
Grotius, 195, 208, 209
Gueroult, Martial, xii, xiii, xiv, 71, 75, 76, 81, 84, 85, 86,

Harrington, James, 223
Hate, 17, 109, 125, 127, 178, 197, 199, 202, 239
Heerboord, Adrian, 128, 154
Hegel, G. W. F., ix, xvii, 4, 5, 7, 9, 10, 13, 65, 66, 67, 69,
71, 72, 73 ,74, 75, 77, 79, 83, 84, 88, 91, 92, 93, 94,
111, 112, 229, 230
Heidegger, Martin, ix, 13, 40, 111, 112, 115
Heraclitus, 185
Hobbes, Thomas, xi, xv, xix, 3, 15, 49, 50, 51, 52, 54, 55,
172, 173, 177, 179, 187, 191, 193, 195, 203, 207, 208,
209, 210, 211, 212, 213, 214, 216
Hope, 102, 103, 104, 148, 178, 184, 188, 190, 199, 215,
230, 242
Hudde, 81
Husserl, Edmund, 12
Huygens, Christian, 31

Idea, x, xi, xiii, xvi, 11, 12, 13, 2, 26, 27, 28, 29, 30, 31, 41,
50, 52, 59, 60, 61, 67, 73, 74, 75, 81, 82, 86, 87, 89, 90,
100, 101, 110, 120, 121, 122, 136, 138, 150, 151, 152,
155, 156, 161, 163, 164, 172, 175, 179, 184, 186, 188,
189, 191, 193, 202, 223, 229, 230, 232, 234, 236, 240
Imagination, 5, 6, 9, 10, 12, 18, 23, 24, 53, 59, 83, 84, 87,
88, 89, 90, 100, 119, 122, 125, 141, 150, 158, 161, 166,
167, 181, 182, 191, 200, 237, 238
Individual, xvii, xviii, xix, 5, 7, 9, 18, 101, 104, 113, 129,
148, 164, 173, 174, 175, 176, 179, 181, 183, 184, 186,
187, 188, 189, 191, 192, 193, 195, 197, 198, 199, 204,
208, 211, 214, 216, 229, 233, 235, 236, 239
Intellect, xi, xiii, 18, 23, 24, 31, 54, 60, 66, 67, 70, 71, 72,
73, 74, 75, 79, 80, 81, 82, 83, 88, 90, 93, 116, 118, 119,
122, 128, 131, 132, 135, 149, 151
Intellectual Love of God, 18, 139
Interpretation of Scripture, 163
Irigaray, Luce, xvii

Jacobi, 109, 110, 111, 112, 113
Joan of Arc, 200
Joy, 12, 18, 19, 22, 23, 26, 27, 31, 124, 125, 126

Kant, Immanuel, 3, 5, 38, 52, 54, 71
Karppe, S., 130, 132

Knowledge, 5, 6, 7, 8, 9, 10, 12, 13, 18, 21, 26, 27, 29, 43, 44, 49, 50, 52, 53, 54, 59, 60, 61, 65, 69, 77, 85, 88, 90, 91, 99, 102, 103, 116, 118, 124, 125, 126, 127, 134, 136, 140, 147, 149, 150, 151, 152, 153, 158, 159, 160, 161, 164, 165, 166, 177, 179, 184, 186, 200, 230

Lacan, Jacques, ix, xvii
Lagneau, Jules, xiii, 30
Law, xii, xviii, 41, 45, 52, 61, 102, 103, 104, 117, 118, 126, 139, 148, 151, 152, 153, 159, 171, 172, 176, 177, 178, 183, 187, 188, 189, 190, 191, 192, 193, 194, 195, 197, 198, 199, 201, 202, 203, 204, 243
Lefort, Claude, 14
Leibniz, Gottfried Wilhelm, 24, 130
Lenin, Vladimir, 6
Lessing, Gotthold Ephraim, 109, 110, 132
Lloyd, Genevieve, x
Locke, John, xv
Love, xviii, 7, 14, 15, 17, 40, 110, 117, 151, 156, 174, 178, 188, 190, 191, 197, 199, 201, 202, 204, 205, 230, 233, 239, 240
Luther, Martin, 149

Macherey, Pierre, x, xiv, xvi, xvii
Machiavelli, Niccolo, xv, 3, 11, 13, 14, 15, 16, 17, 19, 101, 181, 193, 195, 197, 202, 223
Maimonides, 152, 154, 155
Mao, 11, 185
Marx, Karl, 4, 6, 8, 9, 10, 11, 14, 19, 62, 11
Materialism, xvi, 11, 49, 52, 54, 55, 58, 60, 62, 111, 112, 124, 130, 223
Matheron, Alexandre, xii, xiv, xvi, xix, 147
Menasseh ben Israel, xi, 141, 154
Mode, 7, 9, 11, 12, 18, 21, 24, 25, 41, 49, 50, 56, 58, 59, 66, 67, 68, 69, 72, 82, 89, 90, 91, 113, 119, 123, 132, 135, 136, 137, 139, 140, 151, 154, 155, 161, 190
Mohammed, 152
Monarchy, xii, 204, 209, 213, 217, 222, 229
Monism, x, 88, 90, 129
Moreau, Pierre-François, xvi
Morteira, 141
Moses, 152, 178, 181, 182, 183, 186, 189, 191, 192, 194, 196, 197, 198
Multitude, xii, xix, xx, 177, 182, 184, 193, 208, 216, 217, 228, 229, 230, 231, 232, 233, 234, 235, 236, 237, 238, 241

Nature, xiii, xv, xvii, xix, 9, 22, 23, 25, 31, 37, 38, 39, 42, 45, 50, 52, 54, 56, 57, 58, 60, 61, 66, 67, 68, 70, 72, 73, 74, 75, 80, 81, 82, 83, 84, 85, 87, 88, 89, 90, 92, 98, 104, 109, 112, 113, 114, 115, 119, 120, 122, 123, 124, 126, 127, 128, 129, 130, 131, 132, 133, 134, 136, 137, 138, 139, 140, 141, 148, 149, 156, 157, 158, 159, 160, 162, 171, 173, 177, 178, 179, 180, 181, 184, 190, 192, 193, 195, 197, 208, 212, 214, 215, 220, 224, 225, 229, 231, 234, 236, 241, 243
Negri, Antonio, x, xvi, xix

Nero, 125
Nietzsche, Friedrich, ix, 122
Orestes, 125
Orobio, de Castro, Isaac, 133
Osier, Jean-Pierre, 13

Pacchi, Arrigo, 52
Parallelism, 12, 18, 40, 42
Pascal, Blaise, 3, 4, 10
Passion, 12, 16, 17, 18, 26, 27, 28, 50, 59, 110, 125, 127, 139, 140, 157, 166, 167, 184, 199, 201, 202, 204, 216, 234, 239, 240
Paul, Saint, 187, 188, 202
Piderot, 232
Piety, 119, 201, 237, 238, 239, 240, 241
Plato, 30
Pleasure, xviii, xix, 22, 43, 119, 126
Plekhanov, 62
Political Treatise, xii, xv, xvi, xix, 98, 171, 216, 217, 218, 220, 221, 223, 224, 227, 228, 229, 231, 232, 237, 238, 240, 242
Popper, Karl, 8, 9
Power, xviii, xix, 12, 21, 22, 23, 24, 26, 27, 28, 30, 31, 41, 55, 88, 110, 117, 121, 123, 124, 125, 127, 132, 133, 135, 136, 137, 138, 139, 141, 148, 149, 150, 151, 171, 172, 173, 174, 176, 178, 179, 180, 182, 183, 184, 185, 186, 187, 189, 190, 191, 193, 194, 198, 199, 208, 213, 214, 215, 216, 217, 220, 222, 223, 224, 225, 226, 227, 228, 229, 230, 231, 232, 233, 234, 235, 236, 237, 241, 242, 243

Ravaisson, Felix, 115
Rawls, John, xviii
Reason, 5, 50, 51, 52, 53, 54, 71, 73, 78, 80, 81, 86, 89, 92, 98, 102, 104, 112, 113, 117 119, 122, 125, 131, 155, 157, 164, 179, 184, 187, 189, 191, 199, 231, 232, 234, 235, 236, 237, 238
Rembrandt, van Rijn, 26
Right, xviii, xix, 163, 173, 174, 175, 176, 178, 179, 180, 181, 182, 183, 186, 189, 193, 194, 195, 198, 199, 201, 202, 210, 212, 213, 214, 215, 216, 221, 224, 225, 229, 231, 235, 236
Robinson, Lewis, 75
Rossi, 52
Rousseau, Jean-Jacques, xv, 3, 10, 172, 208, 222, 232

Sabbatai, 121
Sadness, 18, 19 22, 23, 27, 124, 125, 126
Sartre, Jean Paul, 140
Sasso, Robert, 29
Savonarola, 17
Schelling, F. W., 109, 110, 111, 112, 113, 114, 115
Schlegel, Friedrich Von, 11
Schleiermacher, 158
Scholem, Gershom, 121
Schuller, 58
Scripture, xv, 53, 56, 80, 119, 156, 157, 159, 161, 162, 163

Servitude, 4, 23, 27, 28, 125, 126, 127, 149, 150, 158, 160, 186, 188

Sign, xvi, 21, 22, 23, 24, 25, 26, 27, 28, 29, 30, 31, 33, 50, 98, 133, 196

Simon, Richard, 158

Socrates, 7

Spinoza, Baruch (starting with Ch. 1), 3, 4, 5, 6, 7, 8, 9, 10, 11, 13, 16, 18, 19, 21, 22, 24, 26, 27, 29, 30, 37, 39, 40, 42, 44, 49, 55, 56, 57, 58, 59, 60, 61, 62, 65, 66, 67, 68, 69, 70, 71, 72, 73, 74, 75, 76, 78, 79, 80, 82, 90, 91, 92, 93, 94, 97, 98, 99, 100, 101, 102, 103, 109, 110, 111, 112, 113, 114, 115, 116, 117, 118, 119, 121, 122, 123, 124, 125, 126, 127, 128, 130, 132, 133, 134, 135, 136, 137, 139, 140, 151, 153, 154, 155, 156, 157, 158, 159, 160, 161, 164, 165, 166, 171, 172, 173, 174, 175, 176, 177, 178, 179, 180, 181, 182, 183, 184, 185, 186, 187, 188, 189, 191, 192, 193, 194, 195, 196, 197, 198, 200, 201, 202, 203, 204, 205, 207, 208, 209, 213, 214, 215, 216, 219, 220, 221, 223, 224, 225, 226, 227, 229, 230, 231, 232, 233, 234, 235, 236, 238, 240, 242

State, xviii, xix, 12, 16, 17, 23, 29, 117, 119, 126, 135, 149, 161, 174, 175, 176, 177, 178, 180, 181, 183, 185, 186, 187, 191, 193, 194, 195, 197, 198, 199, 200, 201, 202, 203, 204, 208, 210, 211, 214, 221, 222, 223, 224, 227, 230, 231, 238

Stolze, Ted, 94, 105, 142, 205, 243

Strauss, Leo, 151, 152, 156, 242

Suárez, Francisco, 128, 136

Substance, xvii, 7, 11, 18, 29, 42, 49, 55, 58, 61, 65, 66, 67, 68, 69, 70, 71, 72, 73, 74, 75, 76, 77, 78, 79, 80, 81, 82, 83, 84, 85, 86, 87, 88, 89, 90, 91, 92, 93, 104, 113, 114, 116, 126, 128, 129, 130, 132, 133, 134, 135, 137, 138, 147, 149, 150, 231

Superstition, xviii, xix, 55, 97, 98, 99, 100, 102, 103, 148, 151, 155, 156, 161, 162, 163, 166, 182, 185, 240

Theologico-Political Treatise, xii, 10, 23, 98, 99, 103, 104, 120, 148, 150, 151, 155, 156, 158, 161, 163, 165, 166, 167, 171, 182, 184, 185, 186, 187, 189, 193, 194, 196, 204, 205, 214, 215, 219, 220, 221, 224, 226, 230, 231, 235, 238, 242

Thomas Aquinas, Saint, 115, 154, 208

Thought, x, xi, xiii, xiv, xvii, 4, 6, 7, 11, 13, 31, 39, 40, 43, 50, 53, 55, 57, 61, 65, 66, 68, 69, 70, 71, 72, 79, 82, 85, 89, 90, 91, 92, 93, 131, 154, 162, 164, 166, 171, 221, 229, 240

Time, xv, xix, 22, 30, 37, 38, 51, 97, 98, 111, 113

Titus, Livy, 202

Tosel, Andréxvi, 242

Treatise on the Emendation of the Intellect, xi, 61, 101

Truth, 5, 6, 11, 12, 31, 56, 60, 61, 68, 69, 72, 113, 116, 117, 118, 153, 156, 157, 158, 160, 164, 171, 224, 236

Tschirnhaus, 57, 58

Vermeer, Jan, 25, 26

Virtue, xix, 12, 14, 15, 16, 28, 117, 119, 120, 124, 125, 127, 139, 162, 179, 189, 230, 237, 238, 240, 241

Voetius, 154

Voltaire, 232

von Baader, Franz, 112

Wittgenstein, Ludwig, 8

Yovel, Yirimiyahu, x